THE
MYSTERY
WRITERS

The Mystery Writers

Edited by
Jean Henry Mead

Medallion Books

First edition March 2012

Book cover design by Bill Mead

ISBN: 978-1-931415-35-4

Medallion Books by Jean Henry Mead:

Diary of Murder
A Village Shattered
Murder on the Interstate
Ghost of Crimson Dawn
Mystery of Spider Mountain
Escape, a Wyoming Historical Novel
Casper Country: Wyoming's Heartland
Westerners: Candid & Historic Interviews
Wyoming's Cowboy Poets and Their Poetry
The Mystery Writers: Their Lives and Advice

Medallion Books
Glenrock, Wyoming

This collection of interviews is dedicated to my fellow members of Mystery Writers of America, especially the RMMWA

Acknowledgement

I'm grateful to the authors who contributed to this book: writers of many subgenres housed under the broad mystery label. They write private eye novels, amateur sleuths, crime, cozies, historicals, humorous mysteries, suspense, thrillers, noir, police procedurals, contemporary westerns as well as traditional mysteries from as far away as Thailand, South Africa, England, Canada and Brazil.

Their interviews originated at my Mysterious Writers blog site and include not only their success stories, but the struggles the authors overcame on their paths to publication. The advice they offer here is invaluable to novice writers. It also gives readers the opportunity to learn how writers function.

Those who people this book range from bestsellers and award-winners to journeyman and independently published authors, who have all been affected in some way by the revolutionary trend that evolved with the advent of the e-book and electronic readers.

It's been my pleasure and learning experience to meet my fellow novelists and feature their stories and advice. I know you'll enjoy them as much as I have.

~Jean Henry Mead

The Authors

Chapter One: Suspense

James Scott Bell

James Scott Bell is a bestselling suspense author. The former trial lawyer was the fiction columnist for *Writers Digest Books* and an adjunct professor of writing at Pepperdine University. His books on the craft of writing are among the most popular today.

Jim, you have led a diverse life as a trial lawyer, lecturer, actor, television and radio commentator, and bestselling author. Which brought you the most satisfaction and pleasure?

Wow, that's quite a list. I hadn't thought about all that in a while. I can tell you I've been very blessed to be able to do a number of things I really enjoyed.

I loved going to court. All the workup before trial, and the 24/7 aspect of thinking about it, is stressful. But standing in front of a jury to argue a case, cross-examining witnesses—all that was supremely enjoyable.

I loved acting. If it were a more secure profession, I would probably still be living in New York, doing Shakespeare and O'Neill and David Mamet.

But I love writing, too, and being able to make my living at it is tremendously satisfying. My office is wherever I can lug my computer or my AlphaSmart keyboard, and my subjects are whatever my imagination can conjure up.

Your *Writers Digest* craft books have all been bestsellers. Has your advice for novice writers changed?

The best advice for today's market is the same advice I gave yesterday and would have given 100 years ago: produce the words. Set a weekly quota, one that is comfortable, and up it by 10%. Then go for it. You still have to show that you can write solid fiction book after book, no matter how it gets to market. And the way you show that is to actually produce.

Yes, study the market, but don't become a slave to it. Trends come and go. Write material that moves you and it will have a chance to move the reader.

How were you mentored by Lawrence Block?

When I called him my first mentor, I meant by way of his columns in *Writer's Digest*. What made those so great is that he knows how a writer thinks. He got into my head and showed me what to do. And he did that for countless other writers.

When I started doing that column myself, I felt like Joshua taking over for Moses. I did finally get to meet and chat with Larry at a convention, and via email, and it felt good to talk as a colleague. But I still reverence those years he was teaching me so much.

Tell us about your latest releases, *Watch Your Back* and *Writing Fiction for All Your Worth.*

I released these two as e-books only. I wanted to supplement both my thriller print fiction and my writing books for *Writer's Digest*. I discussed this with my agent and the publisher beforehand. I see these as volumes to make new readers. And that's what publishers and agents keep telling writers to do. Build a platform. This is one way to build it.

Watch Your Back is suspense fiction, the title novella and three stories. I love the old pulp days when writers like Chandler and Cornell Woolrich were producing great short fiction. But the pulp market died. Now, with e-books, it's back, and I want to be part of that.

Writing Fiction for All You're Worth is a collection of my best blog posts, articles, interviews and reflections on writing. It covers the writing world today, the writing life, and the writing craft. I've also included a section of my "secret" writing notebook. No one but me has ever seen that material, until now.

How do you feel about the e-book revolution?

Of course it's here and it is a revolution. But will it turn out to be the United States in 1776 or France in 1789? Will it be order or chaos? Will it shake out into anarchy or some form of cooperation between traditional publishing and electronic publishing? No one knows!

But it is definitely a heady time and even the professionals—authors, agents, publishers—are wondering how to act and react.

I'm a writer. I write. I write for readers. The readers are out there with e-devices. Why should I not give them material when I've got so much of it?

Suspense/thrillers and inspirational books almost seem polar opposites.

I began in the Inspirational Fiction market because I liked writing about people struggling with faith issues in a dark world. In a way, that's what great thrillers are about. It may not be religious faith, but it's faith in something—in the quest for justice, say—that makes a thriller worth reading on the character level.

So there is no inherent opposition in the thriller/Christian fiction genres. It's true the latter market is dominated by "softer" titles, such as Amish fiction. I have chosen to jump into the mainstream with my Try series and *Watch Your Back*. But no matter where you are, you still have to produce page turning fiction.

Why do you set your novels exclusively in the Los Angeles area?

I just can't get away from it. It's my home, I love it, I know it and it's the greatest noir city in the world. There is a plot around every corner, a great character on every street. You can drive for a mile and be in a completely different neighborhood. And I think there's something cool about being one of the bards of L.A. I love Cain and Chandler and Connelly and Crais and those guys. I like being part of that tradition.

What's the worst thing that has happened to you while researching a novel?

Oh, nothing major. I never got thrown in the clink or anything. I did have some uncomfortable moments when I was researching Skid Row for *Try Darkness*. There's nothing like walking around in a location, but this one is rather sketchy to say the least. Having learned how to walk fast and with attitude when I lived in New York, I did fine.

Do writers really need an agent, or are agents becoming the dinosaurs of the publishing industry?

A great agent is such an asset. And indispensable for getting published the traditional way. I have the best agent in the world, Donald Maass, and I'm also friends with some terrific agents. I know it's a tough deal right now. If an aspiring writer gets with a good agent, that's fantastic. I know the search can be long and difficult. But the discipline of trying to write material good enough for an agent to take on is not wasted should the author eventually try another route. Agents will evolve with the changes in the industry.

Ten Commandments for Writers

by James Scott Bell

1. Thou Shalt write a certain number of words every week.

    This is the first, and greatest, commandment. If you write
    to a quota and hold yourself to it, sooner than you think
    you'll have a full length novel. (I used to advocate a daily
    quota, but I changed it to weekly because inevitably you
    miss days, or life intrudes, and you run yourself down. I
    also take one day off a week.) So set a weekly quota, divide
    it by days, and if you miss one day make it up on the others.

2. Thou Shalt write passionate first drafts.

    Don't edit yourself heavily during your first drafts. The
    writing of it is partly an act of discovering your story, even
    if you outline. Your plot and characters may want to make
    twists and turns you didn't plan. Let them go! Follow along
    and record what happens. I edit my previous day's work
    and then move on. At 20k words I "step back" to see if I
    have a solid foundation, shore it up if I don't, then move on
    to the end.

3. Thou Shalt make trouble for thy Lead.

    The engine of a good story is fueled by the threat to the Lead
    character. Keep turning up the heat. Make things harder.
    Simple three act structure: Get your Lead up a tree, throw
    things at him, get him down.

4. Thou Shalt put a stronger opposing force in the Lead's
    Way.

The opposition character must be stronger than the Lead. More power, more experience, more resources. Otherwise, the reader won't worry. You want them to worry. Hitchcock always said the strength of his movies came from the strength and cunning of the villains. But note the opposition doesn't have to be a "bad guy." Think of Tommy Lee Jones in the *The Fugitive.*

5. Thou Shalt get thy story running from the first paragraph.

    Start with a character, in a situation of a change or threat or challenge, and grip the reader from the start. This is the opening "disturbance" and that's what readers respond to immediately. It doesn't have to be something "big." Anything that sends a ripple through the "ordinary world."

6. Thou Shalt create surprises.

    Avoid the predictable! Always make a list of several avenues your scenes and story might take, then choose something that makes sense but also surprises the reader.

7. Thou Shalt make everything contribute to the story.

    Don't go off on tangents that don't have anything to do with the characters and what they want in the story. Stay as direct as a laser beam.

8. Thou Shalt cut out all the dull parts.

    Be ruthless in revision. Cut out anything that slows the story down. No trouble, tension or conflict is dull. At the very least, something tense inside a character.

9. Thou Shalt develop Rhino skin.

    Don't take rejection or criticism personally. Learn from criticism and move on. Perseverance is the golden key to a writing career.

10. Thou Shalt never stop learning, growing and writing for the rest of thy life.

    Writing is growth. We learn about ourselves, we discover more about life, we use our creativity, we gain insights. At the same time, we study. Brain surgeons keep up on the journals, why should writers think they don't need to stay up on the craft? If I learn just one thing that helps me as a writer, it's worth it.

(James Scott Bell's website: http://www.jamesscottbell.com/ and his blog site: www.killzonauthors.blogspot.com. He can also be found on Twitter and Facebook.)

Hank Phillippi Ryan

Award-winning investigative reporter Hank Phillippi Ryan's work in Boston has resulted in new laws; people sent to prison, homes removed from foreclosure, and millions of dollars in restitution. Along with her 27 EMMYs, she has won dozens of other journalism honors. Her first mystery, bestselling *Prime Time*, won the Agatha Award and was a RITA nominee as well as a Reviewers' Choice Award Winner. A subsequent novel, *Face Time* is a "BookSense Notable Book," and *Air Time* and *Drive Time* were nominated for both the Agatha and Anthony awards. Her latest suspense-thriller is *The Other Woman*. Lee Child said, "I knew Ryan was good, but I didn't know she was this good."

Hank, what has brought you the most pleasure in your professional life?

In the past 30 years, I've wired myself with hidden cameras, chased down criminals and confronted corrupt politicians—and had many a door slammed in my face! But the idea that I can change lives and even change laws is so gratifying. It's a big responsibility, which I take very seriously. But when a tough story comes through and changes are made as a result—the rewards are immense.

How did your TV news program, "Hank Investigates" originate?

It's a segment on the news here in Boston, and airs on the NBC affiliate. I've been a reporter for a long time—starting out as the political reporter in Indianapolis in 1975—then assigned to other beats from the medical reporter (!) to movie critic (!!) to on-the-road feature reporter in Atlanta, Georgia, where every Monday morning I'd close my eyes and point to a map—and then go to wherever that finger pointed to see what I could come up with.

I came to Boston as a reporter in 1982, where for a while I was the "funny one." Whenever the newscast needed a clever feature—what we call a "kicker"—I was the one assigned to the story. They called me "Something out of nothing productions" since I could always find a story anywhere.

In 1988, I was assigned to do the long-form "think pieces" for the presidential conventions. After that, my news director told me he'd realized I was wasting time being the funny one. He said, "you're the serious one." And he made me the investigative reporter. And that's what I've done—with much delight—ever since.

Which of all your many awards do you cherish most and why?

Oh, impossible. My Agatha for *Prime Time* as Best First Novel brings tears to my eyes every time I see it. What a joy! But I love each of the 27 Emmys and 12 Murrows as if it were the only one. Each one of them represents a secret that we discovered and brought to light. I'm very proud of those, and what they represent.

Tell us about your background.

I was born in Chicago, where my dad was the music critic for the old *Chicago Daily News*. We moved to Indianapolis (where some of my family still lives) when I was about six. I went to public schools, where I was a geeky Beatle-loving misfit voted "most original" in high school—much to my chagrin at the time. I majored in English at Western College for Women in Oxford, Ohio, went to work in politics and then radio.

I got my first job in broadcasting because—as I told the news director at the radio station—"Your license is up for renewal at the FCC, and you don't have any women working here." Well, it was 1970! I'm proud to be part of the group of women who began to break down the gender barriers back then.

I worked for almost two years in the U.S. Senate, and a couple of years at *Rolling Stone Magazine* in Washington, DC. And then, TV.

When did you decide to write novels? And how did you come up with your "Time" mystery series?

Well, I decided to write mystery novels when I was about seven—Nancy Drew was my first best friend. But for whatever reason, it took me about 48 more years to come up with a plot I thought was worthy!

That happened when I got a weird email one day at the station. It was clearly a spam, with the subject line "mortgage refinancing." But inside was what looked like lines from a play by Shakespeare. I wondered why someone would send lines from a play in a spam about mortgage refinancing. And it crossed my mind—maybe it's a secret message.

And ding ding ding! (I still get goosebumps telling this story.) I thought—my plot! And that's how it all started. From the moment on, I was obsessed with writing the book. And that was the Agatha-winning *Prime Time*.

What's the scoop on *The Other Woman*?

The Other Woman is about consequences. The idea came to me in the dentist's office. I was reading *People Magazine*, because that's what you do at the dentist. There was an article about Jenny Sanford, the wife of the South Carolina governor—you know, the one who supposedly went off on the Appalachian Trail when he was actually with his Argentinean mistress? I thought, Isn't that astonishing? Why would anyone do that? The mistress, I meant. She was certainly ruining her life, and the life and career of the man she was supposed to love...as well as his wife's life, and his children's and his employees and constituents. It was so awful, on so many levels. And I kept thinking—would there be ANY good reason to do that? And then, in this interview, Mrs. Sanford said, "You can choose your sin, but you cannot choose your consequences." Again, I thought, ding ding. This is my book.

So, *The Other Woman* introduces Jane Ryland, once a rising star in television news until she refused to reveal a source. The consequences of honor? She then lost everything. Now a disgraced newspaper reporter on the lowest rung of the ladder, Jane isn't content to work on her assigned puff pieces, and finds herself tracking down a candidate's secret mistress just days before a pivotal Senate election.

Detective Jake Brogan is investigating a possible serial killer. When a second woman's body is discovered like the first—near a bridge and with no identification—Jake is plagued by a frenzied media, convinced that a Bridge Killer is hunting Boston's young women.

As the body count rises and the election looms closer, it becomes clear to Jake and Jane that their cases are connected, and that they may be facing a ruthless killer who will stop at nothing to silence a scandal. Dirty politics, dirty tricks, and a barrage for final twists, *The Other Woman* is *The Good Wife* meets *Law and Order*. Seduction, betrayal and murder—it'll take a lot more that votes to win this election.

Lisa Scottoline says "Riveting!" And Louise Penny says "Thrilling!" I'm crossing my fingers that you think so, too.

What's your writing schedule and how long does it take to write your novels, from idea to finished manuscript? And do you outline?

Prime Time took maybe two years. The others have taken maybe six months each. *The Other Woman* took a year. Sort of.

Outline? Yes. No. When I started with *Prime Time*, I had no outline. Just one of the many things I didn't understand about mystery writing. My first manuscript was 723 pages long! I had to cut 400 pages!

When we sold *Prime Time*, the publisher initially wanted two books. And they wanted an outline for the second. So I did outline *Face Time*, and although I complained the entire time writing it— it was no fun at all—it turned out to be a terrific tool. Even though the final story was nothing like the outline!

So now, I outline. Sort of. And then I write the real story—however it comes out.

Do you prefer novel writing or investigative reporting?

No way I could decide that. I love them both.

Which novelist most influenced your work? And which writer, past or present, would you like to spend some time with?

I love Edith Wharton's cynical take on the world, and the way she illustrates the social structure even while being dramatic and entertaining. Her stories have such depth and texture, and her characters are wonderful. Julia Spencer Fleming. Margaret Maron's wonderfully authentic dialogue and settings. Sir Arthur Conan Doyle for clever plots. Lisa Scottoline for her contemporary and hip take on the world. John Lescroart for story, story, story. And P.D. James.

Who would I love to spend time with? Shakespeare. I have many, many questions for him. Whoever he was. Oh! And Stephen King. What a genius, on so many levels.

Advice to fledgling writers and journalists?

For journalists: Don't be afraid and be very afraid. Be scrupulously careful. Think. And think again. Never give up.

For writers? On my bulletin board there are two quotes. One is a Zen saying: "Leap and the net will appear." To me, that means: Just do it. The other says "What would you attempt to do if you knew you could not fail?" And I think that's so wonderful—just have the confidence to carry on. Writing is tough, arduous, not always rewarding in the moment—but no successful author has ever had an easy path.

Using TV Techniques to Write A Killer Mystery

by Hank Phillippi Ryan

Here's what you need to produce a successful television story: Develop memorable characters. Build suspense. Show conflict. Tell a compelling story. Create a satisfying ending. Find justice. Change lives.

Here's what you need to become a successful television journalist: Never miss your deadlines. Be fair. Get people to tell you things they won't tell anyone else. Understand how the world works. Work with an editor. Create a brilliant and flawless product every time. Be completely devoted to your job.

As I began to write my first novel, I realized the number of parallels between writing for television and writing a mystery novel. Your primary focus is telling a great story, right? With compelling characters. And centered around an important problem. You dig for leads, track down documents, conduct intensive research and see where the clues take you. You want the good guys to win, and bad guys to get what's coming to them. You want a satisfying and fair ending—and you want some justice. And if you're lucky, you get to change the world.

Here's a new way of looking at your work as a journalist. And it doesn't matter if you've never written a news story in your life.

You won't use every idea every day. Some you won't realize you need—until you do. On those days, there are journalism-based questions you can ask yourself to prod your brain into story telling—kind of a who-what-when-where-why-and-why-not?— that may just get you out of that pre-deadline panic.

Why do I care?

If you're in a scene that seems to be flabby, or boring, or simply not compelling, it may be there's no reason to write it! Set your intention before you start the scene—what's the point of these next 200 words? Why do we care about what's going to happen next? Figure that out. It may be that you're writing a scene that you don't need. You may be writing a scene that needs to move faster, or go a different direction, or wind up in a different place.

Am I in the right place?

Not only the right place geographically, but the right place in time or space. If you've got two guys sitting around talking, or someone looking up a name on a computer, or talking on the phone, or if it's the fourth scene in a row that's taking place in an office—hmmm. Television is all about good video. Can you place your characters someplace more cinematic? What would happen to your story when you do?

Who said that?

Maybe you've got the wrong person talking, or using the wrong point of view. Putting the same scene in the point of view of a different person changes the perspective and as a result, shows you motivation in a different way. What's at stake in your scene? Who has the most to lose? Sometimes even thinking about a scene through a different character's eyes can open your own to some new ideas.

What's the goal?

Are you at the beginning of the book where you need a big compelling hook? In the middle where you need to twist and turn and keep readers turning the pages? Or near the end, when you need to ratchet up the suspense even more and come up with the big finish or happy-ever after ending? Make sure you're clear on your goal—think about what you should write to accomplish that.

What's my deadline?

Do you have time for a cup of tea, waggle your shoulders and look at a magazine? Make an appointment with yourself to return to your computer in say, ten minutes. I promise you—the moment you give up your fear and give yourself a break—knowing you've committed to return at a specific time—your brain will relax and the ideas will flow.

What if you don't have an extra second to waste? Okay, then. Just do it. It may not be pretty, but you can fix it later. Give yourself permission to be (briefly) terrible. It won't be. You'll be surprised at the quality of the words that emerge.

Whose idea was this, anyway?

Remember that day, that moment, when you first thought of your wonderful plot? You were going to have a bestseller, a blockbuster, a knockout of a book. Right? You loved it. Now, after a few months of stubborn characters and stalling vocabulary and various self-criticisms, you've lost some of that lovin' feeling. Take yourself back to the moment you had the wonderful idea. What did you like about it so much? That's still there! Fall in love with your story again.

What, me worry?

You know, every author I've ever met tells the same tale of woe. There are days when you just think—forget about it. I stink, I'm terrible, I'm a fraud, this will never work. Do you feel that way?

Well, join the club. This is how everyone feels.

And yet, there are bookstores full of books and libraries full of books and bestseller lists and daily reports of new contracts on Publishers Lunch. How does that happen? Because writers like you know it's difficult. And then they press on.

There's a motto on my bulletin board: "What would you attempt to do if you knew you could not fail?" Do that. (And then let me know how it works! I can't wait to hear.)

(You can visit Hank Phillippi Ryan at her website: http://www. HankPhillippiRyan.com and her blog sites: http://www.JungleRedWriters.com, http://www.femmesfatales.typepad.com)

Joan Hall Hovey

In addition to Joan Hall Hovey's critically acclaimed novels, her articles and short stories have appeared in a number of diverse publications. She has also held workshops and given talks at various schools and libraries, and taught a course in creative writing at the University of New Brunswick as well as her tutoring with Winghill, a distance education school in Ottawa for aspiring writers.

Joan, your writing has been compared to Stephen King and Alfred Hitchcock. How would you describe your suspense novels?

I'm always flattered to be compared with authors I admire, but I like to think my own writing is unique to me. Of course being a voracious reader all my life, I'm sure my writing has been influenced by many fine authors. We all stand on the shoulders of those who have gone before us and paved the way. I'm a big Stephen King fan. Other authors I enjoy are Edgar Allan Poe, Peter Straub, Ruth Rendell and more than I can list here. It's not easy to describe one's own novels, but I will say that I always strive to give the reader a roller coaster ride and a satisfying conclusion. And characters that will resonate with my reader long after the books is closed.

I like to write about ordinary women who are at a difficult time in their lives, and are suddenly faced with an external evil force. I didn't think a whole lot about theme until I had written a couple of books, but I realized with the writing of *Chill Waters* that my books generally have to do with betrayal and abandonment, and learning to trust again. And more important, learning to trust oneself. Almost any good book will tell you something about the author herself. (or himself.) You can't avoid it.

All my books are generally rooted in childhood. I draw on my life for inspiration and an emotional connection. Then I'm off and running. The seeds for *Night Corridor*, for example, were planted in my childhood. On Sundays, I went with my grandmother to visit an aunt in the mental institution, once called The Lunatic Asylum. She'd spent much of her life within those walls. They said she was 'melancholy'. Though the sprawling, prison-like building has long since been torn down, the sights, sounds and smells of the place infiltrated the senses of the 12-year-old girl I was, and never left. *Night Corridor* is not about my Aunt Alice, but it was indeed inspired by her.

My latest novel, *The Abduction of Mary Rose,* was inspired by a true story as well. After her adopted mother dies of cancer, Naomi Waters learns from a malicious aunt that she is a child of a brutal rape. Her birth mother, a teenager of MicMac ancestry, lay in a coma for eight months before giving birth to Naomi, and died five days later. Feeling angry and betrayed, but with new purpose in her life, Naomi vows to track down the man responsible and bring him to justice.

Are your novels all set in your home territory of New Brunswick?

My novels are set in fictional towns that could be anywhere in New Brunswick or Maine, since the flora and fauna are similar. Although I did set part of *Nowhere To Hide* (Eppie Award) in New York. I researched the city but I also spent time there. But New Brunswick, which lies on the Bay of Fundy, Canada, is part of my

DNA. And the town where I live, whose streets and hills and shops are bred in my bones, is probably in essence where all my novels are set, whatever fictional name I give them.

What have you stressed in your creative writing classes at the University of New Brunswick?

I stress to students (and myself because we teach to learn) to relax and let the story come to them. Not that you don't have to think; you do, of course. But sometimes we think too hard. Imagine, I tell them. Imagine.

Please explain the Ottawa distance education school for aspiring writers.

I have been a tutor with Winghill School for writing for over 20 years. Most of the correspondence is conducted over the Internet, though a few students prefer to correspond by mail. It's a great school. I enjoy my work and get almost as excited when my students publish as when I do, myself. I'm sure I learn as much from them as they do from me.

How has your writing evolved since your first books, *Nowhere to Hide* and *Listen to the Shadows*.

Language is important to me, and I hope my work is always improving in some way. Maybe the dialogue is crisper, the transitions smoother, the characterizations deeper, but always evolving. And that comes simply from being an avid reader of the best there is, both in my own and other genres. And writing and writing and writing. Since I both love to read and write, it's not a chore. Too, I like to think I've grown as a human being over the years. I believe I've become more insightful, more compassionate. And that reflects in your writing.

What constitutes a good suspense novel? And which is more important, character or plot?

With any novel, regardless of genre, characterization is the most important element. Without a character that readers can care about and identify with at some level, the most ingenious plot won't matter. That doesn't mean that your character is without flaws, quite the contrary. Consider the late Patricia Highsmith's Tom Ripley. He is a ruthless killer, but we are fascinated by his complexities and we're happy to follow him throughout the books.

In the end, I don't think you can separate character and plot. They are interwoven. With suspense, I am always aware of the thread in my story and I hold it taut, letting it out a little at a time, but never letting the thread go slack. It should grow tighter and tighter until it fairly sings. This is what constitutes a page-turner and it's a promise I make to my readers and one I take very seriously. Reviews tell me I've succeeded for the most part, and that makes me happy.

How has the e-book revolution affected your own work and are the electronic versions outselling your print editions?

Absolutely. It's totally different now. My first two novels were published by Zebra/Kensington Books, New York, and sold thousands of books. They didn't take the third one and I was suddenly without a publisher. I didn't feel up to doing the rounds of agents and publishers again, so I went with a small Canadian publisher, BWLPP Publishing, mainly an e-book publisher who published authors with a track record, but also bring the books out in print.

With e-books you promote in a totally different way, mainly on the Internet. Although I still do book signings in my local bookstores, I can see that my focus is different now. I'm quite sure I'll not see those big numbers again, and I really don't mind. That doesn't mean I'm not always looking for new ways to promote the books, and without annoying people. Pretty much like most e-book authors. Once, my books could be found in bookstores across Canada and the U.S. That's no longer true. Now they're available worldwide on the Internet. Sounds great, but that means that you're vying for readers with literally thousands more writers showing up every day, many of whom are self-publishing. Some of those books should never have seen the light of day. But I've also found some excellent new authors among them. We have stars like J.A. Konrath, James Scott Bell, Timothy Hallinan, L.J. Sellers and others who are making a very good living selling their e-books. So in the midst of this gargantuan storefront window, you have to somehow find a way to make your books stand out. 'Ay, there's the rub'. But the possibilities are endless.

Describe your writing schedule.

I write in mornings when I'm freshest and the day has not yet had a chance to intrude on the muses. I work on other things in the afternoon—tutoring, promoting and whatever else needs doing.

Advice for aspiring suspense novelists?

Try to write true, whatever you write. Find that truth inside the fiction. Write out of yourself. That's important.

Writing From the Psyche

by Joan Hall Hovey

"Most of the basic material a writer works with is acquired before the age of fifteen." ~Willa Cather

We're told to write with passion or write from the heart, and while this is good advice, I take it further. I suggest you write from the Psyche.

When I say that, I mean writing from those places inside your memory that stay with you, that delight you, and even haunt you. The memory can be a joyful one, like a trip to the carnival at night when you were a child, with all the lights, the smell of candied apples and french fries in the air, the musical rides, the lure of the sideshow barker. Can you still feel that excitement?

Or maybe it was a darker memory—a time when you were chased down the street by a stalker. Can you still hear those running footsteps behind you? Feel your heart thudding in your breast?

What memories haunt you?

The seeds for *Night Corridor* were planted in my childhood. On Sundays, I accompanied my grandmother to visit an aunt in the New Brunswick Provincal Hospital, later changed to Centracare, where she'd spent much of her life within those walls. I don't try to force those connections, but I do invite them, long before I begin the novel. Something that I can grasp in my writer's imagination and make something of—a kind of alchemy, turning lead into gold. At least that's the intention. I'm not aware that I'm working out childhood issues, but I'm sure they play a part. Once I begin to relive that memory, complete with sensory details—sight, sound, smell, taste and touch, I invite the character into that world. It helps that I can remember with more vividness my childhood, then I can tell you what happened last Tuesday.

When you make a connection with that memory from your childhood that is so vivid to you, so present that you can transport yourself back to that time and place in an instant, use it. It is fodder for the imagination. And it makes no difference what genre you're working in—romance, suspense, horror, whatever your cup of tea, you can make something of that memory. It's impossible to say exactly how it all works. Enough that it does. You can take that memory in different directions. Transplant it to a different time and place. Use those emotional memories as a spider uses its spinneret glands to weave a web.

So the next time you're stuck for an idea, what about that memory you could never shake?

Maybe it's time to exorcise it by using it in your next novel. Give it to one of your characters.

(You can learn more about Joan Hall Hovey at her website: http://www.joanhallhovey.com/. She's also on Facebook, Twitter, My Space and Booktown)

Ellis Vidler

Ellis Vidler's love of writing began as a child. While her parents played poker with friends, she and the other children wrote mysteries in the bedroom. Growing up in Florence and Huntsville, Alabama, young Ellis encountered a number of fascinating people and heard various stories that continue to influence her. Although she writes from imagination, she loves research and can easily follow a thread until she forgets the original subject. Her first mystery, *Haunting Refrain*, is now on Kindle. She then wrote a suspense novel, *The Peeper*, with a retired police officer. *Cold Comfort* followed.

Ellis, how did your collaboration with a former lawman, Jim Christopher, come about and do you plan to write more suspense novels with him?

Chris was a speaker at our local Sisters in Crime meeting. We became friends and he asked if I'd be interested in writing something with him. He had the basics in mind, the main characters, setting, and primary crime. It was a great experience, and I learned so much about police procedure and how detectives handle a crime scene—I loved every minute of working with Chris. Both of us were pleased with the book. It's a fast-paced suspense novel, and even though the main character does some bad things, his reasons are understandable.

The book has some explicit scenes.

When did you write your first mystery?

It was a time long ago. Something about horses and jewels, maybe a bridle set with rubies the size of jawbreakers. (Big and gaudy appealed to me at that age.) I do remember churning out pages and pages of printing on those wide-lined tablets. A slightly older friend corrected my spelling. Gee, even children have editors.

How do you conduct your research?

I have stacks of reference books, but most of the research for my books is done on the Internet. I try to verify information, such as going to the Glock manufacturer's site instead of to a gun enthusiast. The Internet is a real blessing—it's always available, whether it's the middle of the night and you're in pajamas or over morning coffee, but you do have to double check.

Has membership in Sisters in Crime helped your writing career?

Through SinC and the online groups, I've learned about agents and publishers, found all kinds of resources, and met some truly great people. Writers are generous and always willing to help. I started out in a vacuum, knowing nothing and blundering my way through. I wish I'd found Sisters in Crime earlier.

Tell us about your latest novel, *Cold Comfort*.

Cold Comfort is old-fashioned romantic suspense. When Claire Spencer, lonely owner of a Williamsburg Christmas shop, becomes a killer's target, she hires burned-out security consultant, Ben Riley, to find out why. He's sworn never to work with women again, but when Claire Spencer lands in his arms after a hit and run accident, he can't walk away. Their investigation reveals political connections to the mob and long-buried secrets, but the truth is *Cold Comfort*.

Describe your writing schedule.

It's sporadic, but definitely mornings—my brain shuts down around 5:00 in the afternoon. I work full time and during the week, it's hard to get focused and work for a couple of hours and then shut it off. Weekends are best. Once I get into the story, I lose track of time and everything else. It's a great feeling.

Has the e-book revolution affected your print book sales?

Yes, *Haunting Refrain,* my first mystery, is now available on Kindle, and it's doing reasonably well. I dropped the price to 99¢ for a week or so before *Cold Comfort* was available. *The Peeper* is still selling in e-book, but the print sales have definitely slowed. I love the convenience of e-books. It's so easy to carry several and to store them—my bookshelves are overflowing.

Advice for novice writers?

Study, study, study. Study your craft. Study grammar. And then keep writing. The more you write, the better you'll be. Just as owning a paint brush doesn't make you an artist, owning a word processor does not make you a writer. Continue to learn and improve. Persist. I'm still working on it.

To Plan or Not to Plan

By Ellis Vidler

I'm trying to make a case for outlining my story before I write. Why are some books easier to write than others? Is it because we already have the plot mapped out in our minds, and it's more like following old Route 66 across country? You can still make small side trips and stop at interesting places, but the main plot is more or less fixed and you know you're going to end up at the Pacific Ocean.

Pantsers are inclined to turn things over to their subconscious to see what happens. Sometimes the result is good, others not so much. One problem, unless you're quite experienced at storytelling is (or your subconscious is), the amount of rewriting usually required. The story is inclined to meander. Often the story sags in the middle and the writer loses direction. It can take a while to get back on track.

People who sit down and begin writing with no plan often see themselves as more creative, or spontaneous. I don't see a difference in creativity—often just when it happens, at the beginning or in spurts as you write.

The fastest and easiest book I've ever written was with a partner who had the basic idea worked out in his mind. It didn't affect the creativity or spontaneity of the writing. The details and lesser events popped up as we wrote. We changed a few things, developed more of the characters and subplot as we went, but the rewriting at the end was minimal. This experience has convinced me to try and make the switch from pantser to plotter. I don't intend to write a detailed outline, more like a synopsis in which I work out the major turning points and highlights before I start. A road map with no details.

The plot points may be like the geographical features of the country, the Mississippi, the mountains, the desert. They present certain obstacles, but each one can be complicated by events and details, the things that come into your head as you get into the story and tap your subconscious.

Complications can be as simple as running out of gas or as challenging as a head-on collision. A landslide may block the road, forcing a detour. Or you may pick up a hitchhiker. Even though you have the main plot more or less established, the conflicts and complications will make the story.

Plotting takes discipline, and for me, a quiet place with no distractions. I like to use paper and pencil (with eraser). I can doodle and jot down ideas more freely, cross out and revise, even go ahead and sketch out a scene or detail without editing myself. Of course, there are no rules. Each of us has to find what works and what doesn't for our particular personality and style. But I'm going to try plotting. I believe the story will be better the first time. And it may be easier to write.

(You can learn more about Ellis at her website: http://www.ellisvidler.com/ and her blog site: http://theunpredictablemuse.blogspot.com, and her profile at: http://profile.to/ellisvidler. She's also on Facebook.)

Cheryl Kaye Tardif

Cheryl Kaye Tardif is a Canadian author well-known for her international bestseller, *Whale Song*. She's also the author of *Divine Intervention*, a suspense thriller. Born in Vancouver, BC, she was both a military brat and a military wife, who now resides in Edmonton, Alberta. Booklist has called her "a big hit in Canada...a name to reckon with south of the border." She also writes techno-thrillers and romantic suspense, and is the publisher of Imajin Books.

Cheryl, how did *Whale Song* come about and had you published anything prior to it?

Whale Song was in my head for two years before I even wrote down the title. In fact, I wasn't even sure I was going to write it. At the time, I had pretty much given up hope on getting published; I had tried for years. But the story of *Whale Song* haunted me. I couldn't shake the characters or the plot. Finally a friend said, "Cheryl, don't worry if it gets published or not. Write it for yourself. Write it because you have to." That was the best advice I've ever been given.

Since *Whale Song*, which was first published in 2003, I've had six more novels published (*Children of the Fog, Divine Intervention,*

Divine Justice, The River, Lancelot's Lady and *Whale Song*: School
Edition), as well as a collection of horror suspense stories, and a
novelette. All of my works are available in e-book editions and all
but the novelette are out in trade paperback. I've also had a short
story published in *What Fears Become: An Anthology from The
Horror Zone.*

You've written in various genres. Which do you prefer?

Suspense is my forte. And any combination of suspense,
mystery and paranormal has been successful for me.

**Why do you think all your novels made the Canadian
bestseller lists?**

In general, readers don't like predictable, formulaic works. They'll
never have that with my novels because I strive to be unpredictable
and I don't use any kind of formula when writing my books. My
stories are a mix of plot-driven and character-driven tales. And I
bring emotion into each story, whether it's fear, sorrow, happiness,
excitement or another emotion. I want my readers to feel like they're
right there in the story, seeing everything, feeling everything.

How do you promote your work?

I have two main websites and a blog, plus I belong to various social
networks. Most of my marketing is done on the Internet through
various websites and promotions. And my books are promoted
via Imajin Books, my publishing company.

**Why did you decide to go the indie route and how long before
you began publishing the work of other writers?**

I began my career as an indie published author, self-publishing
three titles from 2003-2005. With their success I was able to secure
a New York agent and a traditional publisher. But I recognized a
lot of serious problems with my publisher early on and ended up
removing my book just before they went under. The experience

wasn't entirely negative though; I learned a lot from them—
especially what NOT to do as a publishing company.

After leaving my publisher, I decided to return to indie publishing
and set up my books once again under my publishing company,
Imajin Books. Over the next year or so I was approached by other
authors who asked me if I'd ever consider publishing them. I said no,
but it made me think. I realized there was a need for what I could
offer.

So on January 15, 2011, I opened Imajin Books to accept other
authors. We now have a great group of authors on board; some
will be publishing their second book with us this spring/summer.

How do print sales compare with e-books? And when did e-books begin outselling print editions in Canada?

Print sales are a small percentage of what we sell. Our e-books
far outsell our paperbacks. Last time I looked at the numbers we
were selling 50 e-books for every paperback. We have always sold
more e-books than print.

What's your work schedule like?

I work six to seven days a week. My hours vary, but I rarely work
less than eight hours a day and often more. I love what I do and I
take frequent breaks, so it doesn't really seem like I'm working that
long. The great thing is that I can take days off when I need them.

My schedule is divided between answering email, reading
submissions, coordinating editors and authors, assigning
covers to designers, checking back with everyone, arranging our
promotions, updating the website and blog, and anything else
that comes up.

Advice for novice writers?

Learn the business of writing and publishing. Too many writers think all they need to do is write a good story. That's just not true in today's market. If you want to be successful you need to have a firm grasp of the business, of what it takes to make your book shine and stand out amongst all others. So take writing/editing courses, join writers' groups, join a critique group (if you can't take criticism you're in the wrong business), and be sure you have a website, blog, Twitter and Facebook account BEFORE you query a publisher or agent. A book won't sell without consistent marketing on the part of the author.

Indie Publishing - The Good, the Bad & the Ugly

By Cheryl Kaye Tardif

In 2003 I began my career as a published novelist. Previous to this I had published smaller works—articles and poetry—in magazines, newspapers and one anthology. I decided to go the indie route because I was tired of trying to get published and only collecting rejection letters. It was the BEST decision I ever made.

In 2003 my novel, *Whale Song*, was released and it saw moderate success, along with two other titles, and I was able to hone my skills as an avid book marketer. I made the book signing circuit to bookstores in both British Columbia and Alberta, Canada. And I began marketing online as well.

In 2006, *Whale Song* was picked up by a small Canadian publisher. It re-released in 2007. It sold well and I surpassed 5,000 copies in sales, making *Whale Song* a national bestseller. It also made various Amazon bestseller lists, .com, .ca and co.uk, making it an international bestseller. However, the publisher began experiencing financial difficulties, along with other problems, and I pulled out. This was definitely the "bad" period for me in my career.

In 2010 Amazon opened KDP to Canadian authors and I went back to my roots—to indie publishing. For me it's probably the best fit. I am by nature very independent and a strong marketer. Plus I'm "an idea person." Even my former publisher saw this in me and often called me a "guru" or "marketing genius." While I don't consider myself a "genius" I do know that I'm a risk-taker.

It's now 2012 and I have nine e-books published—most have made numerous bestsellers lists—and eight trade paperbacks. I'm also published in another anthology, What Fears Become. And I've moved from bestselling author to publisher, a move that has surprised me yet is so rewarding that it's hard to explain. My company, Imajin Books, isn't like most publishers. We think ahead and out of the box.

I'm still technically indie published as I've published all my own titles now, but Imagin's authors are "traditionally published." We pay them advances and regular royalties. And we pay them more than most publishers. In many ways we treat our authors as if they're indie published. They have more say in their book, title, cover and trailer. We think of them as partners, even though they've put no money up front for the publication of their titles. Like I said, I'm a risk-taker.

During my career I've seen the good, the bad and the ugly. But now I see a wide window of opportunity. Those who go the indie publishing route will be successful if they have what it takes—marketing know-how and determination. What an exciting time to be in publishing! Especially if you're "an idea person" like me.

(Cheryl Tardif's websites: http://www.cherylktardif.com, http://www.imajinbooks.com. She's also on Twitter.)

Chapter Two: Crime Novels

Lawrence Block

Mystery Writers of America Grandmaster, Lawrence Block, has won four Edgars and Shamus awards. The bestselling author's wide range of characters: from private investigator Mathew Scudder, burglar Bernie Rhodenbarr, insomniac Evan Turner to assassin Keller have made him one of the most versatile crime novelists on the planet. He has also published four how-to writing books as well as short fiction and articles in *American Heritage, Redbook* and *The New York Times.*

Larry, what in your background prepared you to write crime novels?

Nothing—outside of extensive reading. After two years of college, I got a summer job at a New York literary agency as an editor. I dropped out of school to keep it, and stayed for a year. Then I went back to college, but I was already writing and selling short stories and novels, and couldn't take school as seriously as it needed to be taken. I wrote full-time, until 1964 when I took a job as an editor with a numismatic magazine in Racine, Wisconsin. After a year and a half I returned to full-time freelancing, and I haven't had honest work since.

How did Mathew Scudder come about?

I developed the character for a three-book paperback original series for Dell, at the suggestion of my agent. Dell didn't do much with the books, but the character remained alive for me, and a few years later I wrote a fourth book and Arbor House published it. *A Drop of the Hard Stuff*, released from Little Brown in April 2011, was the seventeenth novel about Scudder, so I've been writing about him for over 35 years, which I find astonishing when I think about it. He's older now, but who isn't?

How did you feel about the gender change when Whoopi Goldberg played the role in "The Burglar in the Closet?"

Whoopi was by no means the worst thing about that movie. The gender change was something the filmmakers had every right to make; it's not their job to reflect and reproduce the novelist's vision, but to make something that works as a film. Unfortunately, what wound up upon the screen wasn't very good. Whoopi's a fine actress and could have been good if she'd had something to be good in. The writer/director is the genius who gave us the Police Academy films, so what could we expect?

How did Evan Michael Tanner originate and do you plan to write additional novels about him?

I wrote seven Tanner books in the 1960s, then nothing until *Tanner on Ice* in 1998. Tanner seems to have the life-cycle of a cicada, and I figure the next book is due in 2026. I don't think there'll be more Tanner books, but I've been wrong about this sort of thing before. I never know what the future will offer.

What's the best advice you can offer novice writers?

Write to please yourself. And don't expect too much.

What's your writing schedule like and how has it changed over the years?

No schedule. Now and then I write something. Less now than

years ago.

How many writing advice books have you written?

There have been four: *Writing the Novel from Plot to Print, Telling Lies for Fun & Profit, Spider Spin Me a Web, and Write for Your Life.* I figure that's plenty.

Have you ever suffered from Writer's block?

Only in interviews.

How do you overcome it?

Doggedly.

Which writer(s) influenced your own writing and why?

I don't know. I read tons of things early on. Jazz musicians talk in terms of influences, because when they begin they try to sound like someone whom they admire. Writers try to find their own voice, which is different.

How would you like to be remembered?

I don't expect to be remembered. The world has a short memory, and that's fine. Those of us who think we're writing for posterity are deluding ourselves. And why give a rat's ass about posterity? What has posterity ever done for us?

How Quickly Things Change

by Lawrence Block

Funny how quickly things change. Since this interview, I've had three more books for writers published! Now two of them, *The Liar's Bible* and *The Liar's Handbook*, are collections of *Writers Digest* columns written after the ones collected in *Telling Lies* and

Spider; through the miracle of e-publication. Open Road brought them both out early this year, and they consist of material never before appearing in book form. They have had a nice reception, too, which is heartening.

Afterthoughts, the third book in the series, is for both writers and readers. When I arranged for Open Road to bring out forty-plus backlist titles as e-books, I found myself writing afterwords for each of them. Now there was no commercial point to this, as the afterwords would be read solely by people who'd already bought and read the book, so they were by no means a useful sales tool. But I enjoyed writing them, and nobody told me to stop.

And after I'd done twenty or thirty of them, I realized that I was writing a sort of piecemeal memoir of my whole writing life. They added up to a whole book, even though I didn't feel like someone who'd just sat down and written a book. So we put them together, called the result *Afterthoughts,* slapped a bargain-basement price of 99¢ on it...and I've found that it's getting a remarkable reception from writers.

Besides that, last year saw the publication of *A Drop of the Hardstuff,* the 17th Matthew Scudder novel, from Mulholland Books; *Getting it Off,* a novel of sex and violence which I published under the transparent pen name "Lawrence Block writing as Jill Emerson," from Hard Case Crime; and my self-published collection of all the Matthew Scudder short stories, *The Night and The Music,* with two new stories included.

A couple of years ago I figured I was ready to retire. If this is retirement, I have to say that I've made a complete dog's breakfast of it.

(You can learn more about Lawrence Block at his website: http://www.lawrenceblock.com/. He's also on Facebook.)

J. A. Jance

Bestselling novelist J. A. Jance knew from an early age that she wanted to become a writer, after a teacher introduced her to Frank Baum's *The Wizard of Oz* series. Because of her gender, she was denied creative writing courses, and she was forced to learn to write on her own. But, determined and resourceful during her difficult life, she eventually made it to the bestseller list.

Judy, when did you realize that you wanted to become a mystery writer?

I knew I wanted to be a writer from the time I was in second grade. I didn't specifically want to be a "mystery writer," but because I always read mysteries it was a natural fit.

Tell us about *Betrayal of Trust* and *Fatal Error*.

Betrayal of Trust is the 20ᵗʰ entry in the J. P. Beaumont series. It finds him dealing with an old high school classmate who is now the governor of the state. When an apparent snuff film shows up on the governor's grandson's computer, Beaumont and his wife/partner, Mel Soames, are called in to investigate.

Fatal Error: Ali Reynolds number six, finds her helping Brenda

Riley, a friend from Ali's broadcasting days, who has fallen victim
to romantic overtures from a cyber-stalker. When the cyber-stalker
turns up dead, Brenda is suspect-in-chief

**How did J.P. Beaumont, Joanna Brady and Ali Reynolds come
about?**

Until Proven Guilty, the first Beaumont book was published in 1985.
When I wrote it, I thought I was writing a one-time book. I was new
to Seattle, but the character was a Seattle native. I had to do a lot of
research to make that work, and writing from a male first person
point of view was challenging. After writing nine Beaumonts in a
row, I was growing tired of the character.

My editor suggested I come up with some other character so I
could alternate. When I wrote the first Joanna Brady, *Desert Heat*,
I knew I was writing a series but I used my experiences of being a
single parent, of living in the Arizona desert, and of working in a
non-traditional job to create her character. Ali Reynolds grew out
of seeing a longtime Tucson female newscaster pushed out of her
job due to age factors.

**What in your background prepared you to write grisly crime
novels?**

I have the dubious honor of having spent sixty days of my life in the
early seventies being stalked by a serial killer, someone who is still
in prison as I write this. During that time I wore a loaded weapon,
and I was fully prepared to use it. I used some of what I learned
from that investigation to create the background for *Hour of the
Hunter, Kiss of the Bees*, and *Day of the Dead*.

Where do you conduct your best writing, in Seattle or Tucson?

I write in both places. It remains to be seen which writing is best.
And I don't have to BE in Arizona to WRITE about Arizona. It was
in trying to turn the landscape around Bisbee into words when I
finally realized why, with the red shale hills and the limestone

cliffs, that Bisbee High School's colors are red and gray.

Who are your favorite authors and who most influenced your own writing?

I started out reading Nancy Drew by Carolyn Keene. But I read John D. McDonald and Mickey Spillane. Those were the people who showed me it was possible to write a series of books for adults.

What's your writing schedule like and do you aim for a certain amount of words each day?

Since I'm on a two-book a year schedule, I write every day. I don't have a set number of words. I'm also a wife, mother and grandmother. I like having a life.

What are the basic ingredients of a bestselling novel? And how long did it take you to reach the list?

I guess I'd say characters and plots. As for when did I make the list? Fifteen or twenty books ago probably, but making the lists is entirely arbitrary and based on decisions that are made far away from the author's effort. I don't think the books I wrote before making "the list" were of any lesser quality than the ones that have.

When did you start donating some of your bookstore earnings to charities?

Very early on. I don't remember exactly. I've been involved with the YWCA, the Humane Society, the Relay for Life and ALS research.

Advice to fledgling writers?

When I bought my first computer in 1983, the guy who installed my word processing program fixed it so every time I booted up the computer, these were the words that flashed across the screen: A writer is someone who has written TODAY! Those were words I clung to when I was a "pre-published" writer and that still resonate with me today. Today I AM a writer. I'm working on chapter five of the next Ali book.

Women of Mystery Reviews

by J. A. Jance

An editor from New York once told me, and not tongue in cheek: "Original paperback mysteries are where anyone who wants to get published can get published." Not only was I being published in original paperback, I was volunteering to give this woman a ride to a writer's conference. Talk about biting the hand that feeds you. I was not amused.

Once I was published, it was what's often disparagingly dubbed "genre fiction," I soon learned an additional ugly truth: getting mysteries reviewed in the main stream media was and is a tough sell, and it's even more so if you happen to be a mystery author who is female. When Sisters in Crime was started, one of its main goals was to monitor reviewing media and try to make sure female writers get more of a fair shake.

Time has passed and the situation is somewhat better than it was when I started. Even so, it's still not a done deal. My 45th book is due out in a couple of months. I've been on *The New York Times* list numerous times, but I've only been reviewed by them ONCE— and that was back when I was still in original paperback. In other words, I've been writing bestsellers for the better part of 30 years, but *The Times* doesn't exactly come calling on a regular basis.

As for being taken seriously by the Groves of Academe? It used to be I would say, "Forget it!" but that's no longer true. The University of Arizona Library has started a Special Collection called "Women of Mystery." The collection is devoted to the works of contemporary female mystery writers in the U.S. They are collecting the books. They are collecting papers. Someday, when some scholar wants to devote some time to studying the female mystery writers of the late 20th and the early 21st centuries, they'll have a place to go— my *alma mater.*

If you qualify and think you should be on that list, feel free to contact Carla Stoffle at the University of Arizona Library. stofflec@u.

library.arizona.edu. Carla is a lifelong mystery fan and a real champion for women mystery writers.

(You can learn more about J.A. Jance at her website: www.jajance.com. She has a blog there as well as at: http://www.seattlepi.com/blogs/city-brights/.)

Bruce DeSilva

A journalist for over 40 years, Bruce DeSilva retired to write crime novels. He also served as the writing coach for the Associated Press and was responsible for training the wire service's reporters and editors worldwide. He directed an elite AP department devoted to investigative reporting and other special projects. Earlier in his career, he worked as an investigative reporter and an editor at *The Hartford Courant* and *The Providence Journal*. Stories that he edited have won virtually every major journalism prize including the Polk Award, the Livingston, ASNE, and the Batten Medal. He also edited a Pulitzer winner and two Pulitzer finalists.

Bruce, *Rogue Island* has received rave reviews including *Publishers Weekly's* listing as one of the ten best debut novels of 2010. How long did the project take?

The reviews were something of a surprise, not so much because they were all raves, but because there were so many of them—*The Washington Post, Kirkus Reviews, The Associated Press, Library Journal, The Minneapolis Star Tribune, Booklist*, and a whole bunch more. *The Dallas Morning News* review was perhaps the most extravagant, saying the novel "raised the bar for all books of its kind." It's usually hard for a first-time novelist to get noticed, so I'm very grateful. Reviews help sell books, of course, but they have also given me confidence as I work on *Cliff Walk*, the second book in the series.

Writing *Rogue Island* took six months or fifteen years, depending on how you count. Way back in 1994, when I was working for a newspaper in New England, I got a note from a reader praising "a nice little story" I'd written and suggesting that it could be "the outline for a novel." The note was from literary novelist Evan Hunter, who also wrote great crime novels under the pen name Ed McBain. I taped the note to my home computer and started writing; but I was only a few chapters into the book when life intervened in the form of a demanding new job, a new marriage, and a child. In this busy new life, there was no time for novel writing; but each time I replaced my computer, I peeled the note from Hunter off the old one and taped it to the new one, hoping I'd return to the book someday. A couple of years ago, I finally did. Writing nights after work and on weekends, I finished the novel in six months. It was published about a year later.

What prompted your book about Rhode Island's seedier side?

I began my writing career as a reporter for *The Providence Journal*. I arrived in the middle of a New England-wide war between organized crime factions, the most powerful of them run out of a little vending machine office on Federal Hill in Providence, so I knew right away that this would be an interesting place to cover. Rhode Island, as one of my colleagues liked to say, was "a theme park for investigative reporters." I ended up staying for 13 years before moving on to bigger things, but journalism was never quite as much fun anywhere else. One reviewer called my portrayal of the state "jaundiced but affectionate," and I think that's exactly right. Rhode Island has a history of corruption that goes all the way back to a colonial governor dining with Captain Kidd, but it also has a history of integrity and decency that goes all the way back to its founder, Roger Williams.

Those two threads are woven throughout the state's history and are still present today. The tension between them is one of the things that make it such an interesting place. But that's not all. Most crime novels are set in big, anonymous cities. There are also some very good ones set in rural areas. But Providence, where most of the action in *Rogue Island* takes place, is something different. It's a claustrophobic little city where everybody on the street knows your name and where it's very hard to keep a secret. But it's still big enough to be both cosmopolitan and rife with urban problems. I strove to make the city and the state not just the setting for the book but something more akin to a main character. I never considered setting my story anywhere else.

Was *Rogue Island's* plot based on stories you've covered as a journalist?

Some of the minor incidents in the book are based on fact. For example, during the mayoralty of colorful and notorious Vincent A. "Buddy" Cianci Jr., city highway department employees really did steal manhole covers and sell them for scrap for a few dollars apiece. But the central plot of the book, the investigation of an arson spree that burned down much of the city's Mount Hope neighborhood, is entirely made up.

Tell us about your writing background.

I spent 13 years writing for *The Providence Journal*, where I specialized in investigative reporting, and 13 years working at *The Hartford Courant*, most of them as the writing coach. Then I moved on to The *AP's* national headquarters in New York. There, I ran the news service's elite team of national enterprise writers for eleven years and served as the writing coach for another three. Stories I edited won virtually every major journalism prize including the Polk (twice), the Livingston (twice), the Batten Medal, and the ASNE award. I also edited two Pulitzer finalists and helped edit a Pulitzer winner. I retired from journalism in 2009 to write crime novels, and I also continue to review them for the *AP*.

What's the most important ingredient in a crime novel?

If I must pick one thing, it's the characters. If I start reading a book and don't care deeply about the people in it after a few chapters, I toss it aside and read something else. *Rogue Island* is definitely a character-driven novel. But hey, everything matters—the plot, the quality of the prose, and don't forget the setting. As one of my crime-writer friends, Thomas H. Cook, once said, "If you want to understand the importance of place in a novel, just imagine *Heart of Darkness* without the river." For a book to be good, all of these elements must be handled well and fit together seamlessly.

Whose work influenced yours? Your most read novelist?

I discovered crime fiction by reading Raymond Chandler and Dashiell Hammett in my teens, and they remain major influences. I reread their work every year or two. As for current crime novelists, I'm a great admirer of Daniel Woodrell and Thomas H. Cook, two brilliant writers who succeed at everything except making the bestseller lists. I find Dennis Lehane's best work astounding. Laura Lippman, James Lee Burke, Kate Atkinson, and Ken Bruen often take my breath away.

I love Ace Atkins' remarkable historical crime novels and James Ellroy's staccato, high-on-amphetamines prose. To name a few. But the fact is, I'm influenced by everything I read including the bad stuff that teaches me what NOT to do. That said, the opening passage of John Steinbeck's *Cannery Row* is my favorite in all of English.

How difficult was it to acquire an agent, and how did you find the right one?

It's not easy for a first-time novelist to find an agent, but I was lucky. Otto Penzler, the dean of America's crime fiction editors and proprietor of Manhattan's famous Mysterious Bookshop is a friend of mine. He read my manuscript, loved it, then recommended me to LJK Literary Management. Susanna Einstein, one of the top agents in the business, agreed to represent me. Otto calls himself "the godfather" of my first book.

For whom do you write?

It's perilous for a writer to think too much about trends in public taste because it can be so fleeting. Right now, someone out there is working on a vampire novel that will be completed just as teenage girls everywhere lose interest in the subject. So I write for myself, telling the stories I want to tell in the way I want to tell them. The late Robert B. Parker, one of the most successful crime novelists of our time, once told me this: "You write what you can."

How important is humor in crime/noir novels?

Some crime novelists, such as James Ellroy, write great books that are unrelentingly grim. Others, such as Tim Dorsey, write slapstick-noir novels that keep you laughing from beginning to end. Most crime writers, including me, fall somewhere in between, tempering dark stories with flashes of humor. Some writers try to accomplish this with a wise-cracking protagonist, but a smart mouth is not enough. Humor shouldn't be tacked on. It should serve the story. Parker's Spenser has a smart mouth, but his put-downs reveal characters which show us his attitudes toward pretentiousness, authority, and women. In *Rogue Island*, I tried something different. Each line of humor in this dark story is there to reveal the character's world view. But a writer must beware of anything that falls flat. The trouble with humor is that it has to be funny.

Advice to aspiring crime writers?

A. Don't quit your day job. For every bestselling author like Harlan Coben or Chelsea Cain, there are hundreds of writers whose books sell only a few thousand copies—or don't get published at all. I know, I know. I said I quit *my* job to write crime novels; but I worked in journalism long enough to have a decent pension; and my wife, an award-winning poet and college professor, makes more than enough to support our family.

B. Don't even think about trying to write a crime novel without first reading at least a thousand of them. Each time you find something you admire, study it to figure out what the writer did. Read books the way teenage boys of my generation tinkered with cars, taking them apart and putting them back together again to see how they worked.

C. Don't procrastinate. Put your butt in the chair and write. Ignore your email, stay off Facebook and Twitter, forget that your favorite sports team is on TV, and don't ever use writer's block as an excuse. I spent 40 years working as a journalist. Journalists aren't allowed to have writer's block. They get paid to write every day, whether they feel like it or not. They know that writer's block is for sissies.

D. Don't allow yourself to be overwhelmed by thought of writing a whole book. It's not nearly as momentous a task as you might think. If you write just 800 good words a day, which is damned little, you can finish an 80,000-word crime novel in 100 days.

A Writer's Unique Voice

by Bruce DeSilva

Every story speaks to the reader in a voice. When you read, you *hear* the writer talking to you. You may think of reading as something you do with your eyes; but in a sense, you read with your ears.

The writer's voice has everything to do with whether you enjoy the story, stick with it to the end, or ever want to read something else by that writer.

A few years ago, I asked Robert B. Parker, one of the most successful crime novelists of all time, why his books were so popular. Readers love them, he said, "for the same reason they love certain songs."

They love the way the language *sounds*.

A lot of writers, even professionals, have trouble with voice, however. Why?

We are bombarded by bad examples. We read a lot of poorly written stuff every day, and that can make us think it's how writing is supposed to be.

We sometimes misunderstand our relationship with our audience. No matter how many thousands of readers you may have, you must always speak to them one at a time. Never write as if you are talking to a crowd. Reading, after all, is a solitary act.

The voices of the best writers are unique. You should be able to identify a passage by, say, Elmore Leonard or Laura Lippman, even if the name of the author is concealed.

How can you find *your* unique voice as a writer?

For some of you, it's just a matter of giving yourself permission to sound like yourself in print. You already have a voice. You just need to use it.

For others, finding your voice requires experimentation. It may sound counterintuitive, but I suggest that you begin by imitating writers you admire.

When I was starting out, I went through my Hemmingway period. And my Raymond Chandler period. And my Hunter Thompson period.

Through this experimentation, I was learning craft—the techniques these writers used to fashion their sentences and paragraphs. As my technical abilities grew, my own voice eventually was able to emerge.

You've probably heard that you should write like you speak. Don't. Very few of us speak well enough to do that. Writing should have the *feel* of a good conversation, but there are differences between written and spoken language. The most important one is feedback.

When I say something to you, your reaction tells me if I'm boring you or if you don't understand. In written language, I don't get that kind of feedback, so I have to provide it myself by reading my work out loud. Anything that doesn't sound good isn't good. No exceptions.

(Bruce DeSilva's website: http://brucedesilva.com/ and his blog site: http://brucedesilva.wordpress.com/. He's also on Facebook and Twitter.)

Diane Fanning

Diane Fanning writes crime novels as well as true crime. Her book, *Written in Blood*, was an Edgar nominee and featured on the TV program, 20/20. Her research led to the release of an innocent woman from prison, who had been convicted of murder, and among her true crime books is the infamous Caylee Anthony murder case, *Mommy's Little Girl*.

Diane, how did you correspond with serial killer, Tommy Lynn Sells?

I sent my first letter to Tommy Lynn Sells after I acquired an agent and a contract to write about his crimes. In my first letter, I told him I was writing a book and requested a visit with him. At the time, he had been transferred from Death Row to the Bexar County Jail in connection with the murder of Mary Bea Perez. After that visit, at the end of September 2001, the correspondence continued.

I interviewed him face-to-face nearly twenty times at the jail and on Death Row before June 2002, when he wrote the first letter that indicated his possible involvement in the murder of Joel Kirkpatrick. He made additional remarks in another letter two weeks later. I visited him on Death Row that July and he provided additional information.

What prompted Sells' confession to you? And did you believe the boy's mother was innocent all along?

At the end of May, I stumbled across an ABC Prime time show about the Joel Kirkpatrick murder case. I heard Julie and her family and friends claiming innocence. I was highly skeptical. And then the show presented comments from the prosecuting attorney. It was what he said that made me doubt Julie's guilt.

Among other things, he said they knew there was no intruder because they found no stranger fingerprints at the scene and because an attacker would come with a weapon, not use a knife found in the kitchen. I knew the things the prosecutor was saying were not true. Many killers leave no fingerprints; many use a weapon found in the home—including Tommy Lynn Sells. It was after listening to the state's attorney that I tended to believe that someone like Sells could have been responsible for the crime.

I wrote to Sells about the ridiculousness of the prosecutor's statements. I did not name the attorney; I did not name the victim, the city or the time frame or mention Julie Rea Harper. Sells wrote back asking if the murder occurred on the 13th of October, two days before he killed Stephanie Mahaney. It did.

That was the first moment that I thought that Sells might be involved. However, at that point, I only doubted Julie's guilt and also suspected the possibility of Sells' involvement. I was not certain of either.

Three months after the release of the book in July 2003, Bill Clutter, an investigator for the Innocence Project at the University of Illinois at Springfield, found corroborating evidence—three witnesses who had seen Sells in the small town of Lawrenceville on the weekend of Joel's murder. Revelations of botched crime scene processing—no one dusted for fingerprints, for example—along with overlooked and untested evidence and other information were then revealed. After learning more, I became totally convinced of

Julie's innocence and nearly certain of Sells' responsibility for the murder of her son, Joel.

When did you become interested in crime fiction?

I have been an avid reader of crime fiction for decades and have been interested in writing it since before I wrote my first true crime. My first success at obtaining a book contract was in non-fiction but I maintained my interest in fiction. At the time, I had a full time job as the executive director of a non-profit organization and struggled to handle just one genre. Once I was able to leave my day job, I had the time to also write my first love: crime fiction.

Has your college chemistry major served you well when writing crime fiction?

I was a science major because that was what I was supposed to do. My real love was writing and I pursued that instead. I first wrote commercials for radio, television and magazines along with freelance articles and personal essays.

A science background is definitely useful in writing about the increasing complexities of forensic investigation.

Tell us about the Lucinda Pierce crime novel series.

Lucinda Pierce is a homicide detective in Virginia. She bears facial scars from a domestic violence incident that are a reflection of the childhood emotional scars that drove her into law enforcement. She feels isolated from the world because of her physical and psychological injuries but is fighting to overcome those obstacles in her life.

She is tough, but not invincible; demanding but empathetic—a strong female protagonist with flaws and feelings.

There are five books in the series: *The Trophy Exchange, Punish the Dead, Mistaken Identity, Twisted Reason,* and *False Front.* You can read the first chapter of each of these books on the Reading Room page on my website.

For whom do you write?

Primarily, I write for my readers. But if you mean who are my publishers, the answer is that my true crime is through St. Martin's Press, my fiction through Severn House.

Do you outline your novels and true crime books?

When I was seeking my first contract to write true crime, I had to do an outline within my proposal to the publisher. However, once I'd started writing the book, I essentially ignored the outline. I don't outline any of my books from start to finish. I do sometimes outline short portions of the book while the writing is in progress when I feel a need to arrange and solidify my thoughts.

How did you acquire an agent and how long did it take to find the right one?

I spent two years unsuccessfully looking for an agent. When I found the right one, at the right time with the right material, I had an agent within 24 hours of submission.

Advice to aspiring writers?

Read like a maniac. You can learn something new from every genre, no matter what you are writing. And keep writing—practice makes us all better at what we do. Most important of all, never, never, never give up. Approach each rejection as a challenge to overcome—the right material at the right time to the right person can happen if you write with passion and commitment.

SPLIT PERSONALITY

by Diane Fanning

Maybe it's because I was born on a cusp. Or maybe it's because my moon is in Gemini. Or maybe, simply, because I'm just not right. But I find myself very comfortable leading a double life. I feel at home assuming two writer identities—one in non-fiction as a true crime writer, another in fiction as an author of mysteries. I seldom get confused about which hat I'm wearing, except when, like many writers, I forget that my fictional characters are not real people.

My dual authorship, however, seems to befuddle a lot of folks. Some assume that because I've started writing fiction, I will stop writing true crime. In fact, I regularly get email from my True Crime fans pleading with me to continue writing those books. I have no intentions of abandoning that genre. Working in two worlds teaches me something new nearly every day and makes me feel complete and fulfilled.

The first lesson I learned was that writers need to be voracious readers of every genre. I learn something about the craft from every book I read, no matter the genre or area of focus. A writer can pick up a useful tool from a nonfiction book to add uniqueness and complexity to a fiction endeavor. Although constrained by reality, you can learn much about plotting and character development in a novel that can be applied to true accounts to keep the reader turning pages. Most important of all of these lessons, in my opinion, is the value of suspense.

Anything and everything that you read needs a strong element of suspense—something that keeps your reader turning the page because you've raised questions in your readers' minds and made an unspoken promise to provide answers. Take a simple children's book like *Are You My Mother?* by P.D. Eastman. Despite the cute drawings and continuous repetition, the book contains a very existential question about identity. And Eastman promises an answer by the time the book ends.

Another benefit of having a split personality as an author is that it fulfills so many of my loves and needs in life. Writing non-fiction gives me the pleasure of digging with abandon into infinite piles of documents, musty newspapers and vignettes of history.

There are some opportunities for research in writing contemporary fiction but you must always be on guard to not let it consume your writing time. With a True Crime book, the research is the life blood of your work.

Additionally, in writing non-fiction, I have to speak to a lot of different people in diverse walks of life for assistance in the research aspect, for interviews, and for observation in various settings—there is simply no end to the one-on-one contact. And, in general, I really like people and enjoy the social interaction in the work sphere.

Finally, with True Crime, I know that I can make a concrete and positive difference in people's lives. There is nothing more fulfilling than a mother telling me that one of my books saved her daughter's life or getting an email from a domestic violence center which finds one of my true accounts important and an essential read or knowing that one of my books helped obtain a new trial for a wrongfully convicted woman. It doesn't get much better than that.

Fiction writing, however, satisfies different needs. At times, I crave solitude and there is nothing more solitary than working week after week crafting and polishing a novel. It gives me a break from reading autopsy reports, looking at crime scene photos, crying with victims' family members. It's an escape to a welcoming world where I, as a person, cease to exist.

Writing fiction also provides an outlet for limitless expressions of creativity. In my non-fiction world, I am tied to facts, constrained by circumstances, bound tight by the truth. With fiction, the facts are of my choosing, the circumstances of my making and the truth only what I say it is and nothing more. If I don't like the bad news in chapter four, I simply re-write it. If I don't like my main character's new best friend, I cut her from the manuscript. If someone is really getting on my nerves, I bump them off using any method I want without causing any grief to real people.

With a foot in fiction and another firmly planted in non-fiction, it might sound as if I am straddling a great divide. But to me, it feels like one place—a world of my own. I cannot imagine living anywhere else.

(Diane Fanning's websites: http://www.dianefanning.com/, http://dianefanning.blogspot.com/, and her cooperative blog site: http://blogs.forbes.com/crime/. She's also on Facebook and Twitter.)

Craig McDonald

Craig McDonald's novels were called "Ingeniously plotted and executed," by Michael Connelly. "*Print the Legend* is an epic masterpiece from beginning to end. I was riveted by this story of character, history and intrigue." McDonald's books have been referred to as "The most exciting series of crime novels currently on the market." His *Rogue Males* was also nominated for the 2010 Macavity Award and his latest, *Print the Legend*, may be the most intriguing of all. Was Ernest Hemingway murdered or did he commit suicide?

Craig, why your fascination with Ernest Hemingway and could his death have been a homicide?

Hemingway, for me, is the most important writer of the 20th Century, not necessarily in terms of what he wrote, so much as the profound and lasting effect his writing has had on the craft from about 1926 onward. He liberated the language and reinvigorated the American novel, doing more than any other writer, I think, to shake off the dead hand and non-native qualities of the European novel that dominated and distorted American letters prior to Hemingway's arrival.

As to the circumstances of Hemingway's death, I tend to view it as a kind of assisted suicide. If his last wife didn't pull the trigger on Hemingway, she all but loaded and handed him the gun in terms of giving him access to weapons that had previously been locked away from the man.

Tell us about *Print the Legend*.

Print the Legend explores the possibility that Hemingway fell prey to a conspiracy or conspiracies tied directly to his writing, and, chiefly, to the FBI under the direction of J. Edgar Hoover. Hoover made it a priority to spy on and, really, to stalk, a number of key writers including Pearl S. Buck, Rex Stout, Dashiell Hammett, Robert Frost, and, for many years, Ernest Hemingway. In *Print the Legend*, crime novelist and Hemingway friend Hector Lassiter, also a target of FBI surveillance begins poking around the circumstances of Hemingway's death.

What's the biggest difference between crime and mystery novels?

The designation "mystery" places a certain obligation on the author to actually satisfy a kind of puzzle imperative and that such books are typically expected to be more plot than character driven. "Crime novels," to my mind, are squarely focused on character and more concerned with the impulses that lead to crime, and its aftermath. I think it's telling, too, that we—or at least publishers and book designers—attach the word "novel" behind "crime," but you rarely see or encounter the phrase, "a mystery novel."

How do you categorize your work and which novelist(s) influenced your writing?

I consider myself a novelist with a tendency to center books around crime(s). My first two books were published by Bleak House, which touted itself as an imprint of dark literary fiction. In terms of my novels to date, the series was very much inspired by James Sallis' Lew Griffin series.

Why two prominent female characters in your series? Is it because you enjoy writing about women or because there are more women readers?

While I think *Print the Legend* offers two very strong female characters, actually the only consistently recurring major characters (to date) in the series have been Lassiter, Hemingway and Orson Welles. I think women too often tend to be props in genre efforts— and not just in the books of male authors. Conversely, a number of female authors frequently tend to use their male characters as props or as kind of romantic hitching posts. I just try to put fully realized characters on the page, male or female. The next novel, *One True Sentence*, introduces the only major female character to date to appear in more than one book. This particular woman is the one who really shapes Hector into the character we've come to know through the first three novels.

How important is an agent to a fledgling writer's career?

You only get one shot at a debut novel in terms of major awards consideration—which can boost or accelerate your prominence as an author. Self-publishing undermines those advantages. It's virtually impossible to secure a publishing deal with any significant house without representation. As to acquiring an agent, it's a matter of writing worthy material and stubbornly putting it out there to potential agents. There's no secret handshake or club, although it can sometimes seem that way when you're on the outside looking in—a perspective I was well acquainted with...for years.

Do you carefully outline your novels or do you "wing it?"

If I outlined a novel I'd never write it. I really believe that. I have a beginning, an end, and maybe a few set pieces in the middle. It's mostly improvisation.

What constitutes a good crime novel?

For me, character development. I demand a strong character arc when I'm reading a book. And I want a series character who evolves and ages. I don't want to read the same book over and over.

Advice to aspiring writers?

Read good books, and a range of books. And write to your passions. The key is to write material only *you* can write.

What Makes a Writer's Work Endure?

by Craig McDonald

Love of craft. Fierce dedication. Focus. These qualities typify our best writers.

When it comes to genre, I draw a line between "mysteries" and "crime novels."

I regard a mystery as plot-driven. The crime happens and the story kicks in. Nobody seems to get *really* hurt. A world of bloodless murders.

There tends to be very little character arc in these sorts of books. What happens in one book doesn't spill into the next.

In a crime novel, character *drives* plot.

It's been said in a *mystery* novel the detective works the case. In a *crime* novel the case works the detective.

In my second novel, I incorporated my own definition of the kind of writing I value and strive to attain. I gave the words to my author protagonist:

"Character is plot. Obsession is motivation. The quest, whatever else it may appear to be, is always a search for self—a race against time to a blood-spritzed epiphany. When that light bulb goes on, the world goes dark. No happy endings."

Somewhere in such books, a crime occurs. That's all that's necessary to set the character, and by extension, the plot, in motion. By that standard, *The Great Gatsby* is a crime novel. Ditto Hemingway's *To Have and Have Not*. Shakespeare could be called a historical thriller writer.

Mystery fiction tells a story straight up. Crime fiction is novelistic. There's a famous passage penned by an inspiration of mine—an author who had a huge influence over other authors including Michael Connelly, Laura Lippman, Dennis Lehane and George Pelecanos. This writer came out of the Iowa Writer's Workshop before turning from literary fiction to crime fiction.

The line is the opening passage of James Crumley's novel, *The Last Good Kiss*. Mr. Crumley passed away a few years ago. Nearly every tribute and obituary printed about him quoted this opening line, noting its importance to crime fiction and inspiration to authors, everywhere, in- and out-of-genre, including Pete Dexter who often cites it as one of great opening lines in all of fiction, not just *crime* fiction.

Final Version of the Opening line of
The Last Good Kiss
by James Crumley:

When I finally caught up with Abraham Trahearne, he was drinking beer with an alcoholic bulldog named Fireball Roberts in a ramshackle joint just outside of Sonoma, drinking the heart out of a fine spring afternoon.

FIRST DRAFT VERSION:

When I finally caught up with Mr. Vernon Moody, he was drinking beer in the middle of the afternoon with an alcoholic bulldog named Winston in a ramshackle beer joint just outside Sonoma, California.

Generally, they are the same, but I think we can all agree the final version is the superior one. The distance between those two takes on that "same" paragraph? Purportedly, it's eight years.

Love of craft. Fierce dedication. Focus.

That's what makes a writer's work endure.

(You can learn more about Craig McDonald at his website: http://craigmcdonaldbooks.com/)

Geraldine Evans

English crime novelist Geraldine Evans has published nearly 20 novels. Her two series, Rafferty & Llewellyn and Casey & Catt, are written concurrently and are fast-paced, filled with humor as well as plenty of plot twists.

Geraldine, did growing up in the London Council Estate affect your writing?

It was great fun, mostly, as I had lots of playmates, at least on the first estate, though we moved from there when I was about eleven. I suppose, looking back, what strikes me most about it now was the lack of aspiration. I didn't know anyone who'd been to university, for instance, or even anyone who had those hopes. As to how it affected my writing; it certainly affects my main character's family background—not for him an intellectual, educated background of the middle-class writer. DI Joe Rafferty has more street wisdom than the academic sort. I suppose the amazing thing is that I started writing at all. I have no real idea from whence this desire came, but I had it in spades and nineteen published novels later, it's still going strong.

Did working in a library pique your interest in writing?

I don't know if the job itself did so—though the fact that I could borrow as many books as I liked without having to worry about paying fines—must have helped. But I was always a reader. My mother encouraged me and my three siblings to read and we've all kept the habit up, though I'm the only one who ended up as a writer. Like Colin Dexter, I remember one day reading a particularly bad novel and thinking even I could do better. It must have planted a seed, of knowing I could do this—even though, at that time, no publisher agreed with me! It was a matter of persevering and seeking out criticism so that I could improve. Eventually, after my sixth completed novel, I was published.

That was in 1991. The book was a romance entitled *Land of Dreams* and the publisher was Robert Hale. I started my Rafferty & Llewellyn crime series after Hale rejected my next effort in the romance genre. Much to my amazement, *Dead Before Morning*, that first crime novel, was plucked from Macmillan's slush pile and published in hardback and paper-back, both in the UK and in the U.S. I brought it out as an e-book in December 2010.

Does England's class system affect your readership, and for whom do you write your novels?

I suppose it does. I don't write books that are particularly intellectually "clever." I aim to amuse and entertain and have never striven to amaze with my brilliant mind! No *Times* crossword type puzzle for me—I haven't the intellect for it as I left school at sixteen. I simply aim to do what I do best and for what I am best equipped. The humorous sub-plots are as much what my novels are about as the main crime plot. I suppose I write for people much like myself: working-class readers, who like a bit of fun in their crime novels.

How did your Detective Inspector Joseph Rafferty and Sergeant Dafyd Llewellyn come about and how do you research your crime novels?

I think Rafferty's "Ma" came about first and Joe Rafferty evolved from that—a London-Irish lad trying to stop his Ma impinging on every aspect of his life as Irish mothers were—are?—wont to do. I wanted to depict a working-class copper as a bit of light relief from the clever but dull policemen depicted in some crime novels. As for Dafyd Llewellyn, he evolved because I wanted someone who would be a complete foil to Rafferty; someone who was a stickler for the law and morality, in a way that Rafferty wasn't. Although that's not to say that Rafferty isn't a moral person. He is. He's just a little more understanding of human nature and all its frailties (particularly his own).

The need for research varies tremendously, I find. Some books, such as *Deadly Reunion* needed very little, just the normal forensic stuff. Others, such as the two books in my Casey & Catt crime series, required a lot more, mostly Asian religions and customs in *Up in Flames* and cannabis farming in *A Killing Karma*.

I've found the internet very useful for research. I also have an endlessly updated library about forensics, police procedure, world religions, poisons, scene of crime, etc. I'm rapidly running out of room, so I thank God for e-books, though some of my favourite research books are as yet unavailable as e-books.

Tell us about your Casey & Catt crime series.

The Casey & Catt crime series is another series that utilizes plenty of humour. The main characters are Detective Chief Inspector Will (Willow Tree) Casey and Detective Sergeant Thomas Catt. It is set in the fictitious town of King's Langley in Norfolk, England. Casey's parents are a couple of old hippies, Moon and Star Casey. Thomas Catt, an orphan, spent his childhood in various children's homes.

So far, there are two novels in the series: *Up in Flames* about a death by fire in the Asian Community and *A Killing Karma* about two unreported suspicious deaths in Casey's parents' hippie commune, which, for various reasons, they expect Casey to sort out. I really ought to write another one or two books in this series, but my publishers prefer my Rafferty & Llewellyn series, so I don't know when I'll produce the next.

Why is humor important in your work as well as other crime novels?

I've always had a lively sense of humour and suppose I was a bit of a class clown. Anyway, as a reader, I found some crime novels as dull as ditch-water and wanted my own first effort to be a bit more lively. Not just a straight mystery, but a bit of fun and games as well. And, as most writers who know will tell you, humour is regarded as one of the hardest types of writing to do. That fact has never worried me—you either have a natural penchant for something or you don't and humour was, I thought, one of my strengths. I think the use of humour in crime novels adds another dimension. The reader gets more for their money, whether it's my crime novels or Brookmyre's. It's important in other crime novels because it's what I, and many others want to read.

Who's your favorite novelist and who most influenced your own novels?

I can't say that I'm aware of a particular influence. Though since starting my own Rafferty & Llewellyn series, I've found the novels of Christopher Brookmyre, Cynthia Harrod Eagles and Ruth Dudley Edwards strongly to my taste. They're all very witty writers and I admire that. These three figure amongst my favourite novelists. I also like P.D. James, Mark Billingham and the Inspector Wexford novels of Ruth Rendell, though I've never got on with her psychological novels. I enjoy the novels of Dorothy Simpson, Margaret Yorke and June Simpsons.

Tell us about your latest novel, *Death Dance*.

In this one, Detective Inspector Joseph Rafferty has just left his wedding rehearsal when Sergeant Dafyd Llewellyn calls. Llewellyn tells him that a local man has come home to find his wife dead on the kitchen floor. She's been strangled. Adrienne Staveley is a woman with secrets and several lovers. Was she killed by her husband in a jealous rage? Or maybe her stepson, driven by hate and teenage angst has killed her? Or maybe one of her lovers did the deed?

To Rafferty's horror, the fingerprints of Abra, his fiancée, are found in the murder house. What had she been doing there? She'd never mentioned knowing Adrienne. And what were her prints doing in the bedroom of John Staveley? Is Abra guilty of having an affair even before their marriage? Or is she a murder suspect? Rafferty isn't sure which he would prefer. But with only a few weeks till his wedding and honeymoon he has to work against the clock to find the killer and, hopefully, exonerate Abra, before he has to cancel both.

Advice to aspiring writers?

Don't follow the crowd. Last year's hot ticket will have often gone out of favour by the time you finish your effort. Find out what matters to you, what you feel passionately about and write about that. And when you've written your book, don't immediately send it out to agents and publishers. Give it a chance in the marketplace and have it professionally criticised. This is not a cheap service, but nothing worthwhile is ever cheap. It could raise your chances a lot, so don't spend the money on a holiday instead. This is you investing in your future. Don't regard is as an extravagance. It isn't. Nor is it an indulgence. It's getting your career off to the right start. So don't stint. Ask for recommendations from writing friends or consult the writing reference books like *The Writers' Handbook* and *Writers' and Artists' Yearbook*.

E-Book Adventures

by Geraldine Evans

I first started down the e-book route in September 2010. I'd read a lot about it on various lists, like Murder Must Advertise and DorothyL, not to mention the ubiquitous J.A. Konrath, who's an evangelist with a missionary's zeal for e-books and indie publishing.

I didn't find it too difficult to get my first book up on kindle; to format the book I used the services of a lady who had been recommended to me. The books had already been edited. All they needed was for me to thoroughly check through them for formatting errors and correct them. Then, once the e-formatting was done and the book returned to me in mobi format, which is the format required by amazon's kindle, I uploaded it and the cover I had commissioned to kindle's KDP platform. It was a slow start. I sold the grand total of seven books that first month. But I persevered and uploaded a second to which I owned the rights on kindle. Soon my sales had climbed to two figures. Exciting stuff.

As I said, it's been a slow process, but sales have gradually grown. They jogged along until February/March 2011 when they rose from 139 to 316 a month. This huge increase followed my February blog tour, which clearly pushed the figures upwards. The blog tour was hard work, but it was worth it in terms of sales returns. As of November 2011, my sales figures have grown to four figures a month. Not a lot compared to Konrath and Amanda Hocking, of course, but still, a vast improvement for a mid-list author who'd have been doing well to sell that many in a *year*. As Konrath so often says in his blog, why take legacy publishers'17.5% royalties when, instead, you can take 70% from amazon? In 2011 I had to make the decision whether to stick with my publisher who wanted the e-rights to my backlist for the lower royalty rate, or go with amazon. It was no contest.

Countless others have found the road to an income that comes from taking the e-book route. It's worked for me. There's no reason why it wouldn't work for you, too. If you want a recommendation for an e-formatter or cover artist, simply ask for this information on one of the writer lists I've mentioned. There's always someone— usually several someones—ready to give you a name or two. It's where I found my e-formatter and I'm very pleased with her work.

Suffice to say, I can recommend e-publishing to anyone. It's given me the income that has eluded me for so long. I'm grateful to Amazon for giving me the chance to self-publish and for giving me the income that puts an end to the years of scrimping and scraping. Three cheers for Amazon!

(You can learn more about Geraldine Evans at her website: http://www.geraldineevans.com and her blogsite: http//wwwgeraldineevanscom.blogspot.com. She's also on Facebook and Twitter.)

Chapter Three: Police Procedurals

Leighton Gage

Leighton Gage writes the Chief Inspector Mario Silva series, crime novels set in Brazil. His work has been praised by *The New York Times, Booklist, Library Journal, Kirkus* and a variety of other publications as well as numerous online reviewers.

Leighton, why have you traveled to various parts of the world during periods of upheaval? Were you a working journalist?

No, it wasn't journalism. It was curiosity—and wanderlust. My maternal grandfather was a Yankee sea captain, like his father and grandfather before him, and when I was a little kid he used to sit on my bed and regale me with stories about the places he'd been and the things he'd seen. He introduced me to a poem from Kipling, a stanza of which became my mantra:

> It's like a book, I think, this bloomin' world,
> Which you can read and care for just so long,
> But presently you feel that you will die
> Unless you get the page you're readin' done,
> An' turn another likely not so good;
> But what you're after is to turn 'em all.

That was some sixty years ago. I have spent the years since trying to turn all of the pages.

Why did you decide to settle in Brazil and set your novels there?

I'm a Brazil nut. I went there first in the mid-seventies. I was supposed to stay in São Paulo for two years. But, in a sense, I never left. I fell in love with the country. And then, somewhat later, I fell (even more deeply) in love with a girl. She became my wife. She and I have been together now for thirty-three years. She's the great love of my life, my constant companion, my soul mate. Oh, we go away every once in a while. Two years in Australia in the eighties. Nine months last year in Paris. But we always go back. It's our base, our anchor. The language we speak at home is Portuguese. I know Brazil better than any other place and, believe me; I know a lot of places. So, when I sat down to write a crime novel, it just came naturally.

Tell us about your Chief Inspector Mario Silvia crime series.

Mario is a federal cop. In Brazil, there's no DEA, no ATF, no Secret Service, no Customs and Immigration Service and no Department of Homeland Security. Most police departments don't have internal affairs departments, but all of those functions, and more, are within the purview of the Brazilian Federal Police. And their mandate is national. So Silva and his colleagues get to travel all over the country and deal with every conceivable kind of crime. That gives me opportunities to make each one of the books very different. Example: *Blood of the Wicked*, the first in the series, deals with issues like liberation theology, and the land wars, the battles between the haves and have-nots. *Dying Gasp*, the third, deals with the sexual exploitation of minors in Brazil's northeast, while book four, *A Vine in the Blood*, involves a serial killer and is a more conventional mystery.

What prompted you to begin writing? And for whom do you write?

Don't we all want to write books? I always did. It just took me a half-century or so to sit down and get to it.

I originally thought I was writing for a male audience. Then I toured the first book and discovered what I should have known all along. Most mystery fans are women. Discovering that had an effect on what I write. I've toned down the graphic violence, and I've introduced an element of romance.

As to why I write, remember what Samuel Johnson said? "Anyone who writes for anything except money is a fool."

Yeah, that's what I thought too. I wish it were true. But with the pittances we writers earn, I gotta admit, I do it for glory.

Your novel, *Every Bitter Thing*, sounds intriguing.

Every Bitter Thing begins with the murder, in Brasilia, of the son of the Foreign Minister of Venezuela. It's a high-profile crime, with diplomatic overtones. Chief Inspector Mario Silva of the Brazilian Federal Police is under considerable political pressure to bring the case to a speedy conclusion. And, initially, because there is an obvious suspect with a strong motive, that seems likely to happen.

But then it's discovered that similar murders committed with exactly the same (somewhat unusual) M.O. have been committed in other cities in the country. And it turns out that the solution of the mystery isn't simple.

I might add that all four of the big trades (*PW, Kirkus, LJ* and *Booklist*) have chosen to review it and all four responded most favorably. (Yeah. Even *Kirkus*.)

What's your writing schedule like?

I get up in the morning, check my emails, do an hour on an exercise bike and get down to it. I write until about two, have lunch with my wife and take a nap. After the nap, I write some more and knock off at about 7:00 p.m. We dine very late, often as late as ten, and seldom go to bed before one or two in the morning. I don't write on weekends, except for the blog I do with five other writers who set their stories outside the United States. I also blog with a dozen other writers on the Murderous Musings blog.

Have your family members served as first readers or sounding boards during a work in progress?

Never. I believe that good books aren't written. They're re-written, and re-written. So I don't like to plague anyone with my scribblings until an editor gets through with me.

How difficult was it to find an agent?

Probably the toughest thing I've done in this business. In comparison, writing the first book was easy. I shudder to think how much tougher it must be now that the bottom has dropped out of the market. But, ya know, I truly think there's an agent out there for everyone. You just have to find her (him). And that may mean you're going to have to query a couple of hundred people. Seriously. A couple of hundred. If you're a new writer, and you hit the jackpot within the first dozen or so, consider yourself blessed.

Advice to fledgling crime novelists?

I've read the advice of the other authors to whom you've asked this question. All of them are right—in part. You do have to read at lot, write a lot, persist, persevere and be committed. But, if I was sitting down with an aspiring writer, just the two of us, I wouldn't presume to answer the question without knowing:

(a) Whom I'm talking to and (b) What kind of a writer they want to be.

And those are questions, Dear Fledgling Crime Novelist, that only you can answer. Early on, in this interview, I inserted a quote from Kipling. Rudyard, as most of us know, was the poet of an empire, a man of the world, a social lion, who traveled everywhere, met everyone. He was widely-read in his lifetime. Kipling was the youngest recipient (ever) of the Nobel Prize for Literature.

Contrast him with Emily Dickinson. Emily the introvert, the recluse, the woman who led a solitary life, never made close friends, hardly ever traveled at all, never married, lived out most of her life in one small town. If I was sitting down with Emily, and she told me she wanted to write an international thriller, my advice to her would be to steer away from it. Kipling might have been able to do it, probably could have. But Emily? I doubt it. I'd suggest she stick to cozies.

Reality Check

by Leighton Gage

Do you want to be a published author? Here's what you're up against:

Almost without exception, traditional publishers accept submissions only through agents. A good agent averages 100 queries a day and asks for manuscripts from only one out of every 1,500 authors who send her a query. For every 500 manuscripts she receives, she chooses to represent only one. And there's no guarantee she'll be able to sell it.

In my genre, about 2,500 books are published by royalty-paying publishers each year. Only 2% sell more than 5,000 copies, which is not a great result. Sell less, and you run a grave risk of being "dropped."

These days, no author can survive two "flops" in a row and find a new home for her work. Why? Because the first thing a publisher will do, when they're thinking of taking on an established author, is check her "performance" on *Bookscan*. They want *commercial* successes, not *critical* successes.

Advances, these days, are nothing to write home about. One agent remarked recently, "five thousand is the new fifty thousand." Forget about quitting your day job. Most writers have to start out writing for a pittance, in the hope of getting established. Ah, but that's all changed now, hasn't it? Now it's the era of self-publishing? The gatekeepers have been overrun? The citadel of big publishing has fallen?

Don't you believe it!

Self-publishing is *not* the answer, despite what Joe Konrath (http://jakonrath.blogspot.com/) would have you believe. It's true everyone can self-publish their work. But that's just the problem. Everyone can—and far too many people do. For every John Locke and Amanda Hocking, there are thousands who have tried and sunk without a trace. But do we hear about them? No, we don't. Failure interests no one, so it doesn't get much press.

A year or two ago, if you offered your work for 99 cents, the lowest price Amazon will accept from an individual author, you had a good chance of obtaining some significant sampling of your work. Not great sales, mind you, just sampling. But these days, everybody and their brother/sister is offering books for 99 cents. And a lot of good work sinks without a trace.

My advice?

Get yourself established in the "old-fashioned" way: by getting an agent who will find you a "legacy" publisher. Are the odds against you? Sure. They always were. Can you do it? Yes, you can. People do it all the time. Is it ever too late? No. I published my first book at the age of 65, and I've just sold my sixth to the same publisher. Good luck!

(Leighton Gage's website: http://leightongage.com.
He blogs at: http://murderiseverywhere.blogspot.com/ and http://murderousmusings.blogspot.com/)

Alafair Burke

Author Alafair Burke "is a terrific web spinner" who "knows when and how to drop clues to keep readers at her mercy," according to *Entertainment Weekly.* Her two series feature NYPD Detective Ellie Hatcher and Portland Deputy District Attorney Samantha Kincaid. A former prosecutor in the Portland, Oregon, DA's office, she currently teaches criminal law and procedure at Hofstra Law School in New York.

Alafair, what prompted your two series?

I was a prosecutor in Portland, Oregon, for several years. After leaving to move to New York, I missed my office. I missed Portland and my friends. And as a long-time mystery reader, I had always wanted to write a crime novel. I thought I'd finally learned enough about the world to give it a try, so I started with Samantha Kincaid, who is a prosecutor in the very office where I served.

By the time I was working on my fourth novel, I'd been living in New York for a few years. I thought the anonymity that comes only in a city this big was exciting territory for me as a writer. I was also ready to write a faster paced book with an investigator, instead of a lawyer, at the center. I had a story I wanted to tell that involved

Internet dating, and I thought a young New York City detective was the perfect narrator. I actually meant for *Dead Connection* to be a standalone, but I knew when I wrote the final chapter that I'd still be hearing more from Ellie.

How do you write two crime series while serving as a Professor of Law at Hofstra University?

I honestly don't know how anything gets done. I Facebook, Tweet, and eat constantly, yet at the end of the year, I usually have a book and a couple of law review articles on my computer. I do try to write every day, and very rarely miss two days in a row. That continuity makes a big difference. Even if I only write a couple of paragraphs on a busy day, I can jump in the next day, fully aware of where I am in the story, how my characters' voices sound, and how they feel in that moment.

Tell us about your latest release.

I'm very excited about *Long Gone*. It's my first stand-alone thriller. I guess I said that about the first Ellie Hatcher book, too, but this time, I think I really mean it. And it's the first time I've written about a character outside the criminal justice system.

After a layoff and months of struggling, Alice Humphrey finally lands what she thinks is her dream job managing a new art gallery in Manhattan's Meatpacking District. Everything seems perfect until the morning Alice arrives at work to find the gallery gone— the space stripped bare as if it had never existed— with the man who hired her dead on the floor. Overnight, Alice's dream job has vanished, and she finds herself at the center of police attention with nothing to prove her innocence. There's also a missing girl from New Jersey, a rogue FBI agent, and Alice's nightmare family running around the pages, but I promise it's all one story.

This is a higher concept book than my series novels, and sometimes those don't end as successfully as they start. I'm proud of how all the threads come together here, though.

How much of an influence on your own writing was your father, James Lee Burke?

With a father who was writing and mother a librarian, we were a family that not only told stories, but thought it was perfectly natural to write them down. My mother would take me to the library every Saturday for a new stack of books. The rhythms of storytelling and character creation become ingrained when you read all the time.

Advice to fledgling writers?

Read a lot. But don't try to copy anyone. Figure out what you can offer the genre. And then write every single day–without starting over–until you finish. Once you have a beginning, middle, and end, it is much easier to make adjustments than you'd ever believe. The hard part is getting it done.

How do you think the e-book revolution affected major publishers' marketing practices?

I'm a bit like the ostrich in the sand on this one. Or a kid with fingers in ears saying, "La, la, la, I'm not listening to you." I try to focus on the books and appreciate the readers I have instead of figuring out the business. That said, my sense is that publishers were more panicked two years ago than they are today. They still believe that writers need a conduit between them and retailers (whether electronic or paper). In my case, they are really pushing the idea of growing my readership through e-books. For example, they've officered *Angel's Tip* for $1.99. (See how I worked in that plug. Wily, huh?)

What has brought you the most satisfaction?

Knowing that someone is reading your work is a grand high. When I hear from readers who say they stayed up all night because they couldn't put down one of my books, I still want to scream out loud.

Any publishing regrets?

I don't believe in regrets. Maybe my very first book would have been better if I'd cut back on some detail, but debut novels are detailed for a reason. New writers share some of the same habits. I like to think that every book I've written has been better than the rest. As someone who cares more about the longevity of my publishing career than dollars and cents, that makes me pretty content.

Finishing a Book

by Alafair Burke

I just finished my book and I've been in a position to use that glorious sentence eight times. The first seven times, I spoke the sentence immediately after typing the final period on the final page.

I even typed THE END to mark the moment.

Did that mean I was completely done with my work on the book? Of course not. My agent and editor needed to read it. I would listen to their good feedback. I would make changes, some of them big. The book would be better for it. And then we'd do another pass and copyediting. But that's all editing. The book was "finished," as I use that word.

With book eight, I typed an ending a month ago, but, for the first time, I didn't type THE END. I didn't say, "I just finished a book." Instead, I paused a moment to celebrate having a beginning, middle, and an end. Then I opened a new, blank document on my computer and I started again from the beginning.

Yep, I rewrote my book. Now, a month later, I'm willing to say I finished. I even typed THE END. Having to reach an ending twice before typing THE END got me to thinking about what made this time different.

1. Why wasn't the first ending the finish line?

I don't generally tinker and refine on my own. I type THE END and send it away. But I've been able to do that because I force myself to get it right—or at least my own best version of right—the very first time. I nitpick at myself constantly during the first (and only) draft.

For this book, I decided to let all that go. I made myself write, even when I knew a certain scene or a certain plot twist wasn't exactly right. It's not a process I would have been comfortable with seven books ago, but I've learned by now that finishing sooner is better than finishing later. I've seen for myself—seven previous times—how much better a book can be once you finish that first pass of editing. Plus I heard Michael Connelly say it, so it must be true!

2. Why I called it a rewrite

In my previous seven edits, I made some pretty big changes. But I made those changes directly to the document. I cut and pasted if I switched the order of two scenes. I added chapters. I deleted entire pages. Overall, the narrative arc of the plot and characters remained intact.

This time, I decided that an "edit"—even a big edit—would not suffice. I wanted to start with a blank document. I wanted to revisit every decision I had made the first time around. I would reimagine the book with more information than I had months ago. I'd pull over scenes, character, words, sentences, paragraphs, and entire chapters only as helpful. I'd skip the rest. I'd write new scenes and characters as I went.

Two characters completely left the page. One arrived a hundred and fifty pages earlier. An affair that happened suddenly didn't. When I reached the ending of this new book, I knew it was better. I knew I was proud of it. And I knew I was actually done.

I'm not certain I'd recommend this process to anyone else. The messiness of it has me wishing once again that I could outline a book chapter by chapter, scene for scene, prior to writing. But at least I'm able to say that I have finished my eighth book and am very happy with it.

THE END

(You can learn more about Alafair Burke at her website: www.facebook.com/alafairburke-books. She's also on Twitter.)

Martin Edwards

Martin Edwards is a Liverpool solicitor who writes English crime novels. A member of the Murder Squad, he is also chairman of the nominations sub-committee for the most prestigious crime novel award, the CWA Diamond Dagger, as well as the archivist for the Crime Writers Association.

Martin, tell us about the Murder Squad.

It's a group of six Northern UK crime writers, set up by Margaret Murphy. Members include Ann Cleeves and Cath Staincliffe, who have both had their books televised in recent years. We do events either jointly, in duos, or singly, all around the UK. We've produced an anthology, ingeniously entitled *Murder Squad*, and a CD sampler of our work. We have a website, www.murdersquad. co.uk and I'm proud to be part of such a super gang.

How do crime novels in the UK differ from those written in the U.S.?

Difficult to generalise, I think. We have plenty in common, and I am certainly delighted with feedback on my books from the U.S. Americans like Deborah Crombie write very good crime novels set in the UK. Lee Child is a Brit who sets his bestsellers in the

States. I suppose that there are fewer good private eye novels in the UK, and perhaps not quite as many serial killers–though we are catching up!

Did you write as a child and what was it like growing up in Knutsford, Cheshire, England?

I was born in Knutsford, made famous as Elizabeth Gaskell's *Cranford* (a Victorian era novelist and short story writer), though in fact I grew up a few miles away in Northwich. I still live close by. It's a terrifically attractive market town, packed with history and there's plenty of culture too. I've featured the town briefly in one novel, and more extensively in a short story featuring Mrs. Gaskell. I did write as a child. I think my first detective story was written when I was about 10, heavily influenced by Basil Rathbone's Sherlock Holmes films.

Are you still practicing law in Liverpool, and how has your legal background influenced your novels?

Yep, I still have the day job. My first series, featuring Harry Devlin, also a lawyer, was set in Liverpool, a truly unique and fascinating city which everyone should visit! The most recent book, *Waterloo Sunset*, is a personal favourite. My legal background influenced a standalone novel of psychological suspense, *Take My Breath Away*, but it is less relevant to the Lake District Mysteries, although sad to say, a lawyer does meet a very unpleasant fate in *The Serpent Pool*.

Tell us about your crime writer organizations.

I was elected to the Detection Club a couple of years ago, which was gratifying, because of its fantastic history and the fact that all the members—except me—are superstars of the genre. I've been a member of the Crime Writers' Association for over twenty years, and I edit their annual anthology. I'm also chair of the CWA Cartier Diamond Dagger nominations committee. It was via the Northern Chapter of the CWA that the members of Murder Squad first met. It's a very good social organisation.

Why does your informative blog site have the title, "Do You Write Under Your Own Name?" And has your blog increased book sales?

Glad you like the blog! When people—such as clients—meet me and learn that I write books, they often ask if I write under my own name. A polite way of saying they have never heard of my novels! I'm sure blogging has been good for my profile. Since it started I have won a Dagger and been elected to the Detection Club, but I'm not sure it's cause and effect.

Tell us about your series and your latest novel?

My main current series is the Lake District Mysteries. The first book in the series, *The Coffin Trail*, was shortlisted for the Theakston's prize for best crime novel of 2006. The series features cold case cop DCI Hannah Scarlett and the historian Daniel Kind. The developing relationship between them is a key element in the series, and so are the landscape, history and literature of the Lakes. The fourth and latest book in the series is *The Serpent Pool*, which draws on Thomas De Quincey's years in the Lakes and above all on his fascination with murder as a fine art, has received terrific reviews since publication earlier this year.

What's your writing schedule like?

Overloaded! I work full time, so I tend to write whenever I can snatch a few minutes in the evening and at weekends.

Advice to fledgling crime writers?

Keep at it, and don't be disheartened too much by rejection.

Developing Characters and Their Relationships

by Martin Edwards

You often hear it said that "character is plot." I'd put it a little differently. Relationships between the characters in a novel are crucial to building a plot. This applies to novels of all kinds, I believe. It's certainly true of crime novels, even in those where there is a very strong focus on plot–whether a whodunit plot, a "will he get away with it?" plot, or any other.

So a key challenge for writers is not only how to develop a particular character, but also how to develop his or her interactions with other people in the story. It's worth mulling this over before pressing finger to keyboard, but I'm not sure it's a good idea to try to map out everything at the synopsis stage.

When I planned the Lake District Mysteries, I decided that at the heart of the series would be a developing relationship between the two protagonists. Daniel Kind is an Oxford academic, a historian with a troubled personal life, who downshifts to the Lakes as a means of escape. Hannah Scarlett is a detective chief inspector, in charge of the Cold Case Squad. Their shared interest in the past is a bond, as is the fact that Hannah was close to Daniel's father, who abandoned his family and left home forever when Daniel was young.

The relationship between the two characters is established in the first book in the series, *The Coffin Trail*, and moves on in *The Cipher Garden* and *The Arsenic Labyrinth*. There is a strong attraction between Hannah and Daniel–but the snag is, they are honourable individuals and they are already in relationships with other people.

I gave a lot of thought to this set-up before I started work on the first book. It seems to have worked, since *The Coffin Trail* reached the final short-list of six for the Theakston's Prize for best crime novel of 2006, along with books by Ian Rankin and Val McDermid. But I didn't try to map out the detailed course of the couple's relationship in minute detail, or anything like it. It's not so much a matter of letting the characters do as they please, but rather of building an infrastructure for the series and then weighing up how things might develop between the couple as they become involved–in varying ways–with trying to solve one mystery after another. Along the way, they find that solving the mystery of how to live a good and fulfilling life is the toughest challenge of all.

Does this sound as though a modern crime series is rather like a soap opera? Perhaps it's a good comparison. From reviewers and readers alike, I've had more positive reaction to the slow-burning relationship between Hannah and Daniel than to any other aspect of my books–even the complex and, I hope, ingenious plots on which I lavish such care!

(You can visit Martin Edward at his website: http://www.martinedwardsbooks.com/ as well as his blog site: www.doyouwriteunderyourownname.blogspot.com/)

Pat Brown

Canadian native, Pat Brown, discovered Southern California and wrote a number of mysteries based in the City of Angels, although her plots are far from angelic. Her novels, including her latest, *Between Darkness and Light*, are written as P.A. Brown.

Pat, you've published quite a few novels within the last few years. How did that come about?

The first book was published in 2006. I followed that with what was to be book two, but around that time my agent quit agenting and my editor was let go. Book two was rejected. Then, in 2007, I became really sick and ended up in the hospital for six months. I had to learn to walk again and was put on disability. Once I was out of the hospital and could pretty well take care of myself I still couldn't work, but I could write. So I sat down and did just that. I rewrote book two, which became *L.A. Bytes* and wrote another book in the series, *L.A. Boneyard*.

Meanwhile, my book went out of print and around that time e-books were starting to take off so I approached a new e-book publisher I knew and asked if she wanted to release *L.A. Heat*, book one, as an e-book. She did and I wrote *L.A. Mischief* for her too. MLR picked up the series plus some other stories I had been working on, including my vet story.

Why did you leave home in London, Ontario, Canada, for Los Angeles?

I grew up in a family that moved all the time. My father was in the Air Force so he was always being transferred. I lived in four places before I was five. So I think I was bitten by the travel bug. I started writing scripts in my late teens and at 22 I knew if I wanted to do anything with that, I needed to be in L.A. This was decades before the Internet made it possible to write anywhere. To get to Los Angeles, I sold everything I owned—including two motorcycles—and took the Greyhound bus to California. My family thought I was insane, of course, and I probably was—who moves from a city of less than 300,000 to a city of four million total strangers? I was young and indestructible.

What prompted your first book?

My very first book was written when I was 17, and thank goodness it was never published. At that time I was reading books like *Steppenwolf* and *Electric Koolaid Acid Test* and I loved music groups like the Rolling Stones, Iron Butterfly and Wishbone Ash, so even then I was interested in the darker side of things. This "book" was an angst ridden story about a young girl who becomes attached to a jaded rock musician and is led into a world of drugs and sex, which destroy her.

How did your debut novel come about?

L.A. Heat was my first published book. It was also my first mystery. Before that I wrote science fiction. Since then I have written four other books in the series, the latest *Bermuda Heat*, which pays homage to my two years in Bermuda.

My latest novel, *Latin Boyz*, is probably my most daring novel so far. The main character is Gabe, a 20-year old Latino in Cypress

Park, an east side barrio, who is struggling to protect his family from local gang activity. Their mother was killed by gangbangers and in the same drive by, his younger sister was left brain damaged from a bullet. Gabe's life is hard enough, taking care of his feeble uncle and sister. He doesn't need any more complications, like falling in love. Especially after he falls in love with a man, who also happens to be an LAPD patrol officer.

Why the love affair with Los Angeles?

From the first minute I set foot in Los Angeles, I experienced something I've never felt before. I felt more alive and filled with possibilities. There were things here that I'd never seen or experienced. To give you an idea, I had never seen a Mercedes or a Rolls Royce. London, where I grew up, was actually a very wealthy city, but wealthy people in London, at least, didn't showcase their wealth.

I never saw a black person until I was in high school. But I had also never seen the kind of homeless people that filled downtown L.A. at that time. People walking around with three or four coats on and pushing shopping carts full of what looked like garbage to me. London doesn't have slums. There might be a street here or there where there are more drugs or very poor people. There *are* homeless people, but nothing so visible as what I saw there. And while I lived there, I saw it all—I went to Beverly Hills, the gates of Bel Air, Skid Row and everything in between. It was beyond fascinating. It was incredible. How could any writer not fall in love with such a place?

Why did you decide to write gay male mysteries?

A lot of the time I was in L.A. I spent living with, drinking with and making friends with gays. I also had discovered Jonathan Kellerman and his Alex Delaware series, with Milo Sturgis, his openly gay LAPD homicide detective. When I decided I wanted to try my hand at a mystery—and I really wasn't sure I could do it, since I don't plot worth a damn—I wanted there to be a gay cop who was the main character, not a side kick. I wanted to explore how an outsider would fit into an organization that only years earlier had a chief who publicly said there were no gays in the LAPD. What's it like to live a lie every day? I'd never heard of police procedurals, all I knew was I didn't like the soft cozies like Agatha Christie, but the way the police worked fascinated me. I liked grittier fiction. I was also a huge fan of Robert Ludlum back then and later Michael Connelly and Robert Crais as well as newer authors, Stephen Jay Schwartz and Robert Ellis.

What's the best part of writing and the worst?

Best when I'm in the zone. When the words are coming and the story is flowing. Then it's the closest to heaven as I've ever felt. I'm also one of those people who loves the editing part. The worst is when the words won't come, when I can't write a word or think of plot or characters. I've grown in the last few years as an author and those moments are no longer so troubling. I know all I need to do is to give my mind a break. Read a fiction book—which I rarely get to do anymore—have a drink with my daughter, or lounge around watching bad movies. I have a particular fondness for disaster and evil alien movies. Sometimes the cheesier the better.

What's your writing schedule like?

It really depends. If I have a deadline or the writing bug has taken over, I'll write for hours, only moving to eat. I try to get to the library at least once a week to do research and write without interruption. Lately, I've started writing historical novels and now have an agent who is working to sell a two-book series set in the late 1880s in New York and early 1900s in California, so my research needs are greater. Last May I was accepted to the Dorland Mountain Arts Colony, in Temecula, California. It's a writing retreat where I can spend two weeks away from TV and the Internet to focus on my writing projects. While I'm there, I'll be researching the area for future stories. I also have a novel set during Prohibition in Los Angeles, a really wild time in my favorite city—that needs work.

Advice to aspiring writers?

Be persistent. It takes a certain amount of stubbornness to be a writer. To ignore the rejections you will get both from publishers and agents, as well as from family and friends. To date I've had three agents, five publishers and I'm on my 13th published book.

If you want to be a writer, write, keep sending your work out, ignore the naysayers. But also finish what you start. A lot of wanna be writers start any number of great stories, but when the writing stumbles they put the story aside and start another one. Finish a book. Then finish another one. Don't write one book and spend a year submitting it. Send the first book out and write another. When that's done write another one. Always be open to learning and to criticism, at least the kind you get from other authors.

The other thing I strongly recommend is write what you want to read. Don't try to write whatever is big at that moment, thinking it will be instantly snapped up. Chances are by the time you see a trend, it's already waning. You need to find something you are passionate about. A story you need to tell. For this reason I think you should also read a lot. You never know where an idea will come from. Read anything. Even now, I'll go to my library and look through the new books, or the special displays they put up throughout the year. I pick up magazines I would never normally read—science, business, history, psychology, whatever catches my eye—and sometimes reading them will trigger an idea. Your mind should be a sponge, soaking up ideas and details of the world around you.

"Never Give Up, Never Surrender"

by Pat Brown

New writers studiously collect and read how-to articles online, in writer's magazines and in the hundreds of books published on the subject, in the belief that there is some secret that all published writers know and if only they could find it, they'd be published too. I'm afraid it's not true. There is no magic wand that can transform you from unpublished to published. The process is the same for everyone, for some it takes longer than others. Even when the dream is realized, it's not the end. You publish one book, one short story or perhaps an article. The next one is not a shoe-in. You might get more consideration for having been published, but you can just as easily be rejected again.

It took me 33 years between the first unpublished book I wrote at 17 to having my first book published when I was 50. In that time I wrote at least eight novels that were not published, in some cases probably weren't publishable. But each one was a learning experience that I built on until I produced a book that someone wanted. But after that there was more rejection. The second book in the L.A. series was rejected and I ended up taking it elsewhere, to a small, independent publisher, which was a step down from the New York publisher I had started with.

I'm still glad to be published by them and until recently continued with them. But I still want to break back into the New York publishing world. To that end I've been pursuing an agent for the last two years. I signed with one who loved the book, but couldn't sell it. I finished a second book and from that signed with a new agent. All of this was after over 300 rejections between both books. That's 300+ times I've had to read 'Sorry, not for us'. But it hasn't stopped me.

So why do it despite all the rejections? Every writer has to find their own reasons. I do it because I can't NOT write. Whether or not I get published, I will always write because the stories and characters are in me and have to be told. With that compulsion I will keep writing no matter what. And each project I work on will be better than the last one.

As a new writer, only you can decide if this path is for you. No one else can make that decision or stop you from trying. If you want to write, despite the odds, then I say go, write.

My motto comes right out of Galaxy Quest—"Never give up, never surrender."

(Pat Brown's web and blog site: http://gkparkernoir.com/, her journal: http://pabrown.livejournal.com, She's also on Facebook and Twitter.)

Marilyn Meredith

Marilyn Meredith is the author of more than thirty published novels, including the award-winning Deputy Tempe Crabtree mystery series. She writes her Rocky Bluff P.D. crime novels as F.M. Meredith and under her own name for the Deputy Tempe Crabtree series. She's a member of four chapters of Sisters in Crime, including the Central Coast chapter, Mystery Writers of America, and is on the board of the Public Safety Writers of America.

Marilyn, why do you write?

Writing is part of my life, like breathing. I enjoy creating a story and seeing where it's going to go. I love connecting with my readers either by way of the Internet or in person at promotion events.

When did you start writing?

I began creating stories before I could write by drawing pictures in what some might call a story board today. As soon as I began reading real stories, I began writing my own. I've been writing ever since in one form or another.

How do you feel about the e-book revolution?

I've been electronically published for over ten years. Most small presses publish e-books as well as trade paperbacks. There have been e-readers around for years, and now with the Sony e-Reader, Amazon's Kindle and Barnes and Noble's Nook, e-books have really come into their own. Even some of my older books are now on Kindle.

What's your writing schedule like and how long does it take to write one of your novels?

My goal is to write every morning at least three or four hours. It doesn't always work out that way because when I have things that have to be done, that weighs heavy on my mind. My writing will work better if I clear my desk–or computer, as the case may be. If I don't have too many other projects going, I can finish a book in three months. Of course that doesn't count the rewriting. Most books I usually read to my critique group too, a chapter at a time.

Do you outline your books or wing it? And do you have the ending in mind when you begin writing?

I don't outline in the true sense of the word, but I start collecting ideas first. Then I decide on characters–who will be the murder victim, if there is one. In the book I'm writing now, I don't think anyone's going to die or don't know who the murderer could be. Usually several folks have a motive and the opportunity. Then I write something about each of those characters so I can get to know them. When I start writing I think I know how the book will end, usually the final climax scene, but as I write that often changes. I do keep notes along the way as I think of things I want to put in.

Do you visit the actual settings of your books?

In my Rocky Bluff P.D. series, I'm relying on my memories of living near the beach for twenty years. In my book, *No Sanctuary*, the two churches are similar to ones I've gone to in the past–but the ministers are totally made-up. I've lived a long time so I can reach back into my experiences for a lot that I write about.

For my Deputy Tempe Crabtree series, I've done a lot of research about Native American culture and visited the reservation and the casino. My most exciting research happened when I discovered that the Tule River Indians (who I write about but call them a different name) believe in a Big Foot like creature called the Hairy Man, and that there are pictographs of him and his family on the reservation.

I've talked a couple of times to the anthropology class and when I asked the professor about the pictographs he invited me to go on a college field trip to see them. What a wonderful experience! The pictographs are hidden away. To get to them you have to climb down huge slippery boulders. Fortunately, the college kids helped me get down there and back up again. The Tule River Indian who guided us told us some wonderful legends and stories of sightings of the Hairy Man. The Hairy Man is in the Tempe book that was released during the fall of 2009, called *Dispel the Mist*.

Who most influenced your work?

Once I joined a critique group, about 30 years ago, I met a wonderful author named Willma Gore who helped me more with my writing than any other person. Willma wrote and still writes for all sorts of publications and has had several books published, both fiction and non-fiction. She taught me more than any writing class or conference I ever attended.

Favorite author and why?

I have far too many favorites to even list them. Jan Burke has always been one of my favorites. I started with her Irene Kelly series and just kept on reading. I've met her several times, and she's a sweet person as well as a good writer. Betty Webb is another. She's tackled a social issue that has plagued Arizona and now she's changed gears a bit and started a new, lighter series. I admire her courage—and she's also a nice person.

Some men that I really like to read are William Kent Krueger and James Lee Burke, and I love the way both of them describe settings.

Advice to fledgling writers?

Read what you want to write. Learn the basics of writing. Write every single day. When you are done have someone who knows what to look for edit your book. Join a critique group. And when you have begun the submitting process, start writing another book. Do not let rejections stop you. Over the years I've met several gifted writers who were discouraged after one or two rejections. My first book received nearly 30 rejections before it was accepted. Over the years, most of my books have been rejected at least once, some several times. Rewrite when necessary.

Novel Settings

by Marilyn Meredith

I judge a lot of writing contests and read many books by new writers who have self-published. I often see the same problem—a lack of setting. It's very disconcerting to read about two or three people having a conversation or doing something in an unmentioned location. I want to know where people are while they're talking. Are they in a kitchen? If so whose kitchen and what does it look like? What does it smell like? So much can be added to what's going on by including the setting.

Setting is important. Readers like to learn about new places whether they are real or fictional. If you're going to use a real place be sure you are accurate when describing places and how to get there. If you aren't, someone will let you know about your errors.

If you make up a place, be sure to keep track of where you put things, the names of the places, and the geography. If it's in a certain place in a particular state, be sure to have trees and flowers and geographical details that are true to that area.

What's in the location and setting can add another dimension to your story. Think about the obstacles your character will face and what's around him or her.

Don't forget weather. Weather can add to the tension and the atmosphere of the story. Decide on the time of year for your tale and what kind of weather goes along with it in the area you've placed your characters.

Smells can add a lot too. Take a deep breath every time you enter someone's home. What does it smell like? What about when you're in the city? Or the country? You are always surrounded by smells, use them in your writing.

And when is your story taking place? Is it a period piece? If so, be sure to be accurate about the technology that is or isn't available, what is going on politically and historically, what kind of clothes people wear and foods they eat.

If it's present day, let the reader know right away. Have your characters use the technology that everyone uses today—unless of course, one of them absolutely hates cell phones, or won't touch a computer as one of his character traits.

My Deputy Tempe Crabtree series is set in the southern Sierras of California. The town of Bear Creek has a definite resemblance to the town I live in though I've moved it a 1,000 feet higher in the mountains—giving the area better trees and the possibility of more snow in winter. Another reason I wanted to change the name of the town was because businesses change too often in my town. By the time a book came out where I named a particular restaurant it might be closed.

Nearby is the Bear Creek Indian Reservation which is quite similar to the Tule River Indian Reservation that is close to where I live. In *Bears Are Us*, Tempe doesn't have a reason to visit the reservation though she does in several of the other books in the series. I do use some of the Tule River Indian's legends in my books.

Obviously, there are bears in *Bears Are Us*. We have an occasional bear visit at the lower elevations—but placing Bear Creek at a higher elevation makes it more plausible that bears would become a nuisance and in some cases a threat.

Deputy Tempe Crabtree has her hands full when bears turn up in and around Bear Creek, a young teen commits suicide and his parents' actions are suspicious, a prominent woman files a complaint against Tempe and her preacher husband, Hutch. A love affair from long ago comes to light, and a woman suffering from dementia disappears.

(Marilyn's website: http://fictionforyou.com and her blogs: http://marilynmeredith.blogspot.com, http://thestilettogang.blogspot.com and http://makeminemystery.blogspot.com.)

Bob Sanchez

Bob Sanchez is a former Massachusetts technical writer who has written five novels and acquired three agents. One small press went out of business before it could publish his book, *Little Mountain*, so Bob self-published three novels: *When Pigs Fly, Getting Lucky*, and *Little Mountain*. The first is a comic road trip, the others conventional murder mysteries.

Bob, why did you decide to publish independently?

Many people told me they were surprised my work didn't sell to royalty publishers, and I felt confident my novels deserved publication. I became impatient with the long process in seeking the approval of agents and publishers who were all complete strangers. Rather than spend the rest of my life hoping to see my work in print, I decided to publish and take my chances. Given the general reputation of self-publishing, that wasn't an easy decision.

Do you upload your books online or hire someone to do it for you?

After my novel, *Pigs Fly*, went online using iUniverse as an intermediary. I then e-published *Getting Lucky* and *Little Mountain*, myself.

Would you now sign with a royalty publisher if you were offered a contract?

A royalty publisher won't offer me a contract because I won't look for one. Should an offer fall out of the blue I'd consider it, but I do enjoy having control over the process.

How did your novel, *When Pigs Fly*, come about?

I wanted to write a funny novel. My earlier efforts had been serious stories set in the mill city of Lowell, Massachusetts, but after my wife and I vacationed in Arizona a couple of times, I thought it would be fun to move my hero to the Tucson area. A couple of Arizona friends helped with the geographical details.

What's the most difficult aspect of self- publishing?

Knowing when your book is ready. Agents and editors perform a critical service by weeding out work that isn't ready for prime time. On the other hand, some good material gets left behind. It's difficult to be objective about your own work, so you have to get trustworthy and competent peer critiques. Also, you are responsible for everything from proofreading to marketing. That's a tough range of skills to master.

Who has done your printing and have you been satisfied with the results?

iUniverse published my first two novels, and I published *Little Mountain* using Amazon's CreateSpace. I will *not* go back to iUniverse because they are too expensive and maintain too much control. For example, they insisted on my charging $9.99 for an e-book.

How do you promote your books?

Other than a few book signings, I don't promote in bookstores. I tried that and it took much too much time and energy. Mind you,

I live in the Southwest, where everything is spread out, making indie book tours unprofitable. So I am experimenting with mainly online marketing.

How much time do you spend networking?

So far just a few hours per week, but I plan to do more.

Advice to aspiring indie authors?

You are completely responsible for the quality of your work right down to the smallest detail. Ask peers to critique your work but remember that you are the final judge. Take all comments as suggestions, then decide for yourself. Spelling, capitalization, and grammar all matter, though. Get those right. Double and triple check everything. Hire a reasonably priced artist to design your cover.

Tips for Independent Publishers

by Bob Sanchez

We self-publishers fight a lonely battle, finding readers for our wit and wisdom. We write alone, and now we sell alone and search for ways to market our work. How do we entice readers to open their wallets?

Those questions are often premature. Before asking how you're going to cope with all those book orders, you need to make sure you have a quality product. So here are ten tips to make your book, fiction or non-fiction, the best it can be.

1. Use a spell checker, but only as a first line of defense. Then you look for misspellings the spell checker won't catch, such as then/than, to/too/two, tail/tale, or its/it's.
2. Read your manuscript critically, as though you weren't the author. Some things to check for include complete chapters and sentences, well-organized paragraphs and accurate punctuation.

3. Be consistent. If you capitalize a word once in the text, chances are you always want to capitalize it. Decide whether you want one space or two at the end of a sentence, and stick with it. Never change your font or type size without good reason. If your work consists of more than one file, be sure that every file is formatted identically.

4. Get honest, competent critiques. Leave your mother and spouse alone. Your family has better things to do than fawn over your work, but also avoid critiques from anyone who has an emotional stake in making you happy. That's not what you need. An excellent source of constructive, informed criticism is available at The Internet Writing Workshop and can be found at: http://internetwritingworkshop.org.

5. Use your judgment. Even good critiquers may give you conflicting advice. Remember that it's *your* project, so the final decision is always yours.

6. Refer to a style manual such as the *Chicago Manual of Style*, which is the most widely accepted guide for standard writing.

7. Make a style sheet. A novel or other large manuscript can involve lots of small stylistic decisions to be made by the author. Keep a pad of paper with a running list of things you don't want to have to keep looking up. For example, a cartoon I liked showed a bank robber writing a note and asking the teller, "Is holdup one word or two?" Think of words you often misspell or don't know how to capitalize, and write them correctly on the list.

8. Follow your publisher's guidelines religiously even if they don't insist.

9. Repeat tip #2.

10. Review the publisher's proof carefully. When you receive the publisher's proof isn't the time to look for typos; you should have done that already. At this stage, the publisher may even charge you if you fix many of your own mistakes. Instead, look for the publisher's errors. Are illustrations in their proper places? Are pages and chapters numbered properly? Look at every page's overall appearance. Is each one properly

aligned? Is any text missing?

If you follow these simple (but not always easy) tips, I can't guarantee best-sellerdom for your book, but I can promise you this: Your book will be far superior to the vast majority of self-published books. You will have a quality product.

(Bob's blogsite: http://bobsanchez1.blogspot.com.
His books are available at:
http://tinyurl.com/bobsanchezauthor.)

Maryann Miller

A diverse writer of columns, feature stores, short fiction, novels, screenplays and stage plays, Maryann Miller has won numerous awards including semi-finalist at the Sundance Institute for her screenplay, "A Question of Honor." She also placed in the top 15 percent of entries in the Chesterfield Screenwriting Fellowship with the adaptation of her mystery, *"Open Season."*

Maryann, why do you write police procedurals? Do you have a background in law enforcement?

No, I don't, but I have always been fascinated by police and crimes and law enforcement. Maybe I *am* a frustrated cop. I fell in love with the genre when I started reading the 87th Precinct series by Ed McBain, Evan Hunter's alter ego. I liked the ensemble cast and the way he intertwined the personal and social issues with the cases the detectives were working on.

Tell us about Winsboro.com.

It was actually called *WinnsboroToday.com* and an online community magazine. It was in operation for ten years, and we just recently suspended publication. It was a one-person operation and it just became too much for me to try to keep up with and write fiction as well. Since I spent so many years as a journalist, it is hard to give up nonfiction entirely. I love interviewing people and writing feature stories, but I am also really enjoying the fiction now and have been having some small measure of success with it. So it was time to focus on that.

You write in diverse genres. Which writing form brings you the most pleasure?

Now that I'm concentrating more on fiction, I'm remembering how rewarding it is to create characters and then have them take over a story. And nothing can top the high of a really stellar day when the creative juices are flowing and you finish a scene and smile. Between novels and scripts, I really don't prefer one over the other. I find some of the same creative satisfactions in both. But screenplays and stage plays can be written much faster than a novel once you have the story planned out. One of my greatest thrills was when one of my plays was staged at a community theatre, and I had the pleasure of directing it. It is hard to describe how I felt as I stood in the back on opening night and saw those characters I had created come to life.

Tell us about your *Open Season* and your new series featuring Dallas police detective Sarah Kingsly.

Open Season, which actually has two lead characters, Sarah and Angel Johnson, started as a film project when I was active in the film community in Dallas. Alan and Cynthia Mondell, documentary filmmakers, were planning to do their first feature film and wanted the story to incorporate some social issue. They asked me to come up with a story for a possible script, so I started interviewing officers on the Dallas force about the problems of the use of deadly force and racism. That was a big problem in the late '80s in Dallas that got national news attention. I thought it would be interesting to explore that from the viewpoints of two women, one white and one black who are thrown together as unwilling partners. As happens so often in the film industry, the project didn't progress, but I still had all that research I had done, so I decided to write the first book. After working with the characters of Sarah and Angel for the entire book, I realized they are strong enough characters to sustain a series. I am pleased that the second book in the series, **S**talking Season, just went to contract.

How has writing changed your life?

It hasn't. I was born a writer. Seriously, this question always stumps me. Writing has been so much of my life for so long that it *is* my life in many ways. A good friend once said that writing is not just something we do, it is an integral part of us. Perhaps if I ever get rich and famous, that might change my life. I might buy a bigger ranch.

How do you research your work?

I interview a lot of police officers, forensics psychiatrists, and other experts for the mystery series. That comes naturally to me because of my background in journalism. I also have a number of books about the judicial system, weapons, federal agencies, and forensics that I refer to. And now with the Internet, if I have a question I can go to one of the search engines and type it in. Invariably, I will find the answer. I also like to call an expert to check on a detail. For instance, in *Open Season* the victims are garroted with piano wire. I needed to find out whether the police forensics team could determine a particular wire came from a specific piano. So I called several piano tuners to find out what I could about piano strings. The character that Sarah talks to in the book was based on one of the tuners I talked to, and it was such fun to finish that conversation in real time, then turn to my computer and write the scene with Sarah.

What's the most difficult aspect of writing for you?

The hardest part of writing is when I have been away from the story for a while and the characters are no longer talking to me. I'm not much of a plotter, so if the people are not driving the story, I tend to stall out. That problem, however, is not nearly as challenging as the issue of marketing. I really struggle with that as I am definitely one of those writers who wishes she did not have to spend so much time marketing.

Advice to fledgling writers?

Never give up, even if someone says you should. If you were born a writer, you need to write. I had a college professor tell me to take up basket weaving as a creative outlet. I let that hold me back from attempting publication for many years, but I never stopped writing. My other advice is to read, everything, not just the genre you want to write in. We absorb good writing by reading good writing, and you find that in every genre. And finally, those who succeed are those who continue to write and continue to seek publication.

We're Going to be Rich!

by Maryann Miller

When I sold my first short story to a national magazine years ago, there was great excitement in the family and we all happily played Howard Hughes for a while. My husband started planning his retirement, the kids picked out houses in the country, and I had visions of never having to look at another price tag again before I bought a new pair of shoes.

I suppose we're all entitled to our glory dreams, and it sure was fun while it lasted. But once the excitement died down to a dull roar and the rejection slips started to litter my desk again, we had to resign ourselves to the fact that perhaps we would have to wait a while before we started recklessly throwing money around, buying mink coats and hamburgers.

Anjanette had to give up her dream of a new bedroom set with maybe a new bedroom to put it in. David went back to mowing lawns to save the money for his new mag wheels and Michael started collecting cans for recycling to keep himself in spending money. I resigned myself to another year in the bargain basement, and, unfortunately, Carl still had to get up every morning and go to work.

Initially, it took a while for me to cash the check. I was afraid to cash it because I knew it would be gone all too soon. Besides that, it was such a big thrill to go into my office and look at it every now and then. I knew that excitement would pass because it only took me two weeks to stop opening the magazine every five minutes to see my name in the credits. I remember thinking that no other acceptance would ever mean as much or create quite the stir that this one did.

Someday, I wouldn't call my best friend to announce, "You are now speaking to a famous writer person!"

Someday, selling stories would all be part of the routine around here and no one would stop by with champagne to celebrate. The kids wouldn't be announcing it to every creature that moves up and down the block, and my husband would no longer run around the local grocery stores making sure the magazine was prominently displayed.

I told him I didn't get any royalties, but he did it anyway.

(Visit Maryann Miller at her website: http://www.maryannwrites.com/ and her blog sites: http://tinyurl.com/7mg7tsv / http://tinyurl.com/ybhp4r5. She's also on Facebook and Twitter.)

Chapter Four: Thrillers

Robert Liparulo

Three of Robert Liparulo's novels are in various stages of development for the big screen: the film rights to *Comes a Horseman* were purchased by the producer of Tom Clancy's movies; and Liparulo is penning the screenplays for *Germ* and *Deadfall* for two top producers. He's also working with the director Andrew Davis on a political thriller. His novels have been called "Brilliantly crafted thrillers" and "Best of high-octane suspense." His bestselling young adult series, Dreamhouse Kings, debuted last year with *House of Dark Shadows* and *Watcher in the Woods,* which were followed by *Gatekeepers* and *Timescape.*

Robert, how difficult was it to make the transition from journalism to novels to screenplays?

Years ago, I wrote short stories, and fiction has always been my preference. When the fiction market dried up for writers whose names weren't Ray Bradbury, John Updike, and the like, I switched to journalism, primarily magazine articles. I thought then that I'd someday get back to fiction and that my time writing nonfiction would have been a waste. But when I started writing *Comes a Horseman,* my first novel, I realized that writing nonfiction had taught me incredibly valuable skills, which made me a better fiction writer.

Primarily, I'd learned how to research, to find that brilliant nugget of information buried under all the stuff everyone had already heard about; all the interviews I'd done gave me an ear for authentic dialogue; it taught me to write concise, tight prose; and I knew how to write every day and meet a deadline. Also, my magazine articles tended to be filled with metaphors and vignettes, which brought to life some topics that would otherwise have been dry and boring. So moving from journalism to novels wasn't too much of a stretch. I loved that I was able to create my own worlds, to tell the stories I wanted to tell, develop interesting characters, and explore themes that interested me. Of course, journalism and fiction are two vastly different disciplines, but my heart has always beat for fiction, so I was ready.

I started out in college as a motion picture production major. I was comfortable with the screenplay format and all of its limitations compared to novels. With screenplays, everything has to be shown, not told, which is a good rule-of-thumb for novel writing anyway. The story is pared down to its core, with fewer digressions, backstories, along with its internal motivations—again, it's a good place to start as a novelist, as well. I'm a very visual storyteller, and a lot of reviewers have commented on the fact that they could "see" my scenes as though they were watching a movie. For me, switching from writing novels to screenplays isn't much different from reading a book, then watching a movie. It seems natural to me.

What prompted your Dreamhouse Kings series for young adults?

After my third novel, *Deadfall* was released; some schools started reading my second novel, *Germ*. I got a chance to speak to high-schoolers and middle-schoolers about it. I thoroughly enjoyed addressing these kids. They didn't care a bit about the business of writing—how to get an agent, how much money you can make. But they were passionate about story—why characters did certain things, how the plot turned this way instead of that way. For them, it's all about the love of stories, which is exactly why I wanted to be a writer. About this time, my publisher called and asked if I'd ever consider writing for young adults. Of course, I jumped at the chance.

In the Dreamhouse Kings series, a family moves to a small town in northern California, so Dad could take a job as principal of the local middle and high school. They move into a run-down Victorian home, where they find a hidden hallway of doors. Each door leads to a portal and a different time in history. But not only can they go from the house to the past, people from the past can come through into their house. Someone does—and kidnaps Mom, taking her into some unknown place in the past. The family—primarily brothers David and Xander—begin a quest for Mom, which takes them to all sorts of dangerous and fascinating places throughout time. We slowly learn that the Kings are in the house for a very specific purpose, and they must do much more than "simply" find their mother. The entire story—less some details and where in history the Kings go—came to me in a dream when I was eleven years old.

Which do you enjoy most, writing screenplays or novels?

Each has its own pros and cons, but overall I like novel writing better. I like exploring my characters' thoughts and delving into their motivations and backstories in greater detail than screenplays allow. There are those who'd argue with me, but I believe you can create a much richer tapestry with novels than you can with movies. There's a reason most people who've read a book and seen the movie based on it will tell you they like the book better. It doesn't mean the movie was bad, typically; it's just that they enjoyed the depth of the novel and partnering with the author through their imaginations to tell the story.

I also like the control a novelist has over his story. Editors make suggestions, but in the end, it's the author's story, if not 100%, then 99% or 98%. Filmmaking, on the other hand, is a collaborative effort. The movie that hits the screen may be, at most, 50% of the original writer's vision. The rest is from other writers brought into the project, the director's interpretation, even producers' demands for changes based on what they think the audience wants to see, what best suits the market.

Why do you incorporate supernatural elements into your thriller novels?

I've felt nudged in that direction from the very beginning. *Comes a Horseman* has hints of the supernatural—things that may or may not end up being supernatural. Readers really responded to that. But at the time—and through the writing of *Germ, Deadfall,* and *Deadlock*—I wanted to stay true to what I thought of as a pure thriller story: suspense set in a solidly real world in which the events could actually happen.

When I conceived of *The 13th Tribe*, it was like that, a thriller set in the real world. Then I realized I could explore its theme— which is primarily vigilantism, frontier justice—even better if I stretched reality just a bit. It opened up all kinds of storytelling possibilities that I think readers will find entertaining and at the same time intriguing and thought-provoking. I'd already written the *Dreamhouse Kings*, which showed me just how fun a tinge of fantasy could be (through the family's time traveling). Readers made it a bestselling series, so I knew my fans would follow me into that genre, as long as I gave them the other elements that make up a Robert Liparulo story—lots of action, adventure, and realistic characters who fight and love and have strong emotions.

It was never my intention to use the supernatural as a gimmick, as a way to circumvent quality storytelling. I strove to create a character-driven story with an interesting plot and a visual, active writing style. The supernatural element simply adds another layer, another color I could use to paint my story.

Tell us about your latest film project and your latest novel.

I have several projects inching toward production. All of my novels are with producers associated with major studios. They're talking big budgets, which is gratifying because they'll have the money to do it right, theoretically. But the problem with big budgets is they add layers of red tape and decision-making.

Mace Neufeld, the producer of Tom Clancy's movies, hasn't been happy with the scripts he's commissioned for *Comes a Horseman*. Whether he'll move forward and keep investing in scripts, I don't know. Eric Garcia, who wrote the novel on which the film "Matchstick Man" (with Nicolas Cage) was based and the screenplay for the recent "Repo Men" (with Jude Law), is writing the script for the *Dreamhouse Kings*. He really gets the story and I love what he's doing with it. Both *Germ* and *Deadfall* are in the scriptwriting stage, as well. I'm working on the "Deadfall" script for David Zelon at Mandalay. I'm also writing an original script for a thriller with Andrew Davis, the director of "The Fugitive", "The Guardian", and "Holes". Phoenix Pictures will produce it. Between our schedules, it's been slow going, but I'm totally psyched about the story. It's an ambitious project that tackles some pressing issues at play in society today.

As far as my next novel, we're still about eight months from the publication of *The 13th Tribe*, and since it's a slight departure from the kinds of stories readers are used to from me, I don't want to give away too much yet; I'd like it to be a surprise. I can say it takes a close look at vigilantes and how they do what a lot of us would condone or even do ourselves if we had the guts. They go after the child abusers, murderers and thieves who somehow escaped justice, whether through their own deviousness or loopholes in the law. I didn't want to mimic what's already been done so well with this topic—in books like *Death Wish* and even *Batman,* so I decided to explore two aspects of vigilantism that I felt have been underserved in literature: the cultural/societal conditions that could allow vigilantism to flourish—and have in specific times in history; and the feelings vigilantism stirs in people who aren't the vigilantes or the criminals, but average bystanders. How do they sort through moral implications, especially if they become the victims of unpunished crime?

What are the best and worst aspects of writing?

The best aspect is simply being able to do what I love to do. That can be applied to any vocation, so to be more writing specific: I love creating characters, setting them in motion, and watching what they do. I can't think of a better way to explore your own emotions, or to tackle a subject that interests you. I get to say, "What if. . ." and then spend months figuring out the answer. A close second is hearing from readers who enjoyed my story. It's a great feeling to know I was able to take someone out of the hustle and bustle of life for a little while and entertain them.

I think for the worst aspect, it's a toss-up between the subjectivity of storytelling and the "business" of writing. There are so many ways to spin a tale; I think most writers are constantly asking themselves, "Is this right? Will this entertain and communicate my message in the best possible way?" It's the infinite possibilities that keep writers guessing, and sitting down to choose one, to commit it to paper, can be both exhilarating and terrifying.

The business end of things is the least appealing to me. Contracts, marketing, publicity—these are necessary evils, but certainly not what made me want to be a storyteller. I love meeting readers and talking shop with other writers, but the rest of it I could do without.

How do you define your characters in a new project?

I don't write bios or bibles for my characters. I prefer to "know" them, to have walked in their shoes. Once I've decided a few basics—their gender, their occupation, for instance—I try to live their lives for a while. It's sort of like the method approach to acting: I listen to the music they would listen to and figure out why they like it. I think their thoughts, even when they're opinions are contrary to my own. I speak the way they would. I go to businesses where they would work and learn their trade as much as time allows. I order what they would at restaurants. Once I start writing, I usually don't refer to character cheat sheets because I know them so well—where they went to college, what their favorite book is, as well as I know my own tastes and background.

How important are conflict, emotion and humor in a thriller novel?

Thrillers have had a rap for being plot-driven, but nowadays most of them are character-driven. Without sympathy for the characters, readers don't care about their fate, which makes for a weak thriller. So most thriller writers invest a lot in character development, and that naturally drives the plot. And where there are compelling characters, you'll have conflict and emotion. Conflict ratchets up tension, while emotion gives readers some commonality with characters who may be otherwise quirky or caught up in crazy scenarios that are completely alien to readers. Combined, they can pull a reader into a story and hold them in a state of tension that keeps the pages turning.

Good writers use humor to give their readers a breather. Depending on how it's used, it can give gruff characters more charm or tell readers, "Yeah, this is crazy stuff. I know it, you know it, let's have fun." Like the supernatural, it's another color on our palette. Some writers use it sparingly, wryly—someone like Thomas Perry—and others like Carl Hiaasen seem to build their stories around laugh-out-loud situations and characters. My own writing leans toward the Thomas Perry approach to humor.

Advice for fledgling thriller and screenwriters?

Read everything you can get your hands on and finish every writing project you start. Reading exposes you to people and things outside your own little world. It helps teach you about the way other people behave and think and talk. It gives you glimmers of other places and ideas—all things you can incorporate into your own stories. On top of that, you learn what works and what doesn't in storytelling.

"Finish things" is simple to say, but not so simple to do. Discipline is essential to all writers, but as creative people, we're easily distracted, often by other stories we want to tell. But if we get in the habit of finishing things, then we have products to show agents, editors, and publishers when the opportunity comes up. The ability to finish is a big question people in the publishing business have for wannabe writers. They've seen so many people with great ideas who either can't finish a story or can't execute it well. Prove you can right off the bat.

So What Are You Waiting For?

by Robert Liparulo

Write! Nothing takes the place of writing for learning the craft. Not formal education, not seminars or conferences or books about writing, not critique groups or deep conversations with like-minded friends, not studying the markets, not reading. All are valuable, but they're insignificant compared to experientially learning how to get what's in *your* head onto the page in a way that puts your ideas into *another's* head.

Not everything you write will be or should be published, but you have to rack up a *lot* of words to learn the craft well enough to attract editors and eventually readers. In *Outliers*, Malcolm Gladwell uses the Beatles and Bill Gates to validate the "10,000-Hour Rule," which says highly successful people in any field have to put in 10,000 hours practicing their craft before they hit their stride or rise above the competition. An average full-time work year is 2,040 hours, so we're talking about five solid years of writing and only writing. At 500 words per hour, that's 500,000,000 words committed to paper.

But let's be realistic and admit that telling a story requires more than slamming out words. You have to think through a story, maybe outline it; research it; write it; and then edit, revise and polish. If we give equal time to the planning, researching, writing, and editing, 10,000 hours still means 1,250,000 words *on the page*.

The words can take any form of written communication—personal letters, practice stories, blog posts, proposals, articles and short fiction published in magazines. (Sure, you can score some cash during this time; the Beatles, after all, were paid to play in Liverpool and Hamburg nightclubs almost nonstop for three years while they honed their craft). All of it moves you closer to the brass ring: a publishing contract or bestseller. Thing is, it's easy to fool ourselves into believing that a pseudo-writing endeavor like attending a conference and talking about writing *is* writing. It's not.

One million, two hundred and fifty thousand words: How far along are you? If you knew, really *knew* that upon reaching that figure (give or take *some*), you'd be among the best of the best and no publisher would dream of rejecting you, wouldn't you choose to write over doing those has-something-to-do-with-writing-but-isn't-writing things?

So, what are you waiting for?

(Robert Liparulo's website: robertliparulo.com.
His Dreamhouse Kings site is: dreamhousekings.com.
He also has tips for new writers at: getitonthepage.com.)

Vicki Hinze

Multi-award winning, bestselling novelist Vicki Hinze, (aka Victoria Barrett and Victoria Cole) has written more than two dozen novels for some well-known publishers such as Random House, Bantam, Pinnacle, Harlequin Signature, St. Martin's Press and Silhouette as well as four nonfiction books for Spilled Candy Traditional Books. An active lecturer on the business and craft of writing, she also sponsors the Writers' Zone mentoring program and the Edna Sampson Benevolence Fund to assist writers with financial needs.

Vicki, how did growing up in New Orleans influence your writing? And when did you actually begin to write?

New Orleans is colorful, and I would say that it's most significant influence is in the unique individuality of the people, which makes for interesting and complex characters. Too, the bayous and swamps and marshes are full of mystery and folklore that make for intriguing settings.

I began writing before starting grade school. To read the Sunday comics, I had to read and discuss the front page of the paper all week. My dad's rules. I wrote political essays. Later, I moved into poetry, very briefly into short stories, and then settled into writing novels. I wrote my first novel in 1986, first sold in 1992. Much later I added nonfiction and, in 2011, short stories for publication. I don't recall a time when I didn't write, to be honest.

Why do your hats cover your eyes in publicity photos?

I could say it adds to the mystique of writing mystery and thriller elements in my novels, but the truth is I needed new pro photos and I was undergoing a series of eye surgeries. Swelling and bruising are hidden by those hats. Readers wrote in liking them, so I've kept the hats.

What prompted your war games series? And why body doubles?

My husband was in special ops and I'm naturally interested in the topic and missions. Body doubles became intriguing in the first Iraq war when I discovered that Saddam had nearly a dozen known body doubles. The "what if" concept kicked in. What if black-market terrorists used doubles to infiltrate high-level, top-secret positions where people have access to all manner of intelligence and technology? That set my imagination on fire.

How do you research your novels?

The research depends on the subject matter, but often I do what I can on the web and then contact subject-matter experts to confer. The preparation I'd say comes from a lifelong interest in politics sparked, spurred and nurtured first by my father and later by an awareness of the impact of politics on my life, then later still, that impact on the lives of my children. My husband being in the military for twenty-two years generated a deep interest. To better understand the man, I spent a lot of time studying warfare, the history and methods of war, means and technology.

You have a diverse group of women protagonists. Were they patterned after women you've admired?

All of the protagonists—male or female—are people I respect and admire. I might not agree with them, their personal philosophies or their actions, but I still respect them. The females well might be victims but they don't let their past challenges identify them or steal their futures. I can't say they're based on any one woman but they are all composites of admirable traits I see in everyday, ordinary women who find themselves in extraordinary circumstances.

Tell us about your novel, *Forget Me Not*.

Forget Me Not is the story of a woman carjacked, beaten and left for dead. She recalls nothing yet others are trying to kill her. To survive, she must discover why. She's definitely a victim, but she holds fast to faith. That sprang from a question that led me to write the book. If, I wondered, you lost everything—every single thing, including your identity—would you lose yourself? In writing the book, I discovered the answer to that question and more. It wasn't easy to write and some of the explorations weren't comfortable, but they were worthy.

When and why did you start your Yahoo group, Writers Zone?

To be honest, I've lost track of when. It started out as Aids4Writers but one of the long-term members was deeply impacted by AIDS, which was a new term to us after I started the group, so I changed its name. Well over ten years ago. Probably close to fifteen.

Why? Every year, as part of a self-improvement program, I tackle a virtue. That year, I wanted to "do good for goodness' sake." You see, when I started writing, I didn't know another writer. I'd spend days looking for answers to the simplest questions on writing or the publishing business. It was very frustrating, and I promised myself that if I ever learned anything about writing or publishing, I would share. So the program was born for the purpose of sharing while looking for nothing in return. I intended to post every day for a year, and then to move on to the next virtue. But as the year came to a close, I mentioned to the followers that I was going to miss them and their questions which kept me on my toes. The feedback was swift and furious, with followers asking me to please continue the program. And so I have.

For the first several years, I attempted to post every day. As my career took off and I had less time available, I'd post three or four times a week. But a shift has occurred that has required me to change the way I run the program. Many of the questions I receive are ones too author-specific to share with the group. So these days the majority of the work occurs between an author, agent or editor and me privately. I don't and never have claimed to know it all. But I do network, and share what I know or what I can find out from others. So the program started with me trying to do good for goodness' sake and continues because they asked.

Which subjects do you touch on most frequently?

I answer a lot of questions on writing craft, but in the last couple of years, (likely due to the rapidly changing market), the bulk of the questions have been related to the writing business. Within that aspect of our industry, the questions widely vary. Some are basic. (What happens to a book after it's submitted to an agent or editor?) Others are a lot more complex, dealing with agent or editor relations, promotional tips, reading royalty statements, terminating agreements—all manner of things. On craft, character, pacing, and suspense raise common, consistent questions. That brings in conflict, goals, story structure and other intricate aspects of character development that impact other novel elements as well. But I also get a lot of questions on time management, teaching workshops, social networking and making presentations, too.

What's the best way to become a bestselling author?

The short answer: produce consistently high-quality work for a targeted, established genre and market it as though your life depended on it. When you do this, you build a bond with the reader, and s/he comes to trust you. By staying in the same genre, you make it easier for readers to find and follow you. It is increasingly important that authors get involved in marketing their own work. Because it is, it behooves the author to learn to market wisely and well. The key words are discoverability and platform. It's never too soon for an author to start building. I don't know whether that is the best way to become a bestselling writer, but I do know it seems effective.

Who most influenced your own writing and what would you be doing, if not a writer?

My parents influenced my writing. Both of them loved books and read constantly. It wasn't uncommon for my mother to read two or three books a day. Those daily discussions on politics with my dad early on in life taught me a lot more than just about the stories that appeared in the newspaper. Writers are good observers, and they learn to look at things from different perspectives. The habit of doing both is one of many gifts my dad gave me in that little ritual of earning my way to read the funnies.

I have no idea what I would be doing if I didn't write. I remember once early on, I told my husband I was going to quit. He suggested that I really think about it because he couldn't see me being happy not writing. So I did. I locked myself in my office and thought about it for hours. What I discovered wasn't that I was frustrated with writing. I was frustrated with trying to sell what I wrote. I walked out of my office and I told my husband: "When I die, bury me with a pencil in my hand."

The idea of going through eternity and not being able to write down my stories was just more than I could bear. So I really don't know what I would do if I were not a writer. I doubt I'd return to corporate. I'd probably teach writing, or counsel writers, or teach the business end of being a writer. I don't know that anything unrelated to writing would hold my interest long-term. I'd have to be fascinated. One of the things that I absolutely love about writing is knowing I'll never master it. I can study, write my fingers to the bone, and I'm still going to learn new things and try new methods and techniques all the time. The adventurous nature of that makes it hard to beat or even to match.

How to Care for and Feed Your Author

By Vicki Hinze

Sounds silly? We're talking soul food and emotional support. We're talking about content writers. Hungry writers are not happy, which means those around them are not happy. Not so silly, after all. Here are a few tips:

Writers need time. Time to think, to dream, to study, to discover. Show your support by giving them uninterrupted writing time. Don't wait to be asked. Take the kids to the park or cook dinner.

If your author asks for a flash drive, don't buy her a diamond. When a writer craves a tool and gets a bauble s/he's disappointed. It's not a lack of gratitude. You buy the flash drive, you're supporting the writer and the writing. You buy a bauble and you're thoughtful but not validating the writer or writing. Big difference.

Writers don't talk to you about their writing or career challenges so you'll solve their problems. You can't solve the author's problems and s/he doesn't expect you to solve them. Authors write through challenges, they talk through challenges, making sense of the jumble so that they can slot those challenges, assign a value to them, and press on. So just listen and let your author talk.

Authors not yet earning money crave tools to learn more about craft, the business, the writing life. But because they're not earning, many feel they can't justify the expense. They feel guilty spending "our" money on "my" dream things even if logically they know these things are costs of doing business. Show your support. Buy that writer a book on writing. Buy that writer a "magic pen" and tack on a note that says it is 100% guaranteed to be writer's block proof. Give that writer a homemade coupon for an hour of uninterrupted writing time. In other words, follow up well-meaning words with indisputable actions. Watch that author blossom.

Authors get emotionally involved. If they didn't, they wouldn't be able to write because emotion is the means by which authors connect with characters who connect with readers. Emotional bonds are why, when reading a book, a reader stops seeing words on a page and begins living the story. Now that can't happen if the author isn't emotionally involved. You can't get out of a book what the author doesn't put in it, right? So expect your author to emote, to invest, to get involved and to care. Maybe s/he doesn't know anyone involved in a situation, but there are bigger issues at stake. Ones that relate. And those, your author will write about with authority and emotion because s/he got involved.

Remember, for an author, everything is fodder. Writers take in and process that fodder, and they can't turn it off. It's natural, like breathing. So if your writer is devastated or outraged by some event, accept it. That author is emoting. Authors do that.

Some inner-circle non-writers will see an author weeping and turn around and walk out. Some will put an arm around him/her and say not a word. Both are equally supportive, or can be. It depends on the specific author. And that's the final tip.

Know *your* author. If you don't know your author, then you don't know how to support him/her. This greatest tip—and it truly is greatest—is that if you don't know what your author needs, ask. That's absolutely priceless.

Too often authors who need support most feel the least able to ask for it. They get hit with unsolicited suggestions and unintended slurs about their "hobby." When they started earning or earning again, then attitudes change. But by then, they've learned to live without support or they've found it in other writers who understand. This can leave those closest to the author feeling like an outsider, and in a sense, they are. But they need not be.

They need only to learn how to care for and feed their author.

(Vicki Hinze's website: www.vickihinze.com.)

Shane Gericke

Bestselling crime novelist Shane Gericke acquired his first typewriter at age seven and has been writing ever since. A newspaper editor for 25 years, most prominently at the *Chicago Sun-Times,* he retired to write crime novels. One critic has written: "Cross James Patterson with Joseph Wambaugh, and you get Shane Gericke." His novel, *Torn Apart,* was a finalist for the international Thriller Award for Best Novel and named a Book of the Year by *Suspense Magazine.* An original member of International Thriller Writers, he was chairman of the ThrillerFest literary festival in New York and founding director of its agent-author matching program, AgentFest. His novels are in translation worldwide, and *RT Book Reviews* chose his national best-selling debut novel, *Blown Away,* as the nation's best first mystery in 2006.

Shane, why did you decide to write thrillers with a female protagonist when we've been told that male characters sell more books?

I like female characters. They're allowed to be interesting in ways male characters can't. Women can be tough, tender, giggly, stern, ass-kickin', nurturing, gun-shooting and scarf-knitting—all at once. Men who giggle tenderly whilst darning socks are looked upon with great suspicion, if not outright dread, in thrillers; it rattles the stereotype of "he-man tough guy." So, I went with a female lead. Male characters probably do sell more books. But that's only relative—if a male lead sells 20 million books and a female sells 10 million, I'll happily take the latter to tell the story I want with the lead character I adore.

Please explain why your last name is pronounced "Yer-key." Has it caused problems when people ask for your novels in bookstores?

The reason is "Gericke" was "Guericke" in the old country. (In my case, Germany.).That extra "U" provided the "Yer" sound. But when the seven Guericke brothers came to America, some immigration guy decided to "Americanize" it by cutting out the "U." But the brothers kept the sound, so now it's spelled with a G and pronounced with a Y. Talk about headaches. The biggest problem is that anyone hearing "YER-kee"—on a radio show, or at a conference—looks in the Y section at the bookstore, can't find it, buys something else. Same thing searching for me online. I wonder if "John Doe" is available as a pen name . . .

Why did you decide to leave newspaper editing to write thriller novels?

On my 25th anniversary of being a newspaper guy, I was in my mid-40s. I looked around the newsroom, a place I loved deeply for its excitement, personality and aggravation, and said to myself, "Do I really want to turn into one of those ancient, burned-out news nags with green eye shades, or should I try something else." Well, I always wanted to write thriller novels. So I left a perfectly good job where I got paid every Friday, for the stuttering mood swings of commercial book publishing. I've never regretted it—I just love this business.

Two things were tough about the switch, though. Story length was one. Newspapers run stories between 200 and 2,000 words. Novels go 100,000. I had to unclench years of compressing an entire scene into one sentence—better, one pithy phrase—and just let the words flow. Second, big-city newspapers—mine the *Chicago Sun-Times*—

have deadlines by which your work must be done. And more than one deadline a day. Book deadlines are one per year. That is a temptation to let the daily writing slide in favor of distractions, as there's always "I'll get to it tomorrow." Then 300 tomorrows go by, and you have to write 100,000 in four weeks. That's when you go blind sucking caffeine to get to "The End." You need enormous self-discipline to be an effective book writer, because there's no badly dressed city editor screaming at you to turn in your story, goddammit.

When did you begin writing and when and where were you first published?

I began writing in high school. The weekly newspaper in Frankfort, Illinois, where I grew up, needed someone to cover the sports teams at the high school I attended. The editor called the principal and asked who he'd recommend. I was the editor of the student newspaper, so the principal recommended me. The editor was Ed Czerwinski, forever be he praised for taking a chance on me. He called me and held the interview in the town diner attached to the back end of the newspaper office—a setup I highly recommend if you're fortunate to find one!—and I said I'd love to. He said he'd pay me $30 a month. Well, I was in heaven—that was all the money I figured I'd ever need in life. Fortunately, I came to my senses and starting covering high school sports for *The Herald* of Frankfort, Mokena, New Lenox. My first story and photos hit the paper in August, 1973—I was both writer and photographer—so I've been a professional writer now for . . . gawd, nearly four decades.

Which writer would you like to spend time with, past or present? And who most influenced your own work?

John Sandford most influenced—and still influences—my work. He is another reformed newspaper guy, and started his "Prey" series starring Minneapolis cop Lucas Davenport exactly 20 years ago, while writing for the *St. Paul Pioneer-Press*. His series became a monsterous hit, and he left newspapers to write books full-time. His writing is a master class in description, word power and characterization . . . and cop humor. I consider him the single finest novelist working today. I wrote a tribute to him for the new *Thrillers: 100 Must-Reads,* a collection of essays tracing the history of the thriller novel from ancient times—think, *The Odyssey*—to James Patterson. My piece on Sandford is the bonus essay the publisher's using to promote the book, and you can read it for free.

How long did it take to acquire an agent?

To get into big-league book publishing, where I wanted to be, it's mandatory to have a literary agent. Publishers simply won't consider your work otherwise. So I sent a bunch of queries and asked a load of people for advice, and wound up in the hands of Bill Contardi at Brandt and Hochman in New York. The agency represents, among others, Scott Turow, whom I hear puts out some pretty good books. The process of finding an agent, let alone a publisher, can take years off your life. I was fortunate in that it took me only one.

You've received great reviews and accolade's from bestselling authors such as Lee Child and Jeffrey Deaver. Which one means the most to you?

Jeff's. He's just a plain cool guy, and I love his work. I run into him from time to time at ThrillerFest and other book events around the country. We were standing in line for something and I said, "Hey, you want to have breakfast tomorrow? I need some advice." He did, we ate, he suggested a way to handle a scene I was struggling with, and then offered to write a blurb. The rest is history. Lee was the same way when I asked: so generous with his time. Big-time authors are among the most giving people in any profession, in my experience. They don't have to help—they can cite having no time, which is breathtakingly true in their cases. Yet, they do without hesitation. Tess Gerritsen, Douglas Preston, Gayle Lynds, John J. Nance, Erica Spindler, Ken Bruen, Alex Kava, John Lutz and others have so graciously offered testimonials for all three of my books. I am indebted to them.

How important is humor in thriller novels and do you use it often?

Very important. Life is both funny and tragic, leavened with large doses of "meh." So I incorporate humor whenever possible. Not jokes—death is not a joking matter. But wry, dark humor from one cop to another as the bullets fly and Life Itself is at stake? Priceless.

Advice for aspiring writers?

Two things: Read everything you can get your hands on. If you don't know what's going on in the world, how can you write about it? Particularly read in the genre in which you wish to write. Every author has a different style and approach to their stories, and you should absorb them all. Then, you can settle on your own when you begin to write. Which leads to my next piece of advice: Write. Every day. Whether a blog, diary entry, magazine story, three pages of your new manuscript or letter to your mom, write it. All the pros write daily, and you should too. It gets you into the habit of producing words every day—commercial fiction is, at base, factory work, as you're putting out product for people to buy, and your production line needs to run smoothly. If you love to write, that shouldn't be a problem. If you don't love to write, find another business. This one will tear out your brain and stomp it flat if you aren't in love with the process. Oh, and a third piece: buy my books. I need the sales.

Motivation: the Key to Your Characters' Hearts

by Shane Gericke

Would you hate your mom if she shot your dad? Or would you admire her?

Depends.

And that's the key to writing powerful fiction: character motivation.

Whether we cheer—or hiss—characters depend mostly on *why* they do what they do. If mom shot dear old dad because she caught him molesting your sister, then, Yay, mom! But if she shot dad for the insurance money to buy her lover heroin and a Jag, then, yeah, we hate her guts.

So infuse your characters with strong motivations for doing what they do. Your hero rescues people because she herself was rescued as a child. And your villain robs a bank because he has no health insurance but his son has cancer.

And readers applaud.

I was reminded of this recently while watching a 1964 TV sitcom called "Hank."

I needed a TV show for a scene in my novel, and didn't want something as obvious as, say, "Gilligan's Island." So I went with a more obscure one from my childhood: "Hank." It starred the fictional Hank Dearborn (played by Dick Kallman), a teenager who desired a college degree but didn't want to pay for it. So he assumed other students' identities and took their classes when they were absent.

At age nine, I thought that was crummy, stealing from the poor innocent university. So, apparently, did the audience, because the show lasted only one season. (It also didn't help it was in the same time slot as "The Wild, Wild West.")

Fast-forward to a few months ago. I found the show online and watched several episodes. Intrigued at some of the hints that were dropped, I looked up the storyline. It turned out that Hank wasn't nearly the soulless thief I had originally assumed.

Yes, he was stealing other students' educations, and no, he wasn't paying tuition. But his *reason for doing so* is what fascinated me.

It turns out that Hank and his baby sister were orphaned when their parents died in a car crash. Hank was left to raise Sis on his own, and worked a variety of jobs to keep them afloat. But the state found out, and threatened to put Tina in a foster home. Hank figured he'd have a better shot at keeping her if he had a college degree, but he couldn't afford both tuition and food for his sister. Desperate to keep the remains of his family together, he turned to identity fraud.

Which is one hell of a great motivation, and it turned me from someone who thought Hank was a thieving *putz* into a wildly cheering fan. As wild as you can get over a 1960s sitcom, anyway.

So work those intriguing, life-defining motivations into your own characters, and your readers will love you forever.

Oh, and Hank? He got caught at the end of the season. But he'd done so darn well on that final exam that the college awarded him a full scholarship and formal admittance to the U, rather than kick him out and call the cops! Leaving his adoring sis to sigh in the finale:

"There goes my brother . . . the registered student."

Yeah. Only in fiction.

(You can learn more about Shane Gericke at his website: www.shanegericke.com. He blogs with other crime novelists and is on Facebook.)

Timothy Hallinan

Tim Hallinan is an Edgar and Macavity nominated author of the traditionally published Poke Rafferty Bangkok thrillers and his Junior Bender mysteries, which are e-book originals. He also conceived and edited a volume of original short stories by twenty first-rate mystery writers, *Shaken: Stories for Japan*, with every penny of the $3.99 price going to the 2011 Japan Relief Fund. He lives in both Santa Monica and Southeast Asia.

Tim, why did you decide to go the indie route with your new e-book series?

The real answer is that the money we were offered by the publishers we approached wasn't very good. I looked at the offers and thought, "I'd rather own the books." And I'd already put up some of my Simeon Grist series from the Twelfth Century—sorry, the 1990s—and people were actually buying a few hundred copies each month. I figured if those books were selling, new ones would sell even better. And they have. In fact the first one, *Crashed*, sold so well that we got a substantially bigger offer for *Little Elvises* and reprint rights to *Crashed*. But, after a life spent lingering outside publishers' doors in the hope someone would offer me a glass of lukewarm water, it was kind of nice to say no.

What inspired your Junior Bender series?

While I was trying to finish the third Poke Rafferty book, *Breathing Water*, I kept hearing a voice in my ear, trying to tell me a story in the first person, and every time I listened, it entertained me. I finally put *Breathing Water* aside for five weeks and let Junior tell me the story of *Crashed*, which is the fastest I've ever written a book. I put the first draft in a drawer, gave a couple of additional months to the task of finishing *Breathing Water*, and then edited *Crashed* and went straight to work on *Little Elvises*.

Part of the appeal was Junior himself; he's a burglar with a moral code who works as a private eye for crooks. In one sense, he's just a middle-class guy who's unhappily divorced and loves his teenage daughter more than anything in the world, and in another, he's risking his life trying to help clients who will not be good enemies if he fails, and he's trying to catch people who are crazy enough to commit crimes against criminals. He's at risk no matter how things come out.

Tell us more about your e-books.

Well, they're the funniest books I've ever written, and that counts as something for me, because laughing, for me, is right up there with eating. They're meant to be funny and thrilling at the same time, and I'm not the best judge, but the reviews are 99.5% 5-star (only one 4-star in the batch), so that must mean something.

I've always loved to write crooks, and Junior gives me the chance to fill entire books with them. In *Crashed*, the main crook is Trey Annunziato, a beautiful woman in her early thirties who runs the biggest crime family in the San Fernando Valley and is trying to take everything legal because she's looked at the techniques the government has developed in the war on terror, and she knows that when the cops get back to catching criminals, criminals won't stand a chance.

And in *Little Elvises*, we meet an old-time, mobbed up Philadelphia record producer who took handsome Philly kids and turned them into pallid imitations of Elvis, plus the oldest still-dangerous gangster in the world, who is based on a very real person, the California point man for the Chicago Jewish mob. (One of Capone's guys said, "If it wasn't for the Jews, we'd still be hiding money in mattresses.") This man, whom I won't name, was for about 40 years the most powerful person in the state. No contest. Half the banks in Southern California were originally opened to launder money.

How well have your e-books sold so far? Are you pleased with the results?

They've done okay, The reviews have been great and it's a few thousand dollars every month. I'd like them to do better, but I just HATE promoting myself. I can't drop in on every online conversation in the world and say, "Speaking of the economy, my book *Little Elvises* takes an offbeat look at the underground economy." It makes me wince when I see other writers do it, and I won't.

I also loathe Twitter, which is undoubtedly hurting me. I've got like a thousand followers and I have no idea what to say to them.

How have you promoted your e-books?

Well, that's sort of the issue. I really haven't. I accidentally did a very successful promotion for *Little Elvises*. I had two covers and couldn't make up my mind, so I put them on Facebook and asked people to choose. And did they ever. And then I did the same thing on my website and in my almost-nearly-sort-of-monthly newsletter, and literally 800 people stopped their lives long enough to cast votes. So I gave away a bunch of the e-books, and that was the promotion. And *Little Elvises* really took off in its first week out.

My primary promo device is the newsletter. My website is loaded with information for beginning writers–it's about 80% of the site, and people have been writing to thank me or ask questions for years and years. And I also get a surprising amount of fan mail. All those people are on my newsletter mailing list now–about 6,000 of them—and I see a sales jump every time I send one out.

I work hard to make the newsletter more than just a plug–each has a theme and got reviews of good books and nice images, and nobody has unsubscribed, which is saying something. Anybody who wants the newsletter can e-mail me at thallinan@gmail.com.

What advice do you offer writers contemplating the indie route?

Pretty much the same advice I have for everyone. Write the book you want to read and when you're finished, make it better. Proofread everything at least ten times. This book is supposed to be you at your best, so you don't want it to be riddled with dumb mistakes.

And do a better job with promotion than I do.

A Golden Age of Writing

by Timothy Hallinan

I once knew a woman who translated hieroglyphics, and one of the texts she rendered into English was one of the oldest poems known to man, dating from about 3000 BC. It was about how things were better before. It was a lament for having missed the Golden Age. It seems to be human nature to think in terms of lost Golden Ages. The operative word is "lost." It's not even fashionable to suggest that we're living in a golden age.

I think we are. I think this is a golden age for mysteries and thrillers. Sure, some of the great ones are gone: Christie, Hammett, Chandler, Sayers, Tey, Highsmith, McDonald, Stout, Parker and many others. But we have an enormous number of exceptional writers working now, and more titles to choose from than at any time in history. I'd put the best writers working today up against the best working at any time since Poe kicked things off. Who's better than James Lee Burke, Sue Grafton, Louise Penney, Laura Lippman, SJ Rozan, Lee Child, John LeCarre, Donna Leon? I could go on for pages–all writing right now.

I think this Golden Age has come about for three reasons: First, the ubiquity of relatively inexpensive books; until just a few years ago, despite all their moans and groans, the world's publishers put out, in editions of varying costs, more books than at any other time in history. And with all those books being published, good writing usually found a champion.

Second, the durability of the genre. The mystery or thriller is the one of the oldest genres (what is "Oedipus Rex" but a mystery?) and one of the most universal. Mysteries and thrillers help readers work through some of the most difficult aspects of human existence. They present a world in which order, even though it's been temporarily broken down, can be restored. They ignore the fashion of nihilism and despair that mars so much supposedly "literary" fiction.

Third, women have come full circle. Once the royalty of the genre, they faded during the heyday of the pulps, the hardboiled noir, and the five-testicle PI fiction of the '40s through the '60s. And then, starting in the '70s, the entire genre tilted; women reemerged with a vengeance, no longer confined to the classic and/or cozy end of the spectrum, but ranging straight across, from one extreme to another. And in one of the most remarkable shifts in modern marketing history, women became the driving force in mystery writing.

So now we have women writing all kinds of books and also some of the best male writers who have ever worked in the genre. Jackpot. We've also seen a loosening (pretty much an abandonment) of the old restrictions on what people can write about, which has produced some terrible books but also some really serious explorations of the darkest corners of human behavior.

And now we're seeing things open up even more widely. The e-book has broken New York's stranglehold on what we can read—and what we can write, too. Once again, we're seeing a lot of books that should have remained in people's desk drawers, but we're also seeing some tremendous stuff. It's certainly opened things up for me. Like most writers, I've been restricted in what I could write because publishers would only buy a certain kind of book from me. But now I can write literally anything I want and put it out there to sink or swim.

I believe it's a uniquely human experience to be frightened and amused at the same time, and I love writing books that attempt to put the reader in that position. But do I think *Little Elvises* and *Crashed* are golden age material? I doubt it—I can't take myself that seriously. But they're the product of a writer doing what he wants instead of what a corporation wants him to do, and in the long run that has to be good for everyone. When people look back on this particular golden age, I think they'll say the emergence of the e-book both broadened and prolonged it.

(You can learn more about Tim at his web/blog site: www.timothyhallinan.com\, as well as his blog/Finish Your Novel. He's also on Facebook and Twitter.)

Lise McClendon

Lise McClendon has written fiction in Wyoming and Montana for the past thirty years. Her latest suspense novel, *Blackbird Fly*, is set in New York and Southwest France. Her latest mystery, *Jump Cut*, was written as Rory Tate. Born in California, she was raised in Delaware and Nebraska.

Lise, where is the center of your universe and is that where you've set most of your novels?

I have sort of spanned the continent, haven't I? I think moving around as a kid is difficult but it also makes you flexible and tolerant—and most of all for a writer, makes you an observer. A writer has to be able to stand back a little and watch human behavior. I've lived in the Rockies for thirty years now, half my life. I love so much about the mountains and people who choose to live in this wild, beautiful place. I had set my first mystery series in Jackson Hole, Wyoming, when I lived in Montana. Later I moved to Jackson Hole, so I guess life sometimes does imitate art.

How did your interest in writing evolve?

I've always loved writing. I studied journalism and communications, and indulged my love of film and television in the broadcasting programs at the University of Nebraska and University of Missouri Kansas City. I also majored in sociology. I think of fiction writing as a meld of words and the study human nature so the double major worked out.

Tell us about your writing background.

Although I'd written some short stories, reviewed films, and taken classes, I really started writing fiction after the birth of my second son. I wrote a screenplay first, a form I felt comfortable with. Later I adapted that story to my first novel. I didn't sell that one but I met a group of writers, wrote a mystery, and published my second novel. That was in 1994, *The Bluejay Shaman*, Alix Thorssen's first adventure, in Jackson Hole.

What does writing mean to you?

Writing centers me. I tend to bounce around, unfocused, if I'm not writing. My head spins with ideas, lists, stuff, but when I write I download it to the page. Then the fun starts: getting it all organized!

When did you begin to teach?

I taught for the Writer's Voice Project for several years when it first spread out through YMCAs around the U.S. I have also been on the faculty of the Jackson Hole Writer's Conference. A new project is a day-long workshop for fiction writers called "Truly Richly Deeply: Structure and Voice in the Novel." I think very few conferences or workshops teach you how to make your own long fiction better, so my co-leader, Deborah Turrell Atkinson, and I tried to find exercises for that. We're teaching it again this year at the Jackson Hole conference.

What's your day job and when do you find time to write?

My day job is being a publisher these days, as I started a small press with my friend and fellow mystery writer, Katy Munger. It's called Thalia Press. Mostly we publish our own and other traditionally-published authors' backlist, in e-book and paperback, and a select few originals. We've also started a co-op of writers like us. My new novel—published as Rory Tate—is *Jump Cut*. I still find time to write, but have to sandwich it in with stuff under my publisher's hat.

What are the biggest mistakes fledgling writers make?

Most fledgling writers benefit greatly from having agents and editors read and edit their work. I know I have. There have been many times I was too close to the story to see how it worked, or if it didn't work. Submitting to criticism and developing a thick hide are developmental steps in becoming the best writer you can be.

Advice to aspiring mystery novelists?

Write what you like to read. You can never go wrong with that. Don't try to chase trends, they'll be gone tomorrow.

The Juggling Pins of Suspense.

by Lise McClendon

Suspense, like the rich, is different.

I started out as a mystery writer, cutting my teeth on Marcia Muller and Sue Grafton. I wrote my first books in first person, the way of tradition. The detective asks you to tag along on her case; you as the reader see what she sees, know what she knows. The clues are fair, the world is mostly rational and sensible (if a little big gruesome.) There is a strong attraction to this type of novel. It appeals to those of us seeking justice in an unfair world, for ourselves, for others. And especially for the detective, and whoever she is working for in the mystery.

Suspense is a different bag of snakes. I found that out when I started to write more complex novels with multiple points of view. A variety of characters is not really what makes the suspense novel different from the mystery. It's the difference between the rational and the emotional. But it's not that simple either.

When I first started to write, expressing the emotions I felt into words was one of the hardest things. I would be sitting at my computer, crying my eyes out because what I wrote moved me. (Yeah, I know! We all love our own words, right?) But did anybody else feel the same emotion when they read what I'd written? To figure out what moved me, how I felt, was one of my main motivators to write. I was, and still am, a completely intuitive writer. (This means I usually have no idea what my book is truly "about" until I write it. I can outline and plot—a must for thrillers—but the underlying theme is often revealed en route.) And I am emotional. My friends will tell you that I cry during Hallmark commercials. But transferring that feeling inside me to the written page was difficult. It still is.

The cool thing about writing suspense is that creating feeling—emotion—is what it's all about. The Wikipedia defines suspense as "a feeling of uncertainty and anxiety about the outcome of certain actions, most often referring to an audience's perceptions in a dramatic work. . . may operate in any situation where there is a lead-up to a big event or dramatic moment, with tension being a primary emotion felt as part of the situation." In the thriller, suspense becomes the main narrative thrust. (I love that term: narrative thrust! What will happen to the protagonist? Will the bomb go off? Will the world be saved? Usually, a number of unanswered questions, possibilities and mysteries are present as well as plots, subplots, intrigues. The writer must juggle them all to keep suspense going strong.

Organizing the suspense-thriller is challenging. Where to stop a scene for maximum effect? When to show the point of view of the antagonist? In my novel, *Jump Cut*, one of my main challenges was keeping the threads of two seemingly separate criminal cases, plus one terrorist action, from fragmenting the suspense. Plus keeping the focus on the main character, a television reporter in Seattle, who is not actually an investigator but a seeker of truth.

Keeping those balls in the air is tricky. But man, I love to juggle.

(Learn more about Lise McClendon at her website: http://www.lisemcclendon.com, She blogs at: http://lisemcclendon.wordpress.com/ and is on Facebook and Twitter. Her small press is Thalia Press: http://www. thaliapress.com.)

Chapter Five: Private Eyes

Sue Grafton

Sue Grafton published *'A' is for Alibi* in 1982, following 15 years as a Hollywood television script writer. The Kentucky native's 22nd Kinsey Millhone novel, *V is for Vengeance* was released in November 2011, and her work has been published in 28 countries in 26 languages. Her books have sold in the millions.

Sue, does 'V' differ from your previous novels?

It does, indeed, differ from the other novels in the series. In writing these books over a span of some twenty-eight years, I've kept detailed charts, which denote the gender of every killer I write about, the gender of the victim, the motive for the crime, and the nature of the climax. I also keep a set of log lines for each novel, describing the set-up for each book.

In 'A' ... Kinsey's hired to prove the innocence of a woman just out of prison after serving seven years for the murder of her husband.

In 'B' ... Kinsey's hired to find a woman whose signature is required on a minor document.

In 'C' ... Kinsey's hired by a kid to find out who's been trying to murder him.

And so on. This way, I can be certain I'm not inadvertently repeating myself. In 'V,' Kinsey witnesses a shoplifting incident and alerts a sales clerk who notifies store security. The shoplifter is arrested and two days after her fiancé makes bail, she dies from a leap off a 400-foot high bridge. While it appears to be a suicide, the woman's fiancé is convinced she was murdered and hires Kinsey to look into her death. Kinsey's investigation uncovers an organized retail theft ring with which the shoplifter has been working. There are two other subplots woven into the overall storyline and all connect at the end.

How do you and Kinsey Millhone differ and which characteristics do you share?

As for Kinsey, I think of her as my alter-ego . . . the person I might have been had I not married young and had children. We're like one soul in two bodies and she got the good one. The '68 VW she drove (until 'G' is For Gumshoe) was a car I owned some years ago. In 'H' is for Homicide; she acquires the 1974 VW that was sitting out behind my house until I donated it to a local charity that raffled it off. That car was pale blue with only one minor ding in the left rear fender

I own both handguns she talks about and in fact, I learned to shoot so that I would know what it felt like. I also own the all-purpose back dress she wears. Like Kinsey, I've been married and divorced twice, though I'm now married to husband number three and intend to remain so for life. I'm much more domestic than she is and I cuss just as much, if not more.

What's going to happen to Kinsey Millhone when you've finished 'Z' is for Zero?

It's going to take me another eight to ten years to complete the series at the pace I've settled on so I have close to a decade to decide what I'll do after 'Z' is for Zero. I may well continue to chronicle her adventures, but I'll do so as stand-alone novels. No more linking titles!

What's your work schedule like?

I usually arrive at my desk at 9:00 am, check e-mails and Facebook, and then log into the current working journal for the novel I'm in the process of writing. I use these journals to talk to myself about the story, the characters, the pacing, problems I foresee, and any scene that worries me. Any research I do is recorded in the journal as well. I break briefly for lunch and then return to my desk and work until mid-afternoon when I stop and do a walk of three to five miles. My guess is that on a good day, I work productively for two hours. The rest is writer's block and Free Cell. I've been known to work by page count and on that theory; I consider two pages a day a good run. In fact, I consider page count a better way to operate. It's way too easy to claim you've worked for six hours when in reality you've talked on the phone, cleaned your desk drawers, and dawdled the time away.

What do you want your readers to experience from your novels?

I'd like for my readers to experience an entire range of emotions, from laughter to fear, to suspense to anxiety to tears depending on where they are in any given book. I want them to feel connected to Kinsey Millhone, to see the world as she sees it, and to come away from a story understanding how it's affected her. These are the same emotions I look for in any book I read. I want to be touched and moved and I want to come away from a writer's work feeling renewed and refreshed.

(You can communicate with Sue Grafton on her Facebook pages.)

She sent her regrets that her busy schedule of promotions for her latest book, *V is for Vengeance,* prevented her from contributing an article for this collection.)

Randy Rawls

A retired career Army officer and ghostwriter, Randy Rawls fulfilled his lifelong ambition of writing novels. After six published books featuring investigator Ace Edwards, Rawls wrote his first thriller, *Thorns on Roses*, with protagonist Tom Jeffries. He's currently working on a new series with a Florida based PI named Beth Bowman.

Randy, what piqued your interest in writing?

Like many others, I have been a writer my whole life. My first story was written in about the third grade. As best as I can remember, the teacher gave me a C on it. Could have been a C- even. As an Army officer, I spent years as a staff officer. In this capacity, I wrote things for my superiors to claim as their own (ghostwriter). Pick a military subject, and I probably wrote a paper on it. I was also a project leader on some interesting efforts and wrote papers on those. Some of those are still circulating today, setting standards for those who followed.

And, during all those years, I started many works of fiction. A few chapters in, each one died. Life kept interfering. Finally, in about 1990, I was assigned to an office where one of the other officers wrote fiction. When his first book was published, I cheered. When his second was published, I thought, I can do that. So I clicked on the keyboard about a high school student who was a star soccer player. About 150,000 words later, I typed THE END and felt like I'd climbed Mount Everest. Little did I know that it might qualify for one of the worst books every written. Bleck!

However, that story, *David's Game*, planted the seed and it sprouted. Immediately, I began the second book in that series, *Tim's Game*. I'd like to think it was a bit better, even though it, also, was bad, bad, bad. The good news is I learned from my mistakes. I sat back and looked at what I'd written and decided I could do better and would do better. Not long after, the opportunity presented itself and Ace Edwards, Dallas PI, was born. Ace's trips to small towns in Texas took me through six books, each of which achieved its own level of success.

I believe that one of the successes of writing is knowing when you've bombed. I've bombed on several efforts. They rest on my hard drive, waiting to be saved. Maybe someday I'll get back to them. There are few bad stories, just bad writing.

Is Private Investigator Ace Edwards autobiographical?

Ace is part of me and a part of many people I've known over the years. None of my characters are autobiographical or biographical. Some of them may reflect my beliefs, but I'd like to think they are pieces of everyone I've known.

How do we differ? Ace is a smooth operator. Me, I'm a klutz.

Tell us about your latest release, *Thorns on Roses.*

After six Ace Edwards books and a couple of other efforts that did not get published, I decided to see if I could write something with a harder edge. Of course, it would have to meet my basic criteria—blood and guts off-page, no graphic sex, and no gutter language. As I considered the challenge, I visualized a PI in South Florida pulling up in front of the Broward County morgue, invited there to identify a teenage Jane Doe. Tom Jeffries was born.

Tom has good reason not to trust the justice system. It failed his baby sister and, Tom believes, it will fail his best friend whose step-daughter's body is found in the trunk of an abandoned car—dead, nude, and the victim of multiple rapes. Tom vows to track down the people responsible and he discovers the Thorns on Roses gang. One by one, he tracks and disposes of them. But the police are also hot on their trail and may overtake Tom. When he speeds up his operation, catastrophe awaits.

Has your military career influenced your novels?

I don't know. My background has certainly taught me respect for weapons and proper preparation. A military operation launched in haste is doomed to failure, and failure means lives lost. I believe my military background has taught me to insure that every step of my story is logical. I write the same as I would plan a military operation. Every possibility must be considered. To miss one minor step in the path might lead to catastrophic failure. I hope that my readers will find it difficult (hopefully, impossible) to punch holes in my plot line. I do attempt to make them so logical as to be failsafe—but not so logical they're boring.

What does writing mean to you?

Simply stated, everything. I love to write. If I didn't have it, I would be incomplete. Almost every night, I go to sleep thinking about my work in progress. Many times, I awaken in the wee hours with my project in mind. Did I tell you, I love to write?

Has the e-book revolution affected your sales? And how do you feel about publishing's future?

I have resisted the impulse to dive into the world of e-books as a self-publisher. Please don't get me wrong. I respect those who have e-publishing books. I am one of the original Kindle owners and have read a ton of e-books. However, I've been burned so many times by books not ready for publication, I am now gun shy. If I don't see a publisher's name, I probably don't bother.

Yes, this sounds cruel. I don't mean to hurt the thousands of wonderful authors who are self-publishing their excellent e-books. But, as an example, recently, I was looking for a new book. I decided to search in historical fiction, a favorite genre of mine. I dumped the first two downloads I found, both with wonderful stories to tell. In both, the head-hopping was so bad I couldn't keep up. I'm now into a third and hope it will be worth the effort. It breaks my heart that the first two didn't have the benefit of a qualified editor to fix them before they went public. They could have been very good. I am a firm believer that you only have one opportunity to win a fan. Fail, and he'll never come back.

I believe the future of book publishing is bright. Yes, we'll go through several tremors along the way, but when it settles down again, we'll have a solid e-book presence and also an equally solid paper presence. I don't believe that paper books are doomed.

However, I do believe there could be a major change in the publishing world. Some of the major imprints may disappear as the big six struggle to cope with the changes. Or maybe, the big six will break up and we will once again have many publishing houses. The future of independent publishers is bright. They are the ones pushing the e-book revolution. I commend them for doing so. Self-publishing of e-books will stay with us as long as the vendors allow it. Some will be good, but many will be bad. In some instances, as is now the case, writers of bad books will thrive.

How did your first novel, *Jake's Burn*, come about?

Jake's was born at a time I was looking for a new approach to my writing. As I mentioned above, I had written *David's Game* (bad) and *Tim's Game* (not much better) and was flailing around trying to find a fix for my many writing problems. At that time, I lived in Dallas and spent almost every Saturday in a small town in Texas participating in a bicycle ride for charity. I'd built myself up to where I could do 100 kilometers in respectable time. I went to Cisco and did the ride around Eastland County. I fell in love with the countryside and decided I needed to base a book set there. Since I had a major head-hopping POV problem then, I opted to move to first person. For the next year, I read nothing but first person PI stories. During that year, Ace Edwards was born, written in first person, and coming from Cisco, Texas.

It worked. I had found my niche. I liked Ace and Ace was good for me. We went on to write five more books together. And, he's not gone yet. He made a cameo appearance in the sequel to *Thorns on Roses.* Ace solved my POV problem. I now write in both first and third person and feel comfortable doing so.

Advice to fledgling mystery writers?

On the top ten of my list of advice to fledging mystery writers, the first eight are Read, Read, Read, Read, Read, Read, Read, and Read in the genre where you want to write. Nine and ten are Read and Read some more. I am a firm believer in learning from those who have done it. And mixing the pleasure of reading with the education of learning from what you read is a no-brainer. Once you know what you're doing and have decided on what you want to write, DO it. Your first effort may stink, but DO it anyway. Progress can only come by writing and learning from your mistakes.

Number eleven on that list is accept constructive criticism. If someone you respect says your manuscript is ugly, smile and say, "Thank you." Develop a thick skin and select critiques who will be honest with you. A single "it stinks and here's why" from the right person is more valuable than a hundred "it's wonderful" from the wrong people.

Where can we find you on the Internet?

Ouch! My Achilles heel. I'm not good in the world of social media. I only have my website, http://www.randyrawls.com/ and I don't claim it's very good. But I love to hear from people and WILL answer every email. Please contact me at RandyRawls@att.net.

Tired of Flawed Protagonists?

by Randy Rawls

It seems that every mystery I pick up these days has a protagonist that I wouldn't allow to babysit my kids—if I had kids. Three recent reads come to mind.

Number one is a "police procedural." I use the quotes to show my skepticism that he'd be a policeman very long. The hero-cop can't seem to pass a bar without stopping for a shot and a beer—over and over again, bar after bar after . . . And of course, he never starts the car without taking a drink—straight from the bottle of bourbon, scotch, whatever he keeps in the glove box. Yes, this is his department-furnished police vehicle, but no one ever checks it. Yet his drinking never gets in the way of his "only-person-who-can-figure-it-out" investigation. Of course, adding to his drinking, he ignores his superiors, who all but fire him for his off-the-books activities. But, all's well that ends well and he becomes the hero who always solves the case. Everyone can believe that, right? Not likely.

Another recent read has a TV lady who races around like crazy while her bosses back at the station bug her about footage she's supposed to send in of the major catastrophe she was assigned to cover. She doesn't have time for her job, though, because she's too busy getting in everybody's way "investigating" the suspicious death of a body found near the catastrophic area—a body the police believe was not a murder. And yes, she not only proves it was murder, but discovers who did it, much to the consternation of the local authorities, who are, of course, incompetent. All the while, her superiors at the station are threatening to suspend her, fire her, tie her to a stake if she doesn't deliver the footage. She's another heroic, but flawed protagonist who ignores the "rules" and does it her way. Not believable.

Number three was a newspaper reporter. Although he gets assignments from his editor, he thinks, Nah, I don't want to. Instead, he's onto all the crimes committed in the city. Oh, by the way, he's not the crime reporter. He just decides he will be although his stories won't be printed. Of course, he's also an alcoholic, hates the police, and can't commit himself to any woman. Does he solve the crimes the police cannot solve? Of course.

Why do writers invest in such flawed characters? In my latest, *Thorns on Roses,* Tom Jeffries has good reason not to trust the justice system—reasons he tells in the story. He is not an alcoholic. He is not a druggie. He's a straight guy who sets out to avenge the death of the step-daughter of his best friend. Along the way, he does not make a deal with the local drug lord or visit the hot prostitute. He eats his meals without loading up first on martinis. He drinks a beer without a shot of booze beforehand. I didn't ask, but I doubt he's ever had a boilermaker. He doesn't even tell his boss a fat lie. The perfect male? Of course not. He's a tough guy who gets the job done while living a life any of us can identify with. And lest you think he's the lone wolf type, he falls in love and makes a commitment. I'd let Tom babysit my kids—if I had kids.

You can visit Randy at his website: http://www.randyrawls.com/

Mark Troy

Mark Troy lived in Thailand for five years as a Peace Corps volunteer, where he taught English and supervised student teachers. He also traveled extensively in South East Asia, India and Nepal. After earning his doctorate from the University of Hawaii, he worked in education research for several years before joining the staff of Texas A&M University.

Mark, you've lived in some exotic places. Which setting sparked your interest in writing fiction?

The first spark occurred while living in Thailand. I was doing a lot of reading and discussing books with other volunteers. I tried some stories, but they were terrible. I caught the spark again after we had moved to Hawaii and I had finished my dissertation. By that time I decided that I wanted to write mysteries. The fact that there were very few Hawaiian mysteries struck me as something that needed rectifying. I was also inspired by the Halekulani Hotel in Waikiki, which is on the spot where the first Charlie Chan story, *The House Without A Key*, was set. The bar at the Halekulani is named The House Without A Key and is the best place in Honolulu to grab a martini at sunset.

How did you conceive your Hawaiian female private detective, Val Lyon?

My first attempts at mysteries had a main character who was an amateur sleuth and a lot like me. He had a job as a junior researcher at a large university. He wasn't any kind of an action hero, so I added a secondary character, an ex-cop, to supply the action. Thinking there ought to be some romance, I made this character a kick-ass babe. The first smart thing I did with the story was submit part of it to a writing workshop shortly after moving to Texas. The workshop was led by Joe R. Lansdale, whom I was not familiar with at the time. Lansdale hated the main character, didn't think much of the story, but he liked the woman, Val Lyon. His first two suggestions were to keep the story in her point of view and write it in the first person. After talking to him about it and giving it a lot of thought, I decided to try it. It turned out to be the best thing I did.

The Shamus Awards convinced me to make Val a private eye. I was following Lansdale's advice, writing the story from Val's POV when I learned about the Shamus Awards. I looked up the past winners and nominees and realized I'd read most of the books and that the authors were writers I greatly admired. I decided at that point that I should write what I liked to read, so I changed from writing amateur detective stories to private eye stories.

Did your participation in sports convince you to write your recent release, *Game Face*?

I don't participate in many sports. My main sport is running, which I have not written about. I did skydiving for a few years and that inspired one of the stories in the collection, but that's the only one. My wife and I watch a lot of sports, though, especially basketball. When I created Val Lyon, my wife suggested that since so many female sleuths were runners, Val should have a different sport. So, I made her a basketball player who had previously played in college and professionally in Europe. That background and a lot of arm-chair sports-watching led to these stories. Three of them were inspired by articles in *Sports Illustrated*.

Tell us about *Game Face*.

Game Face is a collection of eight short stories, all featuring detective Val Lyon. Seven have been previously published in various magazines, e-zines and anthologies and one story is original to this collection. I wrote that story because I wanted readers who had read the published stories to have a reason to buy this book. There's also some great interior art. It's available for all the major e-book readers and in trade paperback.

Although sports provide the backdrop, I don't consider these sports stories about winning and losing. They are about greed, lust, and murder. More cheating takes place in bed than on the court in this collection. The title refers to Val's dominant attitude of competing to win. The games are afoot and Val had better have her game face on because her opponent is Death and he scores first every time.

How do you support your writing habit?

I do research on institutional effectiveness at Texas A&M University. Most of my work involves surveys of students and faculty, course evaluations, and assessment of academic programs. Eight to five, I'm heavily involved in statistical analysis. Outside of work, I do my writing. I think the two—statistical analysis and writing fiction—are complementary. Statistics is all about people. It's one way of learning about people. So is writing fiction. I write to learn about these characters.

I get up early every morning and write before doing anything else so that nothing can interfere with it. In the evenings I do my research, my editing, or just read for pleasure. I do the querying, submitting and networking at lunch.

Do you outline your books or do you wing it?

Both. I start with a few notes about the story, which usually include some background on the characters and statements about the main plot points and the central idea. As I write, I'll add more information on the characters and list more plot points as they occur to me. From time to time I will look at the plot points and rearrange them as necessary. I used to put the points and the notes on index cards, but now I use Scrivener, which has virtual index cards. By the time I finish the first draft, I have a pretty good outline to aid in the revision.

What's the most difficult aspect of writing for you and what do you enjoy most about the process?

The first draft always seems to bog down at some point. I start to question the story and the writing. Sometimes I find it hard to get motivated. If I didn't have a set time to write, I might not get anything done.

I enjoy revising. Once I have a draft completed, I enjoy turning it into something good and exciting. I also like letting a story take me to new places and discover new things. A lot of that comes with research.

Who most influenced your own work?

Joe Lansdale set me on the path I'm on now. John D. MacDonald, Robert Crais, Robert B. Parker, Greg Rucka, Marcia Mueller are some of the writers I greatly admire.

Advice for fledgling writers?

Don't write what you know.

Write What You Don't Know

by Mark Troy

Every writer and everyone hoping to write has heard the admonition to "write what you know." But is that really how we write? It might be true of memoirists, but not of fiction writers. Fiction writers make stuff up. We don't write what we know, we write what we imagine.

The late Ken Kesey said "Don't write what you know. What you know is boring. Write what you don't know." We need to write about what excites us and what excites us is what's new, the unknown. We want to get out of our comfort zone and explore new territory. Writing is exploring. When we write, we learn new things about characters and what moves them. That's why we write, at least it is for me. Hemingway said that knowledge is found at the point of a pencil. Writing is exploring.

Too many new writers think they have to write what they know. They create characters who are like them; who do the things they do; who have the same ideas they do. I know I made that mistake when I started. My main characters were my surrogates, and, frankly, they weren't all that interesting. It was only when, on the advice of Joe R. Lansdale, that I started writing from a woman's point of view that I was able to create interesting characters.

People ask, "How do you know what it's like to be a woman?" The answer is that I don't know, but I can imagine it. I take risks and get out of my comfort zone. It might seem like a paradox, but the more I rely on my imagination, the more real my characters become.

I can't be lazy when I write from a woman's POV. I admit that I do have a tendency toward laziness in my writing, especially when I write what I know or when I create a character who resembles me or people I know. Creating characters who are *not* like me forces me to call on my imagination and explore what I don't know. When I write what I know, the result is flat and boring.

Recently a friend showed me a story she'd written. This person is an excellent writer, but this particular story was not. The story was about some people we both know. Their names were thinly disguised, but the places and most of the incidents in the story were real. Therein lies the problem. The characters in her story were uninteresting because my friend had confined herself to only visible, surface features and had not gone into their complexities. She had not delved into the unknown.

How often have you heard that a character was taken from real life, that they "really did that," or they "really talk that way" only to find the character was flat and boring? It's not that real life and real people aren't boring, but that to make them come alive on the page we need to get deep into them and explore what we don't know.

So to new writers I say: Take risks. Step out of your comfort zone; Write what you don't know.

(Visit Mark Troy's websites: http://www.marktroy.net and http://hawaiianeye.blogspot.com, as well as his blog sites: http://tinyurl.com/7u733tt, and http://tinyurl.com/7wotwc. He's also on Facebook and Twitter: Sktwritermt)

Chapter Six: Noir

Vincent Zandri

Vincent Zandri is a bestselling, award-winning author who travels the world as a photojournalist. His novel, *As Catch Can,* was called "brilliant" by the *New York Post* as well as "The most arresting first crime novel to break into print this season" by *The Boston Herald.*

Vincent, why the large cross with neon letters on your website?

The Big Cross. That's from a piece I did for RT (Russia Today satellite news network) about New York state going broke. The governor warned the public that in two or three week's time the state would be bankrupt. I had just flown in from an assignment in Moscow and Italy, and promptly drove down to the local mission in Albany, and took that shot. I liked it so much I put it up on my website. Very noir, especially at night. The mission was built by my dad, a local Albany contractor. So he was probably responsible for purchasing and installing that big illuminated cross.

How do you support your novel writing habit?

Lately it's been lots of journalism and pretty good royalties from my releases last year alone: *Moonlight Falls,* and *The Remains,* which has been a bestseller for months in both hardboiled and romantic-suspense fiction. But while I was building back my career, my dad was pretty generous about helping me out. I used to work for him, and he knows how hard this business can be. There's been some movie interest in my *Moonlight Falls* novel, so fingers crossed there.

Tell us about your recent release, *The Innocent*.

The Innocent came about while I was working on a non-fiction biography concerning New York State's first black maximum security prison warden by the name of David Harris. Story goes that he was personally investigated for failure to properly do his job when a cop killer managed to escape. He was eventually exonerated but that kind of thing sticks with you and can make you bitter. No one likes to be falsely accused of anything! While the nonfiction didn't sell, I came up with the idea of a prison warden who not only is blamed for the prison break of a cop killer, but who is also brought up on charges of murder one when said cop killer shows up murdered.

I wanted it to be a paranoid thriller in the vein of Hitchcock, and I hope that I succeeded. It was originally published by Delacorte Press under the title *As Catch Can*, and numerous foreign translations were sold. For some reason Delacorte couldn't really make it do anything even after laying a ton of money on me. But now that it's been re-released, it's an Amazon bestseller in hardboiled fiction, which really pleases me.

How did your transition from journalism to fiction come about?

The transition is never ending in that every day I work on journalism assignments and write fiction. These days, having signed two more contracts for two books with StoneGate Ink (a new noir imprint from StoneHouse Ink), it's getting harder and harder to balance my time. I'm also an obsessed marketer of my work. But I learned long ago not to place all your eggs— golden, rotten, or otherwise—into the same basket. I did that once before and was out of work for more than a year. I don't ever expect to give up journalism, but if my books continue to sell as well as they have, I will be able to choose only the stories

I want to write. Stories that really interest me.

Do you outline your novels or have a vague idea of what you're going to write when you sit down at the computer?

I try and think about the story in my head for a good long time before I begin to write. I used to begin on the story long before it was meant to be written and it would result in the worst frustrations. Nowadays, I might take a month or more to make notes and think about my characters. Only when that's completed will I draw up a prelim outline that's loose enough to allow the story to form organically. When I finish the first draft, which I usually do by hand, that will serve as my formal outline. I'll let that sit for a while before going back to it. At any one time, I might be working on three different novels. In this, the day and age of Kindles and e-books, readers want and expect more work from their favorite authors than they used to. So I plan on putting out two books per year for the rest of my life. Plus a bunch of digital shorts, like my noir short, *Pathological.*

You've traveled to China, Russia, France, England, Italy, Spain, Greece, Africa and a lot of other interesting places. Which country do you most enjoy writing about and why?

The country I enjoy most is Italy. I spend a month there every year just working, thinking, eating and drinking. But the country I most love to photograph and write about is Africa. I was on an assignment there for RT last year and I wrote about 10 pieces and took hundreds of photos. I was stationed on a hospital ship off the coast of Benin, West Africa, during the peak time of piracy. I spent time in the surgery and off ship in the bush, which was an incredible experience, not to mention dangerous. You feel pretty vulnerable when the Land Cruiser you're driving over a dirt road is suddenly flagged down by a soldier standing in the middle of the road waving an AK-47 at you. They demand papers but what they really want is money. You give them money and the first thought that crosses your mind is, "If he kills me, no way anyone is going to find my body." I actually had to bribe my way out of the country. My idea of fun!

How difficult was it to acquire an agent?

Curiously, I've never had any trouble luring agents to my cause. And I've had a bunch of them, from Suzanne Gluck at WMA to my present one, Janet Benrey. What's difficult is finding an agent who wants to remain in the business. And, frankly, a lot of them are sort of crazy. My first big agent, Jimmy Vines, is missing in action, on the lam, or some such thing. Following him I signed with a string of agents who for one reason or another up and quit the business just like that. Their actions literally cost me years and tons of sales. But agents looking for a new line of work seems to be one of the growing trends in the business. In fact, I've been in and out of this commercial fiction thing for more than ten years now, and not a single person I started with—agent, editor, chief editor, publicist, etc.—is still working in the publishing business. Well, that's not entirely true, since Jacob Hoye, the editor who first bought me (and Harlan Coben, by the way), heads up MTV's Pop Culture books division. But hey, I don't write pop culture, whatever that is.

Advice to aspiring writers?

Finish school, learn to live on little while living large. Travel, gain experiences, pay attention to what people say and how they say it. Read all the greats from Hemingway to Robert B. Parker to the great Charlie Huston. Then write as much as you can and rewrite some more. Don't be dismayed when the people you graduated from high school and college with are pulling ahead financially. You will catch up eventually so long as you stick to your guns. Persevering is what this business is about as much as it is about writing well. Oh, and don't get married. For the first ten years of your working life, the writing will be both spouse and mistress. Hope this helps. If anyone has more questions, feel free to email me at Vanzandri@aol.com.

Renewing My Writing Vows

by Vincent Zandri

I've experienced one of the hardest seven days of my life with the unexpected and very sudden death of my dad, who dropped dead while tying his shoes after having jogged his daily three miles and gotten in a full free-weights workout. Being in the possession of a strong heart, even at 76 years of age, he over-exerted himself on this particular morning and his heart stopped. No resuscitation possible, despite a valiant effort on the part of EMTs, who worked on his chest for nearly an hour. By the time he arrived at the hospital in Albany he was DOA.

My dad was a giver and he liked to be involved, even if in a small way, in all the lives of his children and grandchildren. He was also a control man who liked to do things his way, and his way only. So now that he is suddenly gone, I find myself wanting to give him a call regarding matters that have to do entirely with him. The paradox is heartbreaking.

Despite the tragedy of his sudden death, I am nonetheless a better man for it in that I have had a lot of growing up to do this week, not the least of which is deciding how I am going to handle the next thirty to forty years of my life. How I can carry on in a way that will make him proud. Curiously, I find myself looking at my writing in a new light. I find myself wanting to work even harder and better than ever. That means slowing down on certain projects in order to grab the most meaning out of the fewest words possible. It will take concentration and a renewed effort.

I also find myself more committed to traveling to some of those exotic destinations I have not yet experienced. Borneo, Tibet, Mongolia and beyond. Life is a process and, like a story, it has a beginning, a middle and an end. Oftentimes, we don't know when that end will occur. It can come when you least expect it, like when you're tying your shoes for instance. It's your responsibility to live that life to the fullest in the meantime. And living life means discovering things. The world is out there. Go walk it. And while you're doing that, work hard. Very hard.

Starting Monday, I am renewing my writing vows so that I can hit New Year in full sprint. You should too. Here's how I'm going to conduct my days:

1. Get out of bed by 7:00 a.m., and be at my writing desk with coffee in hand by 7:15.

2. I will write two to three pages in the morning (or if editing, 10 to 15 pages).

3. At around 10:30, I'll go for a run and hit the gym.

4. By 1:30, I'll be back at my desk for another two to three pages.

5. When that's done, I'll put in an hour or so of marketing via the social networks and my blog.

6. On Saturdays I will work in the mornings and take the afternoon off.

7. Sundays are days off (unless I have a deadline looming).

I'm going to commit myself to this routine even when traveling, so long as it's possible (I understand it's pretty hard to write sentences on your laptop from the back of a camel.) I think my dad would be proud to hear that I'm renewing my writing vows. Every day he got up, put on his running shoes and hit the pavement in the dark and cold of the dawn, and then he showered up and went off to work. Nothing stopped him from doing what he needed to do for himself and for those around him whom he loved and who depended upon him. He worked to both please himself and to make the world know that he was here, if only for a brief but poignant time.

(You can learn more about Vincent Zandri at his blog sites: http://www.vincentzandri.com/and http://vincentzandri. blogspot.com/. He's also on My Space, Facebook and Twitter.)

Roger Smith

Former filmmaker-screenwriter, crime novelist Roger Smith tells it like it is in his native South Africa. The brutality of his novels will shock most Americans but he writes about a way of life in the country of former apartheid.

Roger, you've been called the Elmore Leonard of South Africa and the shooting star of the crime scene. What sets your work apart from other crime novels?

I'm very flattered to be compared to Elmore Leonard and I can only imagine it's because my books, *Mixed Blood, Wake Up Dead* and *Dust Devils,* are ensemble pieces like most of Leonard's work, with the POV shifting between a number of different characters. But the body count in my books is way higher than in Leonard's—especially his later ones.

International readers tell me they are fascinated by the South African setting of my novels—which is new to most of them—and they are appalled by the brutally of the society I depict.

Why do you write about violence, brutality, exploitation, poverty, gang and prison life?

I live in—and write about—an extremely violent country. When apartheid ended in the mid-90s, South Africa went from being pariah of the world to everybody's darling under Nelson Mandela, but the bubble burst when Mandela moved on: crime and corruption replaced apartheid as our number one social ill.

We now have amongst the highest homicide statistics in the world. One in three South African women will be raped in her lifetime, and nearly 1,500 children were murdered in South Africa last year. Most of those children were also sexually violated. So I don't portray anything that doesn't happen every day in South Africa. I loathe the comic book porno-violence of a lot of European and U.S. crime writing (and movies, TV and video games, for that matter) where bloodshed is used to titillate. People aren't turned on by what I write—they're shocked. As they should be.

What about your own background?

I grew up under apartheid in South Africa. As a teenager in Johannesburg, I watched white cops mow down black school kids my age during the 1976 youth uprising. A few years later I was drafted into a white army fighting a meaningless bush war against older versions of those black kids.

In the 1980s I was a founder member of a non-racial film cooperative that produced anti-apartheid films for foreign TV networks. As a screenwriter I have written for movies and TV in Africa—everything from sitcoms to drama series. No soaps, I'm pleased to say. I now write crime novels fulltime.

Tell us about your novel, *Dust Devils*.

Years ago I stumbled upon an obscure web interview with an ex-CIA operative who was undercover in South Africa in the early 1960s, based at the U.S. consulate in Durban. He claims he got wind that Nelson Mandela—on the run from the South African security police—would be in the Durban vicinity on a certain day. The CIA guy alerted the SA cops and Mandela went to prison for

27 years. True story, or so the man says.

This stayed with me and became the catalyst for *Dust Devils* when, uninvited, a seventy-something-year-old Texan dying of lung cancer elbowed his way into my consciousness. He told me his name was Bobby Goodbread and he'd been in the CIA for years, involved in dirty tricks across the planet, from South Africa, to Vietnam, to Angola. When Jimmy Carter pulled the CIA out of Angola (where they'd been helping the South Africans fight Cuban-backed guerrillas), Goodbread—who was married to a South African woman and had a son by her—found employment with the apartheid state as a hit man, and ended up serving a long stretch in prison for atrocities he committed.

It turned out that Goodbread's son was very different from his old man. He grew up to become a journalist who was a staunch opponent of apartheid and went on to marry a mixed-race woman and father twins with her. Robert Dell hated Goodbread enough to refuse to carry his name and hadn't seen his own father in twenty years.

Dell's wife was having a tryst with the rich guy when the Minister of Justice sent two hit men to take him out, afraid he was going squeal. Rosie Dell escaped, but one of the hit men—a Zulu by the name of Inja Mazibuko—saw her and tracked her down, wanting to kill her, along with her husband and kids, in what looked like a car accident. But Dell survived. So the State framed him for the murder of his family and he ended up on the run. And the only person there to help him was his oldest enemy: his father. Bobby Goodbread.

So, my thriller, *Dust Devils*, a dark and bloody look at contemporary South Africa—and no love letter— grew out of that stray chunk of dialogue.

How important is humor in crime novels?

I'm not a great fan of comic crime novels—"capers" and whimsical cozies leave me cold. But all great crime writers like Chandler,

Leonard, and one of my current favorites, Daniel Woodrell, weave humor into their novels, through dialogue or the dark and outrageous predicaments they contrive for their characters. The criminal world is rich with black comedy.

I think there's a lot of humor in my books, albeit uniquely South African gallows humor. We do it well, because we've had so much practice.

How do you research your books?

Around ten years ago I moved down to Cape Town, and I fell in love with—and later married—a woman who grew up out on the Cape Flats, a sprawling ghetto outside the city, home to millions of people of mixed race, where the rape, murder and child abuse statistics are the highest in the world. The true stories she told me and the world she introduced me to changed my view of Cape Town forever and inspired me to write crime novels.

A few years ago, I accompanied my wife to a prison to visit her brother. He's in his thirties, a human canvas of prison artwork. Since the age of fourteen he has spent a total of two years out of jail. He knows if he ever goes out into the world again he won't stand a chance, will end up where he always ends up: back in prison. I wrote about men like him in *Mixed Blood* and *Wake Up Dead*.

My latest, *Dust Devils*, is set on a wider stage: Cape Town, Johannesburg and a remote part of the Kwa-Zulu/Natal province which is the epicenter of the HIV/AIDS pandemic and has a culture of extreme violence including clan warfare and battles for lucrative taxi routes. I spent time working on a film in this area in the 1980s, so it was familiar to me, but I traveled up there for a research trip just before I started writing *Dust Devils*.

For the rest, it's reading as much as possible—talking to as many people as possible. Dredging things out of the ditches of my memory that I thought (or hoped) I'd forgotten. The usual business of writing.

How important is an agent and how did you acquire one?

I was determined to have an agent in New York and pursued Alice Martell. She read the manuscript of my first novel, *Mixed Blood*, agreed to represent me and was able to get me a two-book deal in a matter of days. She now sells my books to publishers in six countries, so she is indispensable!

Is there a difference in the South African and American reading preferences?

Not really. If you visit a bookstore in South Africa, you'll find pretty much the same books you'd find in the U.S. or the UK. But there is more of an appreciation of noir crime fiction in the U.S. and Europe; South Africans tend to favor more conventional mystery fare.

Advice to budding crime/noir novelists.

Your challenge is to find stories and characters that move, stimulate and excite *you*—material that you are passionate about. If you find yourself shocked, appalled, terrified and moved by what appears on the page, then your readers will be too.

WHY NOIR NOW?

by Roger Smith

Why does noir crime fiction resurface during times of uncertainty, when societies seem to have lost their moral compasses? Perhaps when reassuring parables with happy endings don't ring true, tougher-minded readers reach for books that are, at heart, dystopian and dark, charting the inevitably downward course of doomed losers who are driven to their fate by their own demons.

In noir the protagonists aren't outsiders called in to restore order, but rather people directly connected to the crime: victims and perpetrators. So noir isn't about private detectives (or their frequent surrogates, reporters) where a hero—or anti-hero—may emerge battered and bruised and even more cynical, but restores some kind of moral balance (and restores the reader's faith in society.) And no way is it police procedural, where the workings of law-enforcement—even if they are flawed—triumph over lawlessness.

In noir, if there are cops (or other representatives of the establishment), which are "bent," they're serving their own outlaw agenda. And unlike traditional mysteries, capers and procedurals, where the story is all about the crime, noir is all about the characters.

What I have always admired about noir fiction is the unflinching way the best of it deals with tough social issues, so when I started writing crime novels set in South Africa—one of the most violent and corrupt countries in the world—I found noir to be the most accurate prism through which to view this society in turmoil.

Apartheid is over, but a crime epidemic, poverty and the highest incidence of HIV/AIDS on the planet present new challenges. Last year the ex-commissioner of police was sentenced to fifteen years in prison for corruption. One in three South African women will be raped in their lifetime. Teenage girls are sold into slave marriages in the name of tradition and men believe that raping young virgins—often children—will cure them of AIDS. Noir country, for sure.

American noir, too, has always questioned its society (from James M. Cain to James Ellroy) and it's unsurprising that this dark brand of fiction is the engine-room of radical new crime writing emerging from the U.S. Younger writers like Frank Bill (*Crimes in Southern Indiana*) and Keith Rawson (*The Chaos we Know*), have both recently published anthologies that paint a bleak picture of the heartland of post-9/11 America: stories of unemployment, disintegrating families and rural meth labs.

So, what better time than now—as protests against the established order sweep the globe—for a resurgence of this brand of existential, deeply pessimistic crime fiction?

(Roger Smith's website: http://rogersmithbooks.com/.)

Chapter Seven: Traditional Mysteries

Sandra Parshall

Sandra Parshall's first book, *The Heat of the Moon*, won the Agatha Award for best first novel. Her latest book in the series, *Broken Place*, features Rachel Goddard, a spunky young veterinarian. The novel has earned starred reviews from both *Publishers Weekly* and the *Library Journal.*

Sandra, tell us about your life of crime.

For years I wrote mainstream fiction without selling a word of it. I hadn't grown up reading Nancy Drew and didn't start reading mysteries until I was in my thirties, so I had no great ambition to write them. When I discovered the work of Ruth Rendell and Thomas H. Cook, I was introduced to a whole new world of fiction.

I realized that crime stories didn't have to be formulaic, like the Christie and Sherlock Holmes books. Within the framework of a crime story, a writer could explore the most extreme human behavior and emotions. A story could be "about something" and entertaining at the same time. I still didn't think I had the talent to manage the intricate plot of a mystery or suspense novel, though. It wasn't until the idea for *The Heat of the Moon* came to me in a dream that I drew a deep breath and jumped into the water at the dark end of the pool.

Why do you think you're drawn to crime?

I like dramatic stories about people in crisis, and crime changes lives drastically. I want to see how people cope with the aftermath of a crime like murder—the most extreme action any human can take against another.

When did your writing begin?

I can't remember a time when I didn't write. When I was barely able to form letters into words and sentences, I wrote stories on lined pulp paper pads. I think the urge to create stories is inborn and can't be explained.

Did your parents encourage your creativity? And did you inherit the writing gene?

No, I didn't receive any particular encouragement. I was the weird one, always either reading or writing. One of my aunts was a journalist who had (unrealized) ambitions to write fiction, but I don't know of any other relative with an interest in writing.

Has residing in the District of Columbia influenced your writing in any way?

Other than providing a setting for my first book, *The Heat of the Moon*, I don't think it has. Although I'm keenly interested in politics, I don't read political thrillers and would never write one. But Washington is much more than politics. It's a beautiful area, with glorious natural parks and wildlife refuges up and down the Potomac, and the museums and galleries are among the finest in the world. I love living here, although I'm conscious of being at what could be ground zero in a future terrorist attack.

What does your novel, *Broken Places*, entail?

In this book I mix the characters' personal issues with a bit of history and what I hope is a light-handed stroke of sociology. The murder victims, Cameron and Meredith Taylor, came to the mountains as idealistic youths during the late 1960s, determined to do their part in the War on Poverty and improve the lives of the local people. Like many of the antipoverty volunteers, they were both poorly trained and immature, completely unequipped to deal with engrained poverty and an unsympathetic local power structure. Instead of leaving when their year was over, the Taylors stayed, pursuing activist goals. By the time they're killed, they have plenty of enemies. The case is personal for Rachel Goddard and Tom Bridger because the Taylors' daughter is Tom's old girlfriend. She returns home after her parents' deaths, not only to see justice done but also to win Tom back.

What's the best part of writing—and the worst?

I love creating characters, bringing them to life, and developing stories. Nothing ever goes in exactly the direction I had expected, and I enjoy being surprised by my own story. The worst part is the doubt that goes with marketing. Will anyone like it, will anyone think it's good?

Do you outline your books? How do you categorize them?

I can't "wing it" completely. I have to know where I'm headed. I do outline, but in a loose way. The outline changes as I write, because, as I said, stories tend to go in unexpected directions and I've learned to follow them.

My first book is psychological suspense, the second and third are dark traditional mysteries with Gothic overtones.

Do you have a writing schedule and do you aim for a certain amount of words or hours per day?

I would love to be one of those super-disciplined writers who can sit down every day and turn out a precise number of words, but I'm simply not like that. I think I'm doing well if I can get myself to the computer at a reasonably early hour. I probably sit at the computer for three to five hours a day. But the truth is that I'm always writing. Like most writers, I take the story and characters with me wherever I go, whatever I'm doing, and I'm always working on some aspect of a book at all times.

Advice to aspiring writers.

Be absolutely sure this is what you want to do and that you have the talent to ultimately succeed. You might write for years before you sell anything, and you won't survive if you don't believe in yourself and feel a burning desire to write. Beyond that, never stop learning. Read with a critical eye, and consider every bit of writing advice you come across, in case it contains some nugget of wisdom that will open doors in your mind.

Why We Need Stories

by Sandra Parshall

The next time you're in the fiction section of a library or bookstore, take a minute to really *see* what's around you. Each of those novels holds between its covers a distinct world that was created inside someone's head.

Every year thousands of fictional worlds, inhabited by nonexistent people living out imaginary lives, are written, published, and sold. The human hunger for made-up stories is insatiable—and unique. No other animal feels a desire, a *need,* to live simultaneously in the real world and in a wild variety of alternate, imaginary worlds.

Why do people have such a strong compulsion to tell and to hear, to write and to read, fictional versions of human experience? Why isn't reality enough?

Reading fiction is usually seen as an escape from reality—so much so that many parents worry about children who "read too much" and don't spend enough time with other kids. They fear their children will be isolated and fail to develop the "people skills" necessary to succeed in society. A series of psychological studies done over the past few years, though, should set the parents' minds at ease. In every study, frequent readers of fiction were more understanding of other people's viewpoints, better at reading the moods of others, and more open to new experiences. They suffered less from loneliness and social isolation than people who primarily read nonfiction.

Fiction has social benefits even when it's not in print form and bound between covers. In a 2010 study of pre-school children, a team of psychologists found that the more fictional stories the kids listened to, and the more fictional movies they saw, the better able they were to understand other people's viewpoints and beliefs. Watching television, however, didn't provide the same benefits. The psychologists theorize that TV shows are too simplistic and don't challenge the mind and emotions the way more complex forms of fiction do.

We need stories in order to make sense of human life. While we're immersed in a fictional world, we set aside our own beliefs and concerns and adopt the point of view of the protagonist. The two worst things we can say about any fictional person are "She/He didn't seem real to me" and "I didn't care about the character." Most of us don't read fiction out of mere curiosity, to watch characters we don't care about move through a series of events we can never accept as real. We want to be pulled into the story. We want to lose ourselves in the fictional world. We want to understand it, however different it may be from our own experience. Understanding fictional events and people makes us more open-minded in the real world.

(Sandra's website: http://www.sandraparshall.com and her blog site: http://www.poesdeadlydaughters.blogspot.com.)

Gerrie Ferris Finger

The End Game, Gerrie Ferris Finger's debut book, won the Malice Domestic "Best First Traditional Mystery Novel" competition. The retired news reporter lives on the coast of Georgia with her husband, Alan, and their standard poodle, Bogey.

Gerrie, do you think e-books are going to edge out print editions or eliminate them altogether?

I wish I had a crystal ball, as does every author, publisher, reader, agent and editor. I believe print will be around for a long time, but hard covers will be published primarily for Big Name authors. These same Big Names will be published in every other form: e-book, audio, paperback and anything else lurking around the corner to provoke and delight an author, reader, agent, editor or publisher. Because e-books are surging in popularity, I don't see that slowing down any time soon. What could put a bug in e-book sales is every Tom, Dick and Jane publishing his own poorly-edited book. Every writer needs a professional editor and some would-be writers don't see the rewards of paying $500 to $1,000 to get their project edited.

How did your novel, *The End Game*, come about?

I was a staff writer and editor for *The Atlanta Journal-Constitution*. A lot of foster children were going missing, many in the custody and control of the division of children and family services. Also, at the same time, the Atlanta Police Department was raiding massage parlors and finding under-age children working in the sex slave business. Thus, the genesis of *The End Game*.

Tell us about your writing background.

I have written all my life, since the day at camp when I was five and the counselor asked me to write a letter home to mom and dad. I told them all about a little green snake that lived under the cabin. All made-up, of course. I majored in journalism in college, where I had to stick to the facts. Then, I retired to write fiction.

Did journalism contribute to your award-winning novel?

I have to believe it did. I learned to write clear, concise sentences without a lot of adverbs and adjectives. I write in different genres, so sometimes, adjectives and adverbs have their place, i.e., historicals. But in most mystery genres they lessen the tension.

With so many current subgenres, how do you define a traditional mystery?

Think of Agatha Christie. In my opinion Agatha Christie is not a cozy writer as a lot of genre experts believe. She dealt with very dark aspects of murder and mystery as did P.D. James. A traditional mystery most often has a professional policeman or a detective such as Hercule Poirot or Adam Dalgliesh. While considered a subgenre of the traditional mystery, the current cozy is a departure from Patricia Wentworth's Miss Silver and Josephine Tey's Miss Pym (as she disposes). They've taken a decidedly lighter tone. The amateur sleuth might own a flower shop and, perhaps, have a cat or bird that helps solve the crime.

Traditional mysteries always have a satisfying ending; that's not to say a happy ending. They are more hardboiled but not noir. Both cozy and traditional mysteries are whodunits. The violence and sex aspects are muted in both types. St. Martin's competition states that the protagonist can't be beaten up to any serious extent. My heroine is a runner which gives her the power to jump on and off trains, and she's threatened with death, but we can be sure in this traditional novel she's going to survive.

How difficult is it to acquire the right agent?

I had two very nice agents who were unable to sell my books. I then placed my e-books with Desert Breeze by sending submissions to that publisher and was accepted, and I won the competition by entering the novel in a contest. Neither agent could sell *The End Game* to a New York publisher. I honestly don't know how hard they tried, but it didn't get to the right editor at St. Martin's. I probably could get another agent, but I have no interest now. It's getting more difficult because publishers are offering fewer advances. An agent takes fifteen percent of the advance, which means the advance must meet their needs. Publishers are no longer "bringing along" writers at their houses. They want debut writers to sell like they've been around for ten years, earning more this year than last.

What advice do you offer aspiring mystery writers?

Love what you do because the road is long and hard and it's easy to get discouraged. Mystery writing is a crowded field. Be original and never give up.

Mysteries Don't Need Murders

By Gerrie Ferris Finger

Every mystery writer who has stood at a podium for long gets asked about murder. Why must there be a murder in a mystery? Why is murder so fascinating? Could you actually murder someone? Answer: Only if you keep asking those danged questions.

No, there doesn't have to be a murder in a mystery, but it's the best source of conflict I, and most mystery writers, can think of. That accounts for the fact that murder often appears in books not classified as mysteries. I figured out a long time ago that murder mysteries aren't about murder, per se, and that a murder mystery must possess a plotline that stands alone with or without the murder.

Characters must drive the story and be people with whom readers identify and believe in. Their story (plot) needs to be dynamic, have conflict, and a puzzle they eventually solve. From the pen of a good writer, crime plays an important role in these elements regardless of genre. At the heart of the story, actions are created by a set of circumstances that drive reactions that lead to the inevitable resolution. Different subgenres require different resolutions. The cozy mystery requires at least a satisfactory resolution while a romantic suspense needs a happy ending.

On the other hand, a noir murder mystery lends itself to unresolved conflict and even the death of the hero.

It's axiomatic that readers must identify with the hero or antihero in a murder mystery (and to a lesser degree develop opinions on secondary characters)—again depending on the genre. In the noir the reader may see himself as a beaten down hero trying to resolve his own personality issues, or in the traditional mystery she can see herself as the cop hero out to save the world from evil. In these vehicles, readers will naturally wonder how they would react in the situations, given their own personal peculiarities.

Yet readers play a guessing game with the unknown evil-doers and the heroes. They play every angle to figure it out who did it, but are pleased when they don't. In my novel, *The End Game*, I got this reaction quite often: "I never guessed. Well, I considered everyone, but I overlooked the obvious one. I was shocked."

In the end, for readers to feel fulfilled, everything must be revealed. And reveal styles change. In the modern mystery, the clues are scattered so that the denouement isn't a la Rex Stout's Nero Wolfe. In those stories everyone gathers in his old brownstone where he lays out the conclusion and how he got to it.

So there you have it; the reason the murder mystery isn't about murder after all. You could say it's about how readers process their lives through the most traumatic thing that can happen to characters they've come to know, and with whom they identify, understand, sympathize, love and or hate.

(Gerrie Ferris Finger's website: www.gerrieferrisfinger.com and her blog: http://www.gerrieferrisfinger.blogspot.com/.)

M. M. Gornell

Madeline (M.M.) Gornell published three mystery novels—PSWA awarding winning *Uncle Si's Secret*, *Death of a Perfect Man* and her latest release, *Reticence of Ravens*—her first Route 66 mystery. *Reticence of Ravens* is a 2011 Eric Hoffer Fiction finalist, da Vinci Eye finalist, and a Montaigne Medalist finalist. *Lies of Convenience* follows in the series. Madeline is also a potter with a fondness for stoneware and reduction firing. She lives with her husband and assorted canines in a Mojave Desert town on Route 66.

Why mystery novels, Madeline?

I can't imagine writing anything but a mystery. I grew up with Agatha Christie, Margery Allingham, Dorothy L. Sayers, Martha Grimes, Marion Chesney (M.C. Beaton), etc. So my brain is not only steeped in mysterious doings—but Brits and British mystery traditions have a most special place in my heart and imagination. I've gone on-and-on ad nausea about P.D. James in interviews and blogs. She continues to be my inspiration and my guiding light. To experience England through her character's eyes is a marvelous treat as well as an adventure.

For me, murder mysteries are unique in that the underlying pinning for the story is solving who done it, which in turn provides much of the impetus for the protagonist's emotions, activities, and interactions—while simultaneously offering the reader a tricky puzzle to solve. But, solving the murder and bringing the bad guys and gals to some kind of justice is not the whole story. For me, the sense of place (especially enjoyable in British locals), the layers of back stories, the human emotions exposed, the characters' psychological or emotional advancement—these are the key ingredients in a good mystery—and why I love them!

What's so fascinating about Route 66 that you use it as a backdrop for your novels?

When my husband and I moved back to California from a twenty-plus year stay in Puget Sound, somehow, we ended up in a small town in California's Mojave Desert on Route 66. I'm continually fascinated by the sights, sounds, weather, history, terrain, ruins—and so much more—in the Mojave. Interestingly, I was born and raised in Chicago—where Route 66 starts. So, I've got both ends of The Mother Road covered.

And my imagination is captured by thoughts of those who have come before me—what challenges they must have had. *Reticence of Ravens* and *Lies of Convenience* are both set in fictional towns on Route 66; and their inspiration comes from my immediate area.

Tell us about your latest release.

Here's the book jacket synopsis for *Reticence of Ravens,* which I think not only gives you a feel for the story, but also the Mojave:

"Time and events have turned Hubert James Champion III into a morose man trying for the last year to escape into California's Mojave Desert—somewhere a little north of Route 66 on the road to Arizona. No longer a practicing psychologist and FBI collaborator, Hugh now owns Joey's mini-mart, a half-defunct gas station without gas or supplies and little food for customers. Opening hours are variable.

He's a man hiding out from the world, and himself—trying to seek redemption among the creosote and Palo Verde trees. His main companions these days are an aged desert dog, and the unkindness of sometimes raucous, but usually reticent ravens.

But Hugh soon senses that he can't escape—especially when a "special" young woman with red Medusa-like hair, and covered in her father's blood is brought to him one Sunday evening. Turner Jackson has been murdered, and LoraLee Jackson is the main suspect. In quick order Hugh is drawn into proving LoraLee's innocence by both the locals and unwanted East Coast intruders. Add the sudden appearance of LoraLee's previously unknown brother, a bulldog FBI agent with an agenda of his own, and Hugh's cousin Della's love-sick ex-husband—not to mention multiple shootings, exploding drug-labs, and most importantly, Hugh's past demons rearing their ugly heads once again.

No, Hugh cannot escape having to find a murderer—or his own past."

Have any of your characters shared your pottery avocation?

In my second novel, *Death of a Perfect Man*, the protagonist, Jada Beaudine, and the first murder victim are potters. Several suspects are too.

Advice to aspiring mystery novelists?

I think every author is unique, so I don't have any "rule type" advice. Just never, never, never give up!

Inspiration, Setting, and Reader Enjoyment are integrally Linked

by M.M. Gornell

My initial inspiration for writing came from—and has been reinforced throughout my life—by all the great mystery authors that have led the way. My earliest memories are of falling in immediate love with Agatha Christie—her style, her plots, her murder methods, her protagonists, her characters, her locations. Christie was my rock star! These days, I am continually inspired and re-energized by P.D. James. (I am an admitted and unashamed anglophile.)

Along with characters, a key ingredient for my enjoyment of a book is being "taken away." For example, with P.D., I just love being transported to her wonderful locations in Britain. And seeing London and environs through the eyes of her protagonist, Adam Dagleish, is marvelous.

For each of my own novels, my inspiration and first kernel of an idea has come from a location that has reached out, grabbed me, and wouldn't let go. That sounds a bit silly, and it's not the whole story, but truly, so far, I've been inspired to start a story because a location said, "Me! Me! Write about me!" From the location, I've then wondered who would have lived there, or come that way? What is their story? In the case of my first published novel, "Uncle Si's Secret"—during my many dog walks, a particular place along the Snoqualmie Valley Trail kept calling out, *"What a perfect spot for a murder."* And in the case of my latest, "Lies of Convenience," a near collapsed Quonset Hut near Route 66 never failed to tug at me. Indeed, Route 66 is my current writing impetus, and I think will hold my imagination for a long time to come. *So many stories along the way.*

Consequently, I hope my readers are taken away for a few hours into an interesting world that captures and captivates—either because it's so different from theirs, or because they identify with the characters and location. Especially with Route 66 and the desert, I'm hoping that through my characters' senses, the "feel" of the place comes through and grabs them like it did me.

In my mind, story inspiration and reader enjoyment are tied together by setting. Wonderful locations drew me to mystery fiction, and they now inspire me as an author. And creating that "sense of place"—*through all the senses*—is one of my writing goals. From my writing aspirations comes my *most* cherished hope—that when a reader closes one of my books, there's a smile on their face, and

thoughts, questions, ideas beyond who the murderer was remain—
but most of all—they feel a sense of regret the adventure is over and
they have to leave the world of my novel.

(You can visit Madeline Gornell at her website:
http://www.mmgornell.com and her blog site:
http://www/mmgornell.wordpress.com. You can also email
her at mmgornell@earthlink.net.)

Earl Staggs

Derringer Award-winning author, Earl Staggs, has published a number of short stories in magazines and anthologies, some of them included in his recent book, *Short Stories by Earl Staggs*. His debut mystery novel, *Memory of a Murder*, earned thirteen Five Star reviews at Amazon and Barnes and Noble, and his column "Write Tight" appears in the Internet magazine, *Apollo's Lyre*. He has also served as managing editor of *Futures Mystery Magazine* and president of the Short Mystery Fiction Society.

Earl, when did you know you were a writer and did you receive parental encouragement as a child?

Neither of my parents were writers—or even readers—but early in high school, my teachers told me I was good at stringing words together and encouraged me to write. I liked creative writing and began to dream of becoming a writer someday. I kept putting it off, however, until I'd gotten past a career in sales, marriage, raising children and all those other life pursuits.

How did your first mystery novel come about?

Adam Kingston, the protagonist in *Memory of a Murder* originally appeared in a short story. The response to Adam and his unusual gift was so encouraging that I decided to feature him in a novel. After more than two years of writing, rewriting and rewriting again, the novel was published. Unfortunately, after a promising start, the small press which published it went under, leaving me stranded and my book orphaned. I then happened upon another publisher who was looking for mystery novels set in the Chesapeake Bay area. Mine fit perfectly, and I was thrilled when they republished it.

Did your background lend itself to mystery writing and have you written in other genres?

Not so much my background, but my own predisposition toward mystery. My reading and viewing pleasure has always been primarily in that genre. I suppose it's because I enjoy the challenge of a puzzle and love a good solid whodunit that keeps me guessing all the way to the end. I also love seeing the bad guys get what's coming to them, something we don't always see in real life. I think most people are the same, which explains the popularity of mystery and crime books, movies and TV shows.

For variety, I've also written a few humorous short stories without a mystery or crime involved. One of them, "The Day I Almost Became a Great Writer," is available for a free read on my website. Some people have said it's the funniest story I've ever written.

I've not yet tried other genres such as fantasy, science fiction and such, but I have a few good years left, so who knows?

What's the best part of writing and the worst?

The worst part is when I know where the story needs to go, but I don't know how to get there. It's that tear-your-hair-out, this-story-sucks, or why-did-I-become-a-writer-anyway phase that can come anywhere between the first chapter and the last. Call it sagging middle syndrome, writer's block, or some other phrases I've used to describe it, which cannot be printed in a public forum, but for me, it's the worst part of writing.

The best part of writing for me is when I don't have to worry about the worst part. The story takes off on its own and all I have to do is type it as it happens in my head. The characters know where they're going and what they're going to do and I happily go along for the ride, barely able to type fast enough to keep up. I love the best part of writing. I only wish it happened more often.

Who most influenced your own writing and why?

That goes back to my earliest reading days when I was impressed by Hemingway and O'Henry. Hemingway for his strong, sparse writing style and O'Henry for his magical ability to weave a completely rounded tale into the format of a short story. I'm not at all surprised when people tell me they see influences of those two gentlemen in my writing.

How do you promote your work?

I do a great deal of networking online in various writing groups and I do as many speaking and signing events as I can. I love talking about writing with other writers and will leap at the opportunity to speak before a writers group. Recently, I've given talks on the difference between writing novels and short stories and how to incorporate backstory without boring the reader. I also enjoy very much meeting with readers groups, since, after all, that's who we're writing for.

Advice to fledgling writers?

There are a lot of good writers out there and competition is tough. Being good is not good enough. You have to be better than good to rise above the crowd, and that requires constant work to improve your skills. To sum it up, I like to say, "Always make sure the next thing you write is better than the last thing you wrote."

What's your writing schedule like?

I have the perfect part time job for a writer. I'm more or less retired, but to get out of the house every day, keep in touch with other members of the human race, and keep out of trouble, I drive a school bus. The job requires driving a couple of hours in the morning and a couple more in the afternoon, which leaves the middle of the day—about six hours–free for my writing activities. I hang out in the driver's lounge, plug in my laptop, tune out all that's going on around me, and write. It also helps that I like kids.

In the event of an impending disaster, which three inanimate objects would you save?

I think they would be: My laptop. a flashlight and a book titled: "How to Turn Anything Into Food in an Emergency."

When a Story Comes Together

by Earl Staggs

Sometimes the planets align and all is right with the world. Sometimes your gravy and your biscuit end up at the same time for one last mouthful. Sometimes, for writers, a story idea comes along, you write it, and it all comes together perfectly at the end. That happened to me with a story called "Where Billy Died."

The story idea came when my wife and I took a day trip with friends to the tiny town of Hico, Texas. There I learned a local legend. They have convincing evidence that one of the most famous outlaws of the Old West did not die at the wrong end of a gun as the history books claim.

Nope, they insist he lived out his final years in Hico and died there in 1950, a month after his 90th birthday. I visited the museum devoted to him and stood on the exact spot where they say he dropped dead of a heart attack. Whether the legend is true or not didn't matter. I was fascinated and knew I had to use it in a story someday.

But, I reminded myself, I don't write westerns.

So I came up with a contemporary story about a modern day bounty hunter named Jack who travels to Hico to bring back a young bail jumper named Billy Joe Raynor. Piece of cake, thinks Jack, until he discovers he has a tail. The chief bone-breaker for a New Jersey mobster has followed Jack to Hico. Is it because Jack beat up the mobster's brother, or because of something young Billy did before he skipped town? Jack only knows he's tangled with the hulking bruiser before and will have to again. Jack doesn't know he'll also get tangled up in Hico's legend about another young outlaw named Billy and that the past and present will merge in a surprising conclusion.

I'm sure all writers feel the same when a story comes together as well as this one did for me. I hope it happens again someday.

(You can learn more about Earl Staggs at his website at: http://earlwstaggs.wordpress.com, and email him at: earlstaggs@sbcglobal.net)

Holli Castillo

Holli Castillo is an appellate public defender for the State of Louisiana and a former New Orleans Prosecutor. She has a JD degree from Loyola University and a Bachelor's in Drama from the University of New Orleans. Her first novel, *Gumbo Justice* was followed by *Jambalaya Justice*. Her various jobs have included: gymnast, can-can dancer, stage manager, child support collector, New Orleans prosecutor, appellate public defender and bar owner, with other jobs in between.

Holli, which job/profession have you enjoyed most and have they served as novel backgrounds?

I've enjoyed all of the hats I've worn—it would be too difficult to pick the one I enjoyed most. One that I haven't mentioned before was hostess at a restaurant on the Mississippi River called Algier's Landing, which is on the west bank of New Orleans. On my first day a customer was stabbed during a robbery while walking to the ferry back to the French Quarter. The restaurant is closed now, but I should have seen that first day as an omen, as I only lasted three months at that job. The man ended up okay, but his wife's purse was stolen.

I would have to say all of the positions I have held, whether waitress or prosecutor, have served me well for providing background material for my writing. The legal aspects I have learned being a prosecutor and a public defender appear in my books because my protagonist is a prosecutor, but my other jobs also come into play in some form or fashion. For instance, the Can Can show was in the French Quarter, and I worked there three and a half years, so I know the Quarter like I know my own mama. And the characters that come into a bar on any particular night could spawn a lifetime of novels.

Tell us about *Gumbo Justice*. The title suggests an element of humor.

Gumbo Justice features Ryan Murphy, a New Orleans female prosecutor trying to keep up with the Boy's Club. She's a rule follower to the extent that it benefits her, and has a big mouth that often gets her in trouble. In *Gumbo Justice*, she's vying for a promotion and looks like she's going to get it until someone starts killing the defendants in cases she previously lost. At first she isn't too bothered; after all, bad guys finally getting what they deserve is poetic justice, but eventually the murders affect her job and her safety. She has to figure out the killer's identity while balancing the rest of her life, which includes an overly protective police captain for a daddy, four overprotective cop brothers, and a potential romance with a detective—or two. The subject matter is pretty serious, but I try to put a humorous spin on it. I like my mysteries with a side of funny, so I hope I'm accomplishing that in my novels.

Gumbo Justice is the first in the Crescent City Mystery Series. The second, *Jambalaya Justice,* was released July, 2011, and picks up a few months after *Gumbo Justice* ended. In that one, Ryan is trying to solve the murder of a hooker she befriended, while trying to keep her involvement secret from her family, her boss, and her boyfriend, who is a NOPD detective. These first two are set in pre-Katrina New Orleans, but the third, *Chocolate City Justice*, which I'm working on now, will take Ryan and the gang through Katrina and its aftermath.

What caused the delay of your first book?

After a torturous history of trying to get published—which included evacuating for Katrina—I signed a deal with a small press. As I was discussing a release date with the owner, I was in a head-on collision with a drunk driver. I am very short and sit pretty close to the steering wheel, and the front of my Jeep was pushed up against my legs. The dashboard ended up in my lap, sending my left thigh bone through my skin and causing me to lose two inches of bone. My right ankle was twisted completely backwards between the brake and gas pedals, breaking the fibula and tibia, and my left elbow shattered. I was immobile for seven months, had six surgeries, and lots of rehab before I was able to move around again. I now have a titanium rod in my thigh, because too much bone was missing to grow back, plates in my ankle, and screws in my elbow. My kids were also in the car with me, and also suffered injuries, but, thankfully, much less serious than mine. When I was finally up and around again, my novel was released, one day short of a year from the date of the accident.

Did your first screenplay, "Angel Trap," come about as a result of your accident?

While I was on my down time from those first few months after the car crash, one of the only things I could do was write. I had bought screenplay software a few years before, planning on trying my hand at screenwriting, and now seemed the perfect time to do it. I wrote "Angel Trap" in a few months, and then rewrote it as I entered it in contests. I ended up placing first runner-up in the Acclaim screenplay contest, which is kind of a big one.

I also won a Silver Screen at the Las Vegas Film Festival and I also made the finals of some other biggies like Page, Script Showcase, Exposurama, Writers of the Storm, and a few others. I then placed third in an unrelated screenwriting contest where we were given assignments every few days for elimination rounds, and won an online screenwriting course called the Pro Series, which I think has greatly improved all of my writing.

You're a "junk heiress"? What does that mean?

My family owns a scrap metal yard, now mostly buying and selling recyclables such as cans and other metals. My father and his two brothers ran it until my father and one of my uncles died, and now my other uncle and my cousin run it. When I was growing up it was more of a junk yard for car parts and oddities, and Daddy would also joke with me and my sister, pointing to all of the junk toilets and stacks of tires, and say, "One day, all of this will be yours." Although I was kind of embarrassed as a teenager that my daddy owned a junk yard, recycling is pretty lucrative and one of the few businesses that do well when the economy takes a downward turn, so we should have kept our mouths shut.

Why did you decide to open a bar?

Growing up in the metro New Orleans area, owning a bar is the dream of every little girl. Well, maybe not all of them, but through high school my three dreams were to be a writer, live in the French Quarter, and own a bar. (I eventually gave up on living in the Quarter when I realized that residential parking is a bear.)

In my case, a building that had previously been a bar had not opened after Katrina because the owner had no insurance and couldn't afford to repair it. My husband (who is a contractor, deputy constable, football referee, and movie extra), used to pass by the building every day and thought about how much he would have liked to have a bar there. The owner received other offers, but for sentimental reasons only wanted to sell to someone who would keep it a bar. My daughter's *parran* (godfather), was looking for a building to invest in, and it seemed like fate. He ended up buying it and leased it to us for the bar. We had a lot of issues with code enforcement in Jefferson Parish trying to revoke our parking zoning, we think because my husband—whom the character "Big Who" in *Gumbo Justice* is very loosely based upon—ran against a long-time incumbent for sheriff. Everything is political in the south. In the end, we had to sue and after a year won the case and opened the bar. We are just getting the video poker machines turned on now.

I'd call it a neighborhood bar, eclectically decorated, and it's where I held my book launch for *Gumbo Justice* and *Jambalaya Justice.*

What's the best part of writing and the worst?

The best part is doing something I love, and in the process hopefully entertaining people with it. The worst part of writing is when someone doesn't get what I'm writing. I always consider that a failure on my part, that I wasn't able to make someone see something the way I see it.

When do you have time to write?

I am so not a schedule person, and am a night owl, so I work my writing around what I call my "job-job," my criminal appeal work, which I also do from home. I'm president of the Co-Op (PTA equivalent) at my youngest daughter's school, and I write weekly online articles for a private client, so I have a lot to work around. I am not one of those people who can set a timer and work a certain amount of time. I try to write every day if possible, and tend to be most creative in the middle of the night when everyone else is sleeping.

I get a lot of writing done on weekends, after sleeping late. The only time I absolutely refuse to write is during a Saints game, because it's too nerve wracking.

Advice to fledgling writers?

I have two bits of advice that seem contradictory but they aren't really—the first is to not give up. It's difficult to get published, so you can't let those rejection letters take away your confidence.

On the flip side, if you are getting a lot of rejections, you need to figure out what is wrong. Is it the query letter? Have you not done enough research to make sure you're submitting to appropriate agents or right publishers? If anyone gives you feedback in any form, you need to read it carefully before you decide it's wrong. I was getting some form rejections, but I was also getting a lot of things like, "Serial killers are not for us," and "Too dark for our agency." That meant I wasn't checking out the agencies I was submitting to carefully enough. I also received a handwritten note from a famous agent, who wrote that he could not read more than a few pages because my dialogue was not realistic.

The funny thing was the dialogue was pretty close to a real conversation I had heard, but I realized then that maybe real life isn't what agents want. I ended up taking an online writer's course at Writer's Digest and was lucky enough to get Miki Hayden as an instructor. The first thing she said was that my manuscript was too long, at 140,000 words. I had no clue that was long, having judged my length by Grisham and King and other people who are already famous and can write as much as they want. She said most agents wouldn't bother to read the rest of my query when they saw the staggering length of my novel. That bit of information was gold, and after I edited and rewrote, I finally got interest in *Gumbo Justice*.

To Outline or Not

by Holli Castillo

The writing process is different for each writer. Some start with a rigid outline, going step by step through every plot line and scene that will occur in the novel. Others take a more fly-by-the-seat-of-their-pants approach and just sit down and write, allowing the seed of an idea to grow as they put words down on the page. Still others take a middle of the road approach, starting with a sketchy, bare-bones outline and filling in the meat as they write.

I take a somewhat middle approach, writing a scene-by-scene outline that includes all of the major plot lines and red herrings that need to be planted, but write only short scene descriptions. These are usually no more than a sentence or two containing the bare minimum I need in each scene to accomplish the goal of leading to the novel's conclusion.

I start with a basic idea for the novel or screenplay—for instance, a waitress is murdered and a cop is the suspect. I will contemplate this idea for a few days before I decide what evidence will point to the cop, determine the relationship between the cop and the waitress, and at some point in the thought process come up with the identity of the real killer.

I then decide if the killer pointed to the cop intentionally and if there is some reason the killer wants revenge against the cop. I also start to develop other characters, decide how many other possibilities there could be for the killer, and what other things are going wrong in the cop's life.

There have to be obstacles in the cop's life other than the murder investigation. Are he and another officer competing for a detective position? Is there a suspect he arrested who just bonded out of jail? Maybe the cop was cheating on his wife with the waitress and the wife just found out.

Every choice will make a difference as far as the other characters I write about and the other potential suspects that exist. During this stage, I also decide what big events will occur, as well as decide on the big twist at the end.

Once I finish the outline, I begin to write the story. Inevitably I will come up with new red herrings, additional scenes, and extra characters. As I write, I may come up with better ideas or find unexpected plot holes. At this point, I revise my outline, go back to the beginning of the manuscript and add or delete material as necessary. I repeat the process many times before the first draft is complete and I can start editing to get the finished product.

Discovering the writing process that worked for me was by trial and error, and didn't fully evolve until after I wrote my first novel. But since I figured it out, I am able to better focus on the story, which makes my stories better and writing them almost effortless.

(Holli's websites: http://www.gumbojustice.net/ and http://www.hollicastillo.com/. She also has a blog site: http://www.gumbojustice.blogspot.com/ and she is on Facebook.)

Alan Orloff

Bestselling author, John Gilstrap, said of engineer/novelist Alan Orloff's debut novel, "Make room on your shelves for a fresh new voice in mystery writing. *Diamonds for the Dead* has it all: compelling plot, great characters, and the kind of tension that keeps you screwed into your seat for a one-sitting read."

Alan, how did your *Diamonds for the Dead* concept come about?

I wish I could point to a specific event as the impetus for this story, but, like most of my ideas, it just popped into my head. Out of the eight or nine manuscripts I've written, this one has the most "autobiographical" elements. When I was about ten or twelve, my father found out that we had a cousin in Russia who was being persecuted—in and out of jail for being an outspoken professor. So, I incorporated that background into *Diamonds*.

Tell us about the book.

Talk to anyone in Reston, Virginia, and they'll tell you Josh Handleman's dad, "Honest Abe," was a real mensch. But when Josh returns home to bury his estranged father, he gets the shock of his life: his thrifty dad was filthy rich. Oy!

Who was this man who donated millions to charity, invested in the dreams of Josh's friends, and shared his home with a strange vodka-swilling Russian? Apparently, Abe collected diamonds too. But when Josh can't find the gems, he begins to wonder if his dad's death was truly an accident. Hounded by grief and remorse, Josh resolves to find his dad's diamond stash—which could be his inheritance and proof of his father's love. What he doesn't realize is that this emotionally charged treasure hunt is taking him closer to his dad's killer.

My next book, *Killer Routine,* is the first in a series featuring Channing Hayes, a stand-up comic with a tragic past.

Not many engineers write mystery novels. When did you begin writing and why mysteries?

I didn't start writing fiction until about six years ago. I never liked my English classes in school and I certainly didn't like writing papers (maybe that's why I became an engineer). But I've always been a voracious reader and I guess my latent desire to write a book finally blossomed. As for writing mystery and suspense novels, those are the kinds of books I like to read so it seemed only natural to write them.

You were born in Washington D.C. and still live in the area. Have you ever written about politicians?

Frankly, I read about politics every day in the newspaper (yes, I still read the daily paper), and I hear about them nightly on the news. Boring! Having said that, it figures that my work in progress, the sequel to *Killer Routine,* is about a politician.

You've had a varied career, including working on nuclear submarines. Other than writing, what else have you done?

You probably don't have enough space for me to list all of my careers. Some of my "jobs" included supervising assembly workers in a factory, consulting at a newspaper (on the business side), managing a group of product planners for a TV/radio ratings company, and helping to commercialize spin-off technology from the Star Wars program.

For whom do you write?

Interesting question. Mostly, I think I write for my readers. I want my stories to be entertaining page-turners, full of suspense with threads of humor. Is it a coincidence that those are the same kinds of books I like to read? No. So I guess I write for myself, too.

What's the most difficult aspect of writing and the part you enjoy most?

The hardest part of writing is finding enough time to flesh out all my ideas. If you're talking more about craft, then I'd say I usually have a tougher time with description. The parts of writing I enjoy most are those rare times when I'm in a zone and the words come flowing out too fast for me to type. That's a very cool feeling.

How do you schedule your writing?

I'm a stay-at-home dad (I have an incredibly supportive wife, in every sense of the word). When the kids are at school, I can usually hear myself think. Otherwise, not so much.

Advice for fledgling writers?

I've got a five-pronged strategy I'll pass along. Take classes and workshops. Get yourself into a critique group. Network with writers at conferences and professional organizations. Read, read, read. And, of course, write, write, write. If you want to get published, perseverance is key.

A Few Things Every Novice Writer Should Know

by Alan Orloff

Things move slowly in the publishing world. Be prepared to wait. A lot. For your critique group to get through your manuscript. For your queries to be answered (if you're lucky). For your partial and full manuscripts to be read. For editors to weigh your submissions. For your book to wend its way through the production process as it heads toward the bookstore shelf. Best advice: have some other projects to work on while you wait!

Getting help really helps. Critique groups can help you with your writing. An agent can help polish your submission and will know where to send it. An editor can help massage your manuscript into its optimal form. Ignore these *helpers* at your own peril. Getting published really is a village effort (so make sure you have plenty of food on hand.)

You need a thick skin. Rejections are the norm—don't let them "spin you out." Otherwise, you'll never get any writing done. Persistence and perseverance are key. When it comes to reviews, read them if you want, but remember writing is subjective and a lot of those online reviewers have axes to grind. My conclusions? Reviewers who write good reviews are sophisticated, discerning, and intelligent, while the bad reviews are written by illiterate trolls.

Your book doesn't "belong" to only you anymore. While you were writing your manuscript, it was *your* baby. You could feed it what you wanted, dress it how you wanted, play with it whenever you wanted. Now, you have to share and listen to other people's "baby-raising" advice. Once you sign a contact, your book gets slotted into a release date and is tossed onto the production conveyor belt. Flap copy, cover design, titles, internal and external sales pitches, editing, publicity, sales. It all gets done on schedule, without emotion and (mostly) without you. Get used to it.

Online promotion takes a lot more time than you think. Website, blog, Facebook, Google+, Twitter, list serves, Yahoo groups, nings, and a kajillion other social sites lure you in and won't let you escape. These connections are valuable, but you need to exercise discipline or you'll look up and four hours will have elapsed with nothing to show for your "writing" time except a few Mafia War hits.

Other writers are extremely generous. I've found other writers (published, unpublished, bloggers, Twitters, etc.) to be very helpful with their advice, comments, and time. The sense of community among writers is unbelievably amazing!

Take time to enjoy every bumpy, thrilling, uncertain, joyous, nail-biting, wonderful, anxious minute. No sense getting stressed about stuff you can't control (and that encompasses a lot). Getting your first book published is a very exciting time—be sure to stop and smell the ARCs.

(Alan Orloff's website: http://www.alanorloff.com/ and his blog site: http://www.alanorloff.blogspot.com/)

Chapter Eight: Historical Mysteries

photo by Charles Bush

Julie Garwood

Julie Garwood is the author of more than 30 historical and romantic suspense novels, and 36 million copies of her books are in print. Twenty of them have appeared on *The New York Times* Bestsellers list. She also writes YA novels as Emily Chase.

Julie, tell us about *The Ideal Man.*

It's a story of a young woman who is facing two threats. The first one has been with her from her childhood, and the second one comes from an incident that she is thrown into by coincidental circumstance.

Despite the fear she's faced since she was young, she's managed to become a dedicated surgeon. She's successful and self-assured; yet, there's always that vulnerability inside. She's never really allowed herself to let go . . . until the second threat appears. She accidentally becomes a witness to a crime, and the FBI agent on the case not only helps her resolve her fears but also opens her up to emotions she's never felt before.

How did growing up in a large Irish family lend itself to storytelling?

The Irish are by nature great storytellers I think. It seems to come with the genes. They bring out all the nuances of a situation, and I loved sitting around the dinner table listening to my family talk. Also, growing up in a family of seven children taught me that self-expression had to be quick and forceful.

Why did you begin by writing YA books and historicals?

I had young children when I began, so I was drawn to that genre, but I was also interested in historical novels. I had taken a medieval history class in college that I absolutely loved, so I was following that passion as well. My first book, *A Girl Named Summer,* was published by Scholastic, and shortly after that, *Gentle Warrior* was published by Pocket Books. The historical novels found a growing audience, and the publishers asked for more of them, so that's that direction my writing has taken.

While I really enjoy writing the adult books, I'm hoping to find the time to write a few more for young readers someday.

How have your books evolved over the years?

I haven't changed my themes much. I still write about family and loyalty, and I try to insert some humor into my stories. There's always an element of intrigue or suspense and the romance between the hero and heroine is absolutely key. The setting has changed somewhat. I started with historical novels and I've moved into contemporary settings in the last few years. I enjoy each of them, so my goal is to find the time to write both.

What's your writing schedule like?

I like to begin writing early in the morning. It's a routine I started when my children were young. I'd get up early and work on my book before they were awake. I usually have the TV on, though I'm not watching it. It's just background noise. This is a habit that developed when I was a child doing my homework around a table with my siblings. In order to concentrate, I learned to block out the distractions.

Do you outline your novels and do you aim for a certain amount of words each day?

I know where the story is headed, but I don't follow a rigid outline. I find that if I let the story evolve, there will always be some surprises along the way that make it more fun. I can't predict how much I'll produce. There are times when the words just flow and I'll write one or two chapters in a day. Then there are times when I can't seem to get a scene right and I may spend two or three days on one page.

Why do some books make the bestseller lists while other equally well-written books fail?

That's a million dollar question. If I had the answer to that, I'd be a genius. I do believe, though, that there are a great many elements involved. They include some marketing, some talent, and a great deal of luck.

Advice to fledgling novelists?

First, stay focused and set aside some time each and every day to work on your writing. It's important that you get into a rhythm and have the discipline to finish your manuscript.

Second, let your voice be heard in your writing. If your reader can hear you talking to them in your words, they're more likely to listen to what you have to say.

Third, develop a network. Writers' organizations and conferences give you opportunities to meet agents and editors, and that will help you learn more about the publishing business and perhaps give you a leg up in getting published.

How would you occupy your time if you weren't writing?

Family would probably take up most of my time. I have a large extended family, so there's always something going on.

You can visit Julie Garwood's website at:
http://www.juliegarwood.com/, at Facebook:
www.Facebook.com/juliegarwood and at Twitter:
@JulieGarwood

She regrets that her busy schedule didn't allow her time to contribute an article to this collection.

Ann Parker

Ann Parker is a California-based science/corporate writer by day and an historical mystery writer by night. Her award-winning Silver Rush series featuring saloon-owner Inez Stannert, is set in 1880s Colorado, primarily in the silver-mining boomtown of Leadville. *Publisher's Weekly* has said, "Parker smoothly mixes the personal dramas and the detection in an installment that's an easy jumping-on point for newcomers." *Library Journal* adds, "Parker's depth of knowledge coupled with an all-too-human cast leaves us eager to see what Inez will do next. Encore!"

Ann, how do you conduct your historical research from San Francisco?

I have a pretty good collection of books and photographs of the area now, after more than a decade of writing about Leadville and its environs. My bookshelves include such items as *Leadville: Colorado's Magic City,* by Edward Blair; the humongous two-volume, *The History of Leadville and Lake County, Colorado,* by Don and Jean Griswold (and I have it on a searchable CD!); and *Historic Leadville in Rare Photographs and Drawings* by Christian J. Buys. I love looking at old photos—you can pick out such interesting little details with a close examination!

I also "walk the streets" when I can manage to get up there, and take a lot of photos and scribble down a lot of notes. I peruse the old newspapers at the online Historic Colorado Newspapers, and I am a regular Internet visitor at the Lake County Public Library's Local History site. And I pester the research librarians at the library regularly by email, when I have questions.

Tell us about *Mercury's Rise*.

When the book opens, it's the summer of 1880, and Inez Stannert, part-owner of the Silver Queen Saloon in Leadville, is on a stagecoach to Manitou, Colorado. Many people come to Manitou to "chase the cure" for tuberculosis, but Inez has a different reason for visiting this fast-rising health resort: she is on her way to reunite with her young son, William, and her beloved sister, Harmony. However, the journey turns lethal when an East Coast businessman, Edward Pace, mysteriously dies under the horrified gaze of Inez and Pace's wife and children.

As Inez digs deeper into the wherefores and whys of his death, she uncovers shady business dealings by those hoping to profit from the coming bonanza in medicinal waters and miracle remedies, medical practitioners who kindle false hopes in the desperate and the dying, and deception that predates the Civil War. Then Inez's husband, Mark Stannert, reappears after a year-and-a-half unexplained absence. Even as she fights to hold on to her child and the life she has built for herself, Inez comes to realize there is no "cure" for murder I know that many readers of the Silver Rush series have been curious as to what happened to Mark Stannert, who mysteriously disappeared before the start of the series. *Mercury's Rise* answers that question, at least in part!

You named your protagonist for your grandmother. Was Inez Stannert the strong woman that you portray in your series?

Granny was definitely strong, in her own way, but not the gun-carrying, whiskey-drinking, card-playing Inez portrayed in my fiction. She must have had a rough childhood—she never talked about her years as a child and a teenager, so I believe that says something in itself. My grandmother raised three children during the Depression, when my grandfather couldn't find work (not an uncommon story back then, I'm afraid). What's more, even though she never finished high school, she made sure her children got good educations and entered worthwhile professions; my uncle was a mechanical engineer, my aunt a legal secretary (back in the days when women didn't generally do that sort of work), and my father became a physician.

Why would someone with a degree in physics decide to write a series about the Leadville mining town?

My decision to write about Leadville is due to a family history mystery: Granny was raised in Leadville, and never talked about it, but loved telling us grandkids stories about her later life in Denver. My Uncle Walt urged me to research Leadville and think about setting a novel there. I took it on as an assignment, and before I knew it, I'd fallen in love with Leadville's rich history and its current-day incarnation. As to how this ties to the degree in physics—I've always been fascinated by science and technology, and that led me to research topics such as silver mining and assaying in 1880s Colorado (for *Silver Lies*). From there, it was easy to apply the same research skills to a host of historical subjects for the other Silver Rush books: Colorado railroads, the Reconstruction, women's rights in terms of divorce and property law, the medical views/research/treatments of tuberculosis, and so on—all in the proper time frame, of course.

What's your day job and when do you find time to write an historical series?

I'm a science and technical writer/editor and I write about darn near any topic you want to throw my way, from nanotechnology to solar energy to cosmology or hydro-dynamics or the latest and greatest in supercomputer architecture for data-intensive computing. I also do regular "corporate" writing projects: developing employee hand-books, safety manuals, website content, proposal writing—if it has to do with words, I'll tackle it. I'm self-employed, for the most part, so I take on whatever comes my way.

As for finding time to write fiction, yes, it's difficult. I don't have a regular writing schedule—work comes first, because it pays the bills. The fiction I write to "feed my soul." I joke that I'm driven by deadlines and panic, but it's actually more truth than not. I'm a caffeine addict, who prefers writing late at night when things are quiet around the house. Sometimes, I will take a weekend and go hide in the guest room of good friend and fellow mystery writer, Camille Minichino. I can pound out up to 30 to 50 pages on such a weekend, sometimes even more. I don't write an outline, but I'm required to write a synopsis for each book before starting, and my synopses tend to run about 10 pages long, so if I get stuck, I turn to the synopsis or brainstorm with other mystery writers.

How has the e-book revolution affected your print book sales?

I think the jury is still out on that. My publisher, Poisoned Pen Press, has the first three out in various e-book formats, so that's great. I can't say I've gotten rich off the sales, but I'm pleased that the books are available in so many ways, including in audio format, for the most recent two: *Leaden Skies* and *Mercury's Rise*.

Which historical author influenced your own writing?

Since I read so much nonfiction, I'm hard put to name a most-read historical author. I always look forward to books by Martin Cruz Smith, and I very much admire his writing and how he can put me right into any time and place! Right now, the historical fiction book I'm looking forward to reading next is Michelle Black's *Séance in Sepia*. I'm also a closet fan of steampunk, and thinking I'd like to try my hand at that genre someday.

Advice for fledgling historical writers?

Write, write, write. Remember to use all the senses in your writing.

Have some honest and blunt "beta readers" who will let you know when you've let your research take over your book (a definite hazard of being an historical write.).

"Telling Details" Bring the Past Alive

by Ann Parker

In historical mysteries, often "the devil is in the details." The right details can pull your reader into your scene and story, and hold them there. The wrong ones—or even too many of the right ones—can yank them out as they wonder "Is that right?" or lose themselves in a welter of information, shattering the magic bond between reader and writer. Since I write historical mysteries set in Colorado in the early 1880s, primarily in the silver-mining boomtown of Leadville, details are all important, and when researching, I'm always looking for those "telling details," the ones that bring the era and area to life through all the senses.

Historically accurate details lurk in many venues. If your era includes newspapers, you have a gold (or perhaps I should say silver) mine of details that can be used as "fodder for fiction." Examine the quotes in the articles to get a sense of the spoken language. Read the descriptions closely for information about clothing, attitudes, locations, slang, and more. Advertisements are wonderful for highlighting everything from shoe styles to popular patent medicines and names of local businesses. Letters and journals can also yield the same kinds of information. Another venue for digging up details is Google docs.

While researching consumption (tuberculosis) for my fourth book, Mercury's Rise, I found the 1880 Transactions of the American Medical Association, which yielded a mountain of specifics on the medical treatments and attitudes of the day.

If you have the option of going to where your story is set, do so. Even if your story is set centuries in the past, you can glean useful material from the present. Once you are there, employ all your senses, searching out elements that "don't change" over time (the weather, the quality of light, and geological landmarks, for instance) and marking the things that do (which may include the day and night sounds, smells, and so on). Walk the area and see it through your character's eyes. Take notes, take photos, make recordings. Then, later, when you are writing, be aware of the temptation to "info dump" all you've learned. Instead, choose those details that reveal something about your story, character, your setting, and/or your theme. Those are the bits of description that will draw your reader into the world you have created, and bring the past to life.

(Ann Parker's website: http://www.annparker.net/, She's also on Facebook and Twitter)

Nancy Means Wright

Nancy Means Wright is the author of 15 books, including five mysteries from St. Martin's Press. She was a Bread Loaf Scholar, an Agatha winner, and she's published stories in *American Literary Review, Level Best Books, Ellery Queen Mystery Magazine*, et al. She lives in Vermont with her spouse and two Maine Coon cats.

Nancy, why did your mother destroy your writings when you were nine, and why did you later write depressing opening novel chapters?

Like most girls of that age, I was inspired by Nancy Drew. I liked her spirit, longed for adventures, and secretly envied her because she only had a father (my mother had a very dominant personality). I'd always walk to school making up dialogue and scenes, like the kidnapping of a pesky older brother.

The scenes played out, and soon I was writing them down. I had some fifty pages before mother found them and thought she had a juvenile delinquent living in her attic. That was my first rejection. And then my beloved father, who brought home licorice and hugs each night from work, died suddenly when I was twelve. The depressing novel chapters came when mother put me in a girls' boarding school for five years, and because she was a housemother there, I was supposed to be a model student and obey all the rules. I wasn't and I didn't.

Your first novel concerns a young woman trapped in a boys' school, who anesthetizes herself with sherry. How much of *The Losing* is autobiographical?

Definitely the boys' school, myself, and the sherry. I wasn't allowed to teach English because the headmaster claimed it was a man's subject. So I taught remedial reading which was boring, and the sherry became ever more inviting. Finally I got an MA in French and put on plays that weren't the headmaster's "cup of tea," so I felt vindicated. And I cut back on the sherry.

Did you actually write by kerosene lamp while living in a 1795 vintage house, without plumbing or electricity?

Winters we lived in dormitories at that school (I'd married a Vermonter, a paragon of "the simple life" and of civil disobedience.) We bought the 1795 house for $3,000 and named it the Broken House. During the summers I was studying French—did my homework while the diapers spun in the laundromat machines. The same jug of water was recycled for cooking, washing hands, dishes, rinsing out stinky diapers, and finally dumped into an unflushable toilet. This went on for five summers until my husband succumbed to indoor plumbing and electricity. I never did get a bathtub to ruminate in or spin plots.

When did you decide to write mystery novels? And who inspired you to write them?

I divorced in the early nineties and taught in a liberal arts college in Poughkeepsie, New York. On a weekend home in Vermont, I read about two elderly farmers who were assaulted one night for the cash they refused to bank. When the police caught the perps spending bills that reeked of barn—I knew I had to write a mystery. I put that assault into the first chapter of *Mad Season*, and Ruth Cavin at St. Martin's Press bought it.

You have some unusual book titles. Do your books have a common theme?

They're all mysteries, somewhere between cozy and noir (I call the St. Martin's series "rural noir.") And each title alludes to a theme in the novel. For instance, *Poison Apples* is set in a vandalized orchard, and *Stolen Honey* refers to the thirties' Eugenics Project in which so called "degenerates" (often simply illiterate folk) were sterilized in order to "breed better Vermonters." Horrible! The law was on the books until 1973. Not only in Vermont. In my novel a young professor is strangled when she writes a paper, comparing the project to the Holocaust. If there is any theme common to all, it's the plight of small farmers today, as my sleuth is an impecunious single mother dairy farmer.

Your novel, *Midnight Fires*, features eighteenth-century feminist, Mary Wollstonecraft. Do you identify with her in any way?

She has been an alter ego to me since I first read her work and letters in the sixties in a consciousness raising group. Her *Vindication of the Rights of Woman* (1792) blew me away with its radical call for the right to divorce, for equal education with males, and for females to think for themselves and not be the pawns of fathers and husbands. Like me, she left home in her teens, taught school (is a rebellious governess in *Midnight Fires*), and above all, wanted to be a writer. And like me, her desire for independence conflicted with her sensuality—head versus heart. She made ill-fated choices in men— until her late thirties when she found the right one (writer William Godwin) but she died, alas, shortly after childbirth.

What's the most important characteristic a writer can possess?

I dare say curiosity. A driving curiosity to discover what makes people tick, and to virtually become real or fictitious people, who vicariously live their lives. Perseverance is important (it's the name of my wonderful new publisher!) but I do think writing talent is equally key. Without the "drive" you won't succeed, but without good writing, a book won't go beyond your doting mama's eyes.

How do you spend your day and when do you write? Do you aim for a certain amount of words per day?

Like Pavlov's dogs in that long ago experiment, the saliva flows round 8 a.m. and I head for my computer. Until I (recently) broke my right arm, I seldom have writer's block, so I keep at it until noon and then return in the evening for a second sprint—or revision. Afternoons I shop, walk, read, do workshops—whatever. No, I never aim at "so many" words. I'm disciplined, but I don't outline, and I take what comes. I let it surprise me.

Advice for fledgling writers?

Vermont writer, Howard Frank Mosher, nails up rejection slips and adverse reviews on the side of his barn and shoots holes in them. I just leave mine in a cardboard box and let my Maine Coon cats make a nest or pee on them. So send that manuscript out again!

Which three inanimate objects would you save in the event of fire or flood?

First my latest manuscript, be it fiction, play or poem. Then my glasses, since I'm hopelessly near sighted. After that, I'd probably save my wallet with its preponderance of identity, credit, insurance cards, photo IDs, and my good luck 18th century Piece of Eight.

How to *Become* Your Character

by Nancy Means Wright

Have you ever been in a play and tried to become the person you've been cast to portray? If so, you've probably familiar with the Stanislavski method: how to make your character wholly believable through a recall of your own anger, envy, or grief. And how to transfer that emotion, through words and action, to your onstage persona. I recall the struggle I was having to play Mrs. Hardcastle in Goldsmith's She Stoops to Conquer. I couldn't get into the head of that foolish female, until one evening my adolescent son drove my car into a snow bank, which made me late for a rehearsal, and his smirks and nonchalance turned me into that irritable, jaded mother.

The Stanislavski method works for fiction, as well. As I write, I try to visualize each scene as if it's on a stage: I see my protagonist laugh, weep, shriek, strike out. I try to get into the heads of both villain and sleuth, for as Umberto Eco wrote regarding his classical mystery, The Name of the Rose, one must learn "to think and to reconstruct in one's own set up my props and act the scene aloud, switching characters off and on with hat, cane, whip, or sword. And the technique of becoming one's character works not only for the author, Eco allows, but should be "an experience of transformation for the reader."

In nine mysteries to date I've morphed into a dairy farmer (I even learned to milk and birth a cow), and an adolescent sleuth (I had four offspring and seven grandkids on whom to eavesdrop). I've attempted to become both male and female secondary characters, and most recently, the real-life, conflicted Mary Wollstonecraft. The latter has been my greatest challenge, for she lived in the 18th century, and I have only my imagination as time machine.

But in order to enter into the mindset of a character, one must also be familiar with the language and events of that person's times. To be comfortable in Mary's head, I read six biographies, her own writings; and most helpful of all, her collected letters. As I read, I could hear her voice sigh or sparkle in my inner ear. Novels by other period writers, along with long, slow walks in Mary's footsteps in Ireland, London and Paris, have all offered entry into her world.

Of course 18th century buildings have been razed, ancient cobbles torn up, and even letters have telling omissions and unanswered questions. It's here, then, that our writerly imagination comes into play: filling in the blanks, adding fiction to fact. In venting or reinventing a character: hearing, visualizing, dreaming him or her (I guarantee you will!)—and finally, becoming that sleuth—or that villain. As Shakespeare's imprisoned Richard II exclaims, attempting (like the writer) to create a link between his solitary self and the "populous" world: "Thus play I, in one person, many people."

(You can visit Nancy Means Wright at her web and blog site: http://tinyurl.com/6voogsb. She's also on Facebook.)

Chapter Nine: Contemporary Western Mysteries

Vickie Britton and Loretta Jackson

Sisters, Vickie Britton and Loretta Jackson, collaborate on two mystery series featuring Wyoming Sheriff Jeff McQuede and archaeologist Ardis Cole. They have co-authored forty-two novels and over a hundred short stories and articles, and have traveled to Russia, China, Scotland and other foreign countries for research.

When did the two of you decide to collaborate?

We first joined forces to write a mystery-romance entitled, *Path of the Jaguar.* Although we had always critiqued each other's work, we had written solo for a number of years. Then, while on vacation in the Yucatan, we were struck by the same idea for a story and were interested in using this exotic place as a setting. Although we were accustomed to editing each other's work, writing a book together was an entirely new concept. However, we were pleased with the results, and we've been collaborating ever since.

Does one of you begin the book and then pass it on to the other? And what happens when you disagree on the plot?

One of us rough-drafts a section of the book, generally a chapter, and the other edits. This method allows each to have input into every chapter and gives our writing unity. Luckily, our writing goals and styles are very similar.

We don't often run into big disagreements because we use a detailed plot outline and discuss the characters in depth, Of course, sometimes the book takes an unexpected turn, and when that happens, we talk and compromise. We have often been asked, "Do you have to sacrifice creativity to write with another person?" The answer for us is a definite no. Working together increases the flow of ideas. We learn from one another and have as a result expanded our interests. The merging of our individual creativity produces a novel neither one of us would have created alone, yet one that is uniquely our own.

Tell us about Sheriff Jeff McQuede.

In our first full-length McQuede novel, *Murder in Black and White*, Wyoming sheriff Jeff McQuede becomes suspicious when someone breaks into the Coal County Museum and steals only one item—a black and white class photograph. Under the name Jerome Slade the photographer had printed two ominous words: Never Graduated. Then, when a body is unearthed beneath the newly-demolished school, McQuede realizes Slade had not left Black Mountain the night of the spring dance. He uncovers hidden rivalries between Slade and his classmates. When he discovers that Heather Kenwell and the woman of his dreams, Loris Conner, were rivals for Slade's affection, McQuede fears finding out the truth. Theft, blackmail, and another brutal killing lead to photographs taken by Black Mountain's eccentric photographer, Bruce Fenton. While others see an innocent collection, McQuede sees murder in black and white.

Why did you decide to place the series in Wyoming?

We share a love for the Old West. Loretta taught English and creative writing on the Pine Ridge Reservation in South Dakota. Vickie lived in Laramie, Wyoming, for fifteen years, where she took courses on forensics and history at the university. We were fascinated by the heroes, the outlaws, and the legends of the area. This resulted in the completion of our three-book Luck of the Draw western series: *The Devil's Game, The Fifth Ace,* and *The Wild Card,* published by Avalon Books, and Robert Hale's *Stone of Vengeance,* which concerns the legend of Tom Horn.

Jeff McQuede, a rugged, but appealing, contemporary sheriff grew out of this body of work—westerns with their strong elements of mystery. Sheriff McQuede first appeared in a collection of short stories, *A Deal on a Handshake,* released from Whiskey Creek Press in Casper. He is the star of the High Country Mystery series purchased by Avalon. The first three novels are *Murder in Black and White, Whispers of the Stones,* and *Stealer of Horses.*

How did your Ardis Cole mystery series originate?

Ardis Cole is our first series character, an archaeologist who travels to exotic places around the world. In the course of investigating an old mystery, a new crime develops. To make our settings authentic, we traveled to Russia, Scotland, China and other locations. The first book, *The Curse of Senmut,* is set in Egypt. Books in Motion published the eight books as an original audio series. They will all soon be offered in hardback and paperback from Rowe Publishing.

Our interest in archaeology inspired us to begin another series for Solstice Press, the Arla Vaughn: Pre-Columbian Treasure Series. The first two books in the series are *The Mayan Mask of Death* and *The Lost City of the Condor.*

What are the best and worst aspects of writing?

The most important advantage to the creative life is the continuing possibility for growth. In his old age right before his death, Michelangelo stated that he wished he could begin his work at the point that he was ending it. A writer always has plans and goals and that makes his or her life happy and meaningful.

With so much to learn, the worst part of writing is the long apprenticeship. In addition, the same people who write could make more money in some other field, for, although good at times, the pay for most part is never steady or dependable. Writers must be concerned with other compensation—they provide instruction and entertainment for others.

Who most influenced your own writing?

While we often enjoy reading the same author and types of books, our influences were very different. Loretta reads Erle Stanley Gardner and many western authors such as Louis L'Amour. She loves the vivid, terse style of John Steinbeck and Ernest Hemingway. On the other hand, Vickie grew up loving gothics, which were very popular at the time, so writers such as Phyllis Whitney and Virginia Coffman were a big influence. She is also intrigued by Somerset Maugham and Ruth Rendell, whose works contain such excellent characterization. Authors shared in common include Aaron Elkins, Margaret Coel, and Tony Hillerman.

Advice to fledgling collaborators?

When writing a book together, it is most important that both writers have the same vision of the finished novel. Even then, they must make compromises. Many partnerships fail because one writer stubbornly clings to a chapter or idea that doesn't fit with what the other author is writing or which doesn't quite fit into the book as a whole. You must build on the other writer's work and not go off in a different direction or destroy or "unwrite" what the other has accomplished. Fortunately we share similar backgrounds and experiences, which make co-authoring much easier.

We have just completed a guideline for creative writers entitled, *Fiction: From Writing to Publication,* one we hope will be of use to others in the exciting journey of creating a novel.

How to Create a Workable Plot Outline

by Vickie Britton and Loretta Jackson

A good plot outline is your blueprint for the finished novel. Having a chapter-by-chapter outline not only gives your work order and direction, it will ensure that you have enough material to complete a novel.

Before you can begin an outline, you must know in addition to characters and setting, the major theme of the book, the obstacles the protagonist will face as well as the outcome. Keep in mind that every chapter and scene is taking you closer to the all-important conclusion. If you understand this, the outline will be an invaluable aid in enhancing suspense and in forming a natural progression of events.

A plot outline does not need to be long. Four to six pages is often enough. A linear chart is often used because it's important to be able to see all the chapters at once. For the same reason, it's better not to write on the backs of pages.

Do the math first. Decide on the length of the book, how many chapters it will have and approximately how many pages per chapter. For each chapter jot down the characters that will appear and events that will happen, then allow a few lines for notes. An average-sized novel runs 65,000 words and is about 260 pages. This can be roughly divided into eighteen chapters of fourteen pages.

It helps to look at books similar to the one you are writing to get an idea of overall length and chapter length. Allow a little "growing room." Most books have a tendency to expand rather than shrink in the actual writing. Some chapters will turn out to be shorter than others, because of faster action or impressive points, but it's always good to have a target chapter length in mind. Generally most chapters will not exceed seventeen pages.

Carefully plan each chapter. The purpose of chapters is to make your book easier to read. A good plan is to end each chapter by leaving a question in the reader's mind, one that will make him want to read on. For each chapter list all the characters that will appear and all action that moves the story forward. Introduce a subplot if there is one, and indicate in which chapter it will start, how the action of it will rise and fall like the main plot, and how it will be resolved. If the book is a mystery, be sure you have planted clues and "red herrings." If you don't have a good idea of where events will happen, or where clues will be planted, you run the risk of having to go back and plant them once the book is written, and this is a long and tedious process.

After you have completed your outline, view the entire book as if it were a three-act play. This will help you give the work balance and will make it easier to assess whether or not strategic scenes are correctly placed.

You should see when you've finished the blueprint of a workable book. If you don't, go back and revise it until you do. Remember, the amount of work you do on an outline will save you tedious steps later on and is time well spent.

(You can visit both Vickie and Loretta at their website: http://www.vbritton.blogspot.com/ and http://tinyurl.com/7s5vegn.)

Curt Wendleboe

Curt Wendelboe was a lawman long before he wrote his first Berkley Prime Crime novel. The Wyoming resident was befriended by another Wyomingite and former lawman, Craig Johnson, who served as his mentor.

Curt, how did your friendship with bestselling author, Craig Johnson come about?

I first met Craig while he was promoting his first book, *Cold Dish*. He was scheduled to give a talk at our local library, but I was an hour away investigating an accident and missed him. I emailed him later and we met in Buffalo. He offered me direction as to how to proceed with marketing once my novel was as good as it could be. Several years later, he asked that I "go over" the Vietnam sections in his book, *Another Man's Moccasins*. He agreed to look at my manuscript after that and made suggestions for revisions. I polished it until it reflected moonlight, and he sent the book up the chain where it eventually landed on the senior editor's desk at Berkley Prime Crime.

How long were you in law enforcement and do you plan to write about some of your experiences?

I was in law enforcement for thirty-eight years. I guess you could say I was one of the last of the dinosaurs in that profession, the last professional peace officer in Wyoming who never attended a police academy. I started in South Dakota in 1972, and the academy wasn't built until a couple years later. I was "grandfathered" in and so never had to go. Many of my experiences, and most of my characters come from places I've worked, people I've worked with, or arrested, and they lurk within the pages of my books just waiting for someone to turn the page and release them.

Tell us about *Death Along the Spirit Road.*

Death Along the Spirit Road forces Lakota FBI Agent Manny Tanno to return to his home in Pine Ridge to investigate the murder of a prominent Oglala land developer. He resents being ordered back to the Indian reservation he fled eighteen years ago, the place where he escaped the poverty and despair. Several attempts on his life throw boulders in his path. But his brother, ex-felon and American Indian Movement enforcer in the 1970s, manages to reconnect Manny with his roots. In the end, Manny established a relationship with a woman, makes a friend, and solves the crime, even if there was no prosecution. And he realizes positive things also roam the reservation.

Your second novel, *Death Where the Bad Rocks Live*, has also been well received. Tell us about it.

FBI agent Manny Tanno thought he had left his tribe and the Pine Ridge Reservation behind him, but now with a cold case unearthed in the hot desert sun, he knows that the past never really goes away. In Badlands National Park, there is a desolate area the Lakota refer to as the Stronghold. General Custer called it hell on earth. During World War II, the Army Air Corps used it as a bombing range. At the end of the war, many unexploded ordnances were swallowed up in its sweltering sands. But that's not all that's buried there.

Fifty-five years after the war, the Sioux tribe has contracted an ordnance removal company to defuse any remaining ammunition in the Stronghold. When the company finds a human arm near a live bomb, Tanno and the Tribal police are called to investigate. As the body is exhumed, two more are discovered. The remains are close together, but the murders were decades apart—and the story behind them is about to blow up.

I know that you wanted to write as a child, but when did you actually begin writing?

My first recollection of writing was in the seventh grade after my teacher asked each person what they wanted to be. That was the first I thought of it, and the first I started writing. I read every journal and book on writing I could. But where I really learned to write was by reading. See, a writer reads differently than most folks. A writer slows down, analyzing how the author sets his scenes, how plot twists add or take away from the story, how the author uses dialogue to advance the story or reveal character. Reading like a writer has allowed me to write short stories and numerous books.

How was your protagonist, FBI agent Manny Tanno conceived? And why a Native American?

FBI Agent Manny Tanno was conceived when I first started working in law enforcement, although Manny's nine-month developmental phase lasted a bit longer. In the 1970s and 1980s, I was policing in an off-reservation town in South Dakota. Tribal officers, BIA officers, and FBI agents working the reservation would come into town, and we'd talk shop over coffee. Manny's a composite of many of those men plus a little of me thrown in.

I've had a fascination with Plains Indian culture all my life, and Manny naturally became a Lakota. As a member of the Oglala Sioux Tribe, Manny returns to work on what is arguably the Indian reservation in the west with the most history and controversy, Pine Ridge.

Who most influenced your own work and why?

As a kid I practically lived in the Carnegie Library, devouring every

Gentlemen Jim Corbet adventure and Ken Robeson's Doc Savage pulps. As I got older, I read Mickey Spillane and John D. McDonald, both which got me hooked on mysteries. George Orwell's *1984* and *Animal Farm* developed in me a certain cynicism, while John Steinbeck's *Of Mice and Men* and *Grapes of Wrath* dragged me into the Depression-era culture that I grew to love. And when I could sneak it, I read Erskine Caldwell's *Tobacco Road* 'cause good Christian boys didn't read such things.

How do you research your books?

Being a career lawman all my life, I don't have to research police procedure or forensics or the way law officers react in certain situations. If I describe a crime scene, for example, it's accurate and believable because I've probably been directly involved investigating such a crime. The research that I do is into Indians in the last century and how they've evolved. I'm lucky to live close enough to several Indian reservations that I can drive to, researching contemporary issues, researching the paths my characters follow during their day. If they stumble and trip into a dry creek bed, I want to make certain that creek bed is there, dry and treacherous.

Advice to aspiring mystery writers of the West?

Read. Successful writers and those that are not so successful. Harry Steven Keeler was a mystery novelist in the 1940s and 1950s who wrote so badly that there are Harry Steven Keeler fan clubs around the country today—trying to figure out how he could have possibly published so many novels, writing like he did. Reading him, like reading many less-than-stellar writers, teaches how not to write.

And don't be afraid to get dirty learning the craft. Western writers typically have dirt under their chipped nails, thumbs swollen black where they've missed fence staples, manure seeping past holes in the soles of their worn boots. Get dirty to get authentic.

Rookie Writer's Police Education

By Curt Wendleboe

As a writer of western murder mysteries, I have a distinct advantage: I do not have to research most aspects of police procedure, weapons and equipment, or forensics. Thirty years in law enforcement allows me to be accurate and plausible, freeing me up to concentrate on characterization, setting and plot structure. But what can other mystery and police procedural writers do: watch non-stop television and movies to get an education in the various aspects of law enforcement? You do if you want to be entertained; you don't if you want to be true to your craft. Or go on a sabbatical and work at a police or sheriff's department?

Apart from a sabbatical, how can an author be believable? Much of the way police function daily can be learned by "ride alongs." Many smaller agencies in particular offer citizens a chance to ride with patrol officers. Having a set of questions to ask officers in down times, and taking notes on seemingly mundane things, will educate the writer better than anything learned on the screen. Be forewarned though: police often experience eight hours of boredom punctuated by that brief period in their shifts when their hearts jump to their throats. Bring coffee and No-Doz to such ride-a-longs!

CPAs (Citizen Police Academies) have become popular across the country the last decade. Citizens meet usually one night a week for six-twelve weeks, each session familiarizing students with a different area of police work. CPAs can give a writer insight into how police function.

Many agencies have PIOs (Public Information Officers) that are willing to visit with writers who need accuracy in their plots. And if asked, tours of agencies and corrections facilities are frequently conducted.

No area recently has been the subject of more inaccuracies than forensics. Few cases are solved in the manner of CSI, where whiz-bang techniques come through to identify and convict the killer. Most investigators use their LPCs (Leather Personnel Carriers) to beat the pavement and talk with people, running down leads that tie in with the crime or need to be eliminated.

Coroners and MEs (Medical Examiners) will rarely allow a civilian to tag along, but they often agree to talk about their profession, especially if a writer has a particular scenario to run by them. And contacts gained from "ride alongs" or attendance at CPAs can give the writer valuable resources to call upon when it comes time to writing forensics into the story.

If you immerse yourself in the varied research techniques, you'll soon develop a system whereby you can present your story accurately, and in the process enhance your stories. Now when I start writing romances, I'll need to develop a different system.

(You can learn more about Curt Wendleboe at his website: www.spiritroadmysteries.com.)

Chapter Ten: Humorous Mysteries

Lois Winston

Lois Winston is a designer and award-winning author as well as an agent with the Ashley Grayson Literary Agency. Her latest book, *Death By Killer Mop Doll*, is the second book in her critically acclaimed Anastasia Pollack Crafting Mysteries series. *Assault With a Deadly Glue Gun*, the first book in the series, received starred reviews from *Publishers Weekly* and *Booklist*. Her work has been compared with that of Janet Evanovich.

Lois, what advice do you give to fledgling writers seeking literary representation?

If I had to pick one piece of advice, it would be: Don't submit your manuscript until it is ready. Too many unpublished authors make the mistake of thinking their work is ready for submission when it's far from ready. They start their agent search the moment they type THE END, without first learning how to write a publishable manuscript. Today, it's harder than ever to sell a manuscript. Editors are doing the work of four and five people. They don't have time to mentor writers with promise. The manuscripts agents submit must be near perfect. Likewise, agents aren't in business to mentor writers. So before a writer wastes her time and ours, she needs to make sure her manuscript is the best it can be.

Tell us about your Anastasia Pollack mysteries.

Anastasia Pollack is a women's magazine crafts editor, a reluctant amateur sleuth, and she's the star of the Anastasia Pollack Crafting Mysteries. The series begins when her husband permanently cashes in his chips at a roulette table in Vegas, and her comfortable middle class life craps out. Suddenly, she's juggling two teenage sons, a mountain of debt, a communist mother-in-law, and her dead husband's loan shark. And that's before she becomes the prime suspect in the murder of a coworker she discovers hot-glued to her office chair.

How important is humor to the mystery genre? And who, in your opinion, has best combined the two?

Humor is very subjective, which is one reason it's so hard to write. As a writer of humorous fiction, I know that not everyone is going to "get it." Some people think humor doesn't belong in mysteries. However, I believe that it's easier to get through anything if you have a sense of humor. A good humorous mystery doesn't make fun of murder and death. The humor lies in how the protagonist approaches life and deals with all the caca thrown at her.

Personally, I love Janet Evanovich's Stephanie Plum series because Stephanie never fails to make me laugh. Being favorably compared to Evanovich by several reviewers has me floating somewhere over the rainbow. Another favorite series of mine is Lisa Lutz's Izzy Spellman books.

You've received some great reviews. How important are reviews and do bad reviews diminish book sales?

Great reviews certainly give a boost to an author's career, but many books that have received mediocre or even lousy reviews have gone on to become bestsellers. Word-of-mouth is the author's best friend. If people like a book and talk, tweet, and blog about it, other people are going to buy it, no matter what the critics have said.

How do you manage to balance design art with writing and your agenting job?

[Laughter] I thought I was doing a pretty good job of juggling designing, writing, and agenting careers—until last Saturday at a conference when someone said, "See you next week." As far as I knew, I had nothing scheduled for this weekend. Turns out, I'd agreed to speak at a Sisters in Crime meeting and had completely forgotten about it. I guess the scheduling gods were looking out for me, because if this other author hadn't said, "See you next week," I would have stood up several dozen mystery writers.

I've decided I need a personal assistant, but first, I need to be making enough money to afford a personal assistant. Either that, or I need to win the lottery—which means I'd better start buying lottery tickets. I wonder which has better odds.

You've won a number of awards. Which one means the most to you?

The award that means the most is the one I didn't win. I was the first runner-up in Dorchester Publishing's inaugural American Title contest. Even though I came in second, I was offered a publishing contract. That first sale launched my career as a published author.

How important is blogging? In your own experience, has it increased book sales?

It's very hard to quantify how successful blogging or any social networking is in regard to actual book sales. All author promo is a crapshoot, whether it's blogging or giving away tchotkes and doodads with your name and website printed on them. For that matter, even the promo done by publishers and independent PR firms is a crapshoot. What works for one author may lay a ginormous goose egg for another.

In an ideal world, authors would sit at their keyboards and write while their publishers handled all the promo. However, today's world of publishing is less than ideal, and authors are expected to flak their books. In the three years between publication of my last book and my current book, much changed, especially the way authors use social media for promo.

I knew it was time for me to have a blog, but I didn't want to compete with all the well-established author blogs already populating the blogosphere. So I decided Anastasia should blog, not Lois. Since Anastasia works as editor for a women's magazine, it seemed a natural extension that the magazine should have a blog.

Has Killer Crafts & Crafty Killers resulted in more book sales for me? I don't know. What I do know is that every week I have more blog visitors and a growing following. Hopefully, that's extrapolating to more book sales.

How has writing changed your life?

Writing enriched my life in so many ways. I've discovered a talent I never knew I had. I've met many incredible people, some of whom have become extremely close friends. My life would be wanting in so many ways without these supportive, wise, and knowledgeable women and men. I've also enriched my mind, accumulating knowledge that I otherwise wouldn't now have. And I've learned that it's sometimes possible to have dreams come true if you work hard enough toward your goals and don't give up on yourself and those dreams.

A Fat Manuscript is a Dead Manuscript

by Lois Winston

Whether you're writing mystery or another genre, your manuscript needs a great story, great characters, and great writing. The quality of the writing determines the difference between an offer and a rejection. As an agent and an author, I see too many submissions where the writer needs to put her manuscript on a diet.

Before you submit your manuscript, make sure it's not bloated with excess wordage that drags down the pacing and bores the very people you want to impress. Your writing must be crisp as well as succinct to catch an editor's or agent's eye.

The Bloated Manuscript Diet

1. Reread your manuscript. Is every scene essential to the plot or goals, motivations, and conflicts of your characters? Does each scene advance the plot or does it tell the reader something she needs to know about the characters? If not, the scene is filler, and you need to get rid of it. Each scene must serve a purpose. No purpose? No scene.

2. Repeat #1 for all dialogue. If the dialogue is nothing but chit-chat, ditch it.

3. Do a search of *ly* words. Wherever possible, substitute a more active, descriptive verb to replace your existing verb and the adverb that modifies it.

4. Instead of using many adjectives to describe a noun, use one all-encompassing adjective or a more descriptive noun.

5. Say it once, then move on. It's not necessary to repeat an idea or image in different words in the next sentence, the next paragraph, or on the next page.

6. Identify needless words and eliminate them. Every writer has at least one or two pet words she overuses.

7. Avoid a laundry list of descriptions by substituting more descriptive nouns and adjectives.

8. Do a search for *was*. Wherever it's linked with an *ing* verb, omit the *was* and change the tense of the verb.

9. Choose more descriptive verbs and omit the additional words that enhance the verb.

10. Omit extraneous tag lines. If it's obvious which character is speaking, a tag line is unnecessary. Use tag lines only when there are three or more characters taking part in the dialogue scene.

11. Show, don't tell. Wherever possible, you want to "show" your story through dialogue and active narrative, rather than "telling" the story.

12. Let your characters' words convey their emotion, not the tag

line. Also, keep to the unobtrusive *said* in tags. You can't *grimace*, *laugh* or *sigh* dialogue. The character can grimace, laugh, or sigh before or afterward but not while speaking.

13. Avoid non-specific words like *it* and *thing*.

14. Describe body movements only when they're essential to the scene. Don't break up dialogue every other sentence by having your characters shrug, smirk, giggle, glance, nod, or drum their fingers.

15. Don't fill dialogue with interjections. We might have the bad habit of peppering our speech with *well* and *like* but having a character constantly adding those words makes for lousy dialogue.

(Lois Winston's website: http://www.loiswinston.com/ and her blogsite: http://www.anastasiapollack.blogspot.com/ She's also on Twitter.)

J. Michael Orenduff

Former New Mexico Governor Bill Richardson wrote of one of Michael Orenduff's mysteries: *"The Pot Thief Who Studied Pythagoras* has all the components of a great read—an intricate plot, quirky characters, crackling dialog, and a surprise ending. What's more, he successfully captures the essence of New Mexico through humor, romance, and even a little philosophical musing. New Mexico's rich history, people, food, and landscape come alive on its pages. . ."

Orenduff is the 2011 Lefty-Award winning author of *The Pot Thief Who Studied Einstein.*

Mike, how did your review from Governor Richardson come about?

I served as president of New Mexico State University in the nineties while he was one of our congressional representatives. He was supportive of higher education, and I worked with him (mostly his staff) on several projects, including one for Hispanic-serving institutions that tied NMSU with the University of Puerto Rico and some other universities in a federal project. So when I retired and started writing books, I asked him for the review and he graciously consented. And it doesn't hurt that my books attract attention for the state.

Tell us about your award-winning Pot Thief series.

The protagonist was a "pot hunter" in his early days, digging up and selling ancient pottery. When the practice was outlawed, he was rebranded as a pot thief, but he rationalizes what he does. Unfortunately, his clandestine excavations often tie him to a murder which he must solve to clear himself. He's somewhat clueless but often gets inspiration and assistance from his sidekick, Susannah, who acquired her mystery solving skills by reading murder mysteries.

How important is humor in a mystery series?

I think every mystery, no matter how noir, must have some humor if, for no other reason, than to break the tension. In my books, even the tension is funny. At least I hope it is.

Your Pot Thief books have been described as a "thinking man's series." How would you describe them?

The protagonist is part thief and part social critic, who finds popular culture unfathomable. He cherishes the naïve belief that reason works.

What else have you written, other than scholarly papers such as "Are Modal Contexts Referentially Opaque?"

Dozens of other such papers. Were you to be stranded on an island with them as the only printed material, the chances are you would burn them for cooking fires rather than read them.

Why does someone with your advanced education decide to write mystery novels?

Because writing fiction is fun.

What's your work in progress?

I also write plays. I have written two comedies, but now I am trying my hand at a serious play.

Who most influenced your own work?

Michael Bond, Lawrence Saunders and Lawrence Block.

Advice to fledgling writers?

I wish I had some sage advice to pass along, but I don't. One learns the craft of writing like one learns most skills—long hours of practice. Write, write, write. Then take a break and read—you'll see things in what you read that you would not have noticed before you started writing. Repeat the cycle for a few years, always getting people to read your work and give you feedback. At some point you will look at your early attempts and shudder. That means you are making progress.

Dialogue Tags

By J. Michael Orenduff

Robert Parker was one of the most successful crime writers of all time, having penned almost seventy books in the Spenser, Jesse Stone and Sunny Randall series. He wrote a thousand words every day, no more and no less. His many books in the pipeline led me to quip a year after his death that he had published more books dead than I have alive.

In a review of one of Parker's books shortly before he died, I was surprised by the reviewer's criticism of Parker's reliance on "he said" and "I said" in dialogue. I had read all his books and never noticed any overuse of dialogue tags. So I grabbed a Parker off the shelf and started reading. The reviewer was right. Parker ended most sentences in his dialogs with "he said," "she said" or "I said." I was astonished that I had never noticed. I finally put it down to Parker's prose being so good that he could get away with it.

If I could miss that in Robert Parker, maybe I could also miss it in my own writing. So I reviewed my own use of dialogue tags. I found that I didn't use them as frequently as Parker. But I did notice in my review of my dialogues that my most successful ones used fewer or no tags at all.

In the time since I read that review, I've given a lot of thought to dialogue tags. I always notice them when I read. I have come to believe the best dialogue has no tags:

"I can't believe this is happening to me."

"It's the restaurant syndrome, Hubie."

"Restaurant syndrome? I've never heard of it."

"Maybe you know it by its original name, *le syndrome de restaurant.*"

I groaned. "Please, no more French words and phrases."

"But that's it. That's the syndrome. You start working in a restaurant, and you have to learn all those French terms. It begins to affect your thinking, like the twins thing."

"The twins thing?"

"Yeah. You know, like how twins have this special language that makes it easy for them to communicate with each other, but it messes them up when they try to deal with normal people. Restaurant workers are like that. We may start out normal, but after you begin using words like *prix fixe, hors-d'œuvres, à la carte, escargots,* and *raison d'être,* you get a little crazy."

"*Raison d'être?*"

"I think it's a raisin soufflé."

This passage is a conversation between my protagonist, Hubie, and his sidekick, Susannah. The context makes it clear they are alone at a table in their favorite watering hole. How does the reader know that the first speaker is Hubie? Because he is the one having problems. But even if the reader didn't make the connection, it is clear that Hubie is speaking because the response mentions him. I could have started the dialogue with: "I can't believe this is happening to me," I said.

That would not be bad. But I like it better without the tag. People don't use dialogue tags when they speak, so keeping tags out of your dialogue makes it easier for the reader to fall into that perfect state of mind when reading dialogue—thinking you are there listening to the characters.

(You can visit J. Michael Orenduff at his website: http://www.orenduff.org/)

Rebecca (R. P.) Dahlke

Rebecca Phillips Dahlke operated her father's crop dusting business in California during the early 1980s, and began writing her mystery series following the death of her son, a career aero agricultural pilot. Rebecca refers to her books as "murder mysteries with some laughter."

Rebecca, why did you take over the family business? And was flying part of your job?

I sort of fell into the job when my dad decided he'd rather go on a cruise than take on another season of lazy pilots, missing flaggers, testy farmers and horrific hours. After two years at the helm, I handed him back the keys and fled to a city without any of the above. And no, I was never a crop-duster.

Tell us about your writing background.

A few short stories got printed in a now defunct magazine and I was hooked. They say you should write what you know and, at the time, I was able to use what I'd gleaned from my own experiences along with stories that my son, John, a career crop-duster, shared with me. When he died in a work related accident in 2005, I was unable to go back to it until 2010.

How important are writer organizations such as Sisters in Crime to a mid-list mystery writer?

SinC is like a big fat favorite granny. She's warm and comforting and tells you you're wonderful when everyone else tells you your writing is crap!

What's your writing schedule like and do you aim for a certain amount of words each day?

Well—if I'm very good, I can smack out 2,000 words a day—but then life gets in the way, like the Monument fire this last week. We were evacuated and living in our RV with two dogs and I was nervous about our home burning to the ground instead of writing. I'm happy to say that the house survived and so did we.

What is the most important ingredient in an amateur sleuth novel?

I'm glad you asked that question because in *A Dead Red Cadillac* and *A Dead Red Heart,* I write about a tall, blond and beautiful ex-model turned crop-duster who, to quote Lalla Bains, says: "I've been married so many times they oughta revolk my license." I wanted to give readers a peek at the not so-perfect life of a beautiful blonde. Lalla Bains is no Danielle Steele character and she's not afraid of chipping her manicure. Scratch that, the girl doesn't have time for a manicure, what with herding a bunch of recalcitrant pilots and juggling work orders just to keep her father's flagging business alive.

Between a philandering famous Puerto Rican baseball player husband and her long time widowed father's triple by-pass, Lalla is now content to run her dad's crop dusting business in Modesto, California, and avoid the paparazzi hounds who feast on the remains of those who aren't famous anymore.

In *A Dead Red Cadillac,* Lalla is once again brought into the unwanted limelight and, as she sees it, the only way she's ever going to get her life back is if she can solve the mystery. As luck would have it, along the way she finds the man who becomes the love of her life.

How do you promote your books? And how much time do you devote to online networking?

I believe that authors must use as many avenues as possible to promote their work. Branding is a term that comes from major corporations, like Pepsi and Ford and these companies understand that one ad in one magazine is not necessarily going to equal one sale. Your name over and over again, along with the name of your series; like *A Dead Red Cadillac* and *A Dead Red Heart* gives you an edge on that branding.

Advice to aspiring mystery writers?

Self-publish because it encourages you to write instead of pinning all your hopes on that New York publisher. Besides, the more you write the better you get. And you're branding your name, developing a fan base. Who knows, you may get an offer from that New York publisher—which you can then accept or not. Which reminds me; I gotta get busy and finish my latest book, a romantic sailing mystery set in exotic Mexico. I hope to have *A Dangerous Harbor* ready for publication by the end of this summer.

Self-Publishing is No Longer a Dirty Word

by Rebecca Dahlke

Facebook, Twitter, My Space, blogging, and that newest, if somewhat puzzling buzzword—BRANDING—sorta smacks of burning flesh from a red hot poker, doesn't it? Still, in a very literal sense, it hits the mark. So, how's an author supposed to juggle all this new stuff and find the time to write books? Some suggest we ignore the message, keep to the "tried and true" and this fad will pass. Well, my little buckaroos, I'm here to tell you that the only thing that will pass is the herd of savvy authors charging ahead, if you happen to get this message.

Eons ago, back in the day, the dark ages—was it really only five years ago?—all we authors could hope for was a good agent, a decent publisher, a slowly growing fan base, and a list of book stores that might, or might not, keep our books on their shelves for three to six months before returning the unsold copies to the publisher. We could send in Advanced Reader Copies to a prestigious reviewers or magazines and hope they would say nice things about our books, or pay a publicist to tout it, take our dog and pony show on the road, eat bad food, stay in crappy hotels, be at that next book store, book fair, conference, and smile till our cheeks ached.

Then Amazon did the unthinkable, they created an Internet book store devoted to e-books. And, better yet, they allowed anyone, yes, *everyone* who had written a book and presented it to Amazon in the right e-book format to sell it under their minimal terms with nice commissions. Suddenly, self-published was no longer a dirty word. Writers presented their words directly to the people who deemed them worthy, or not. And, then surprise, surprise, stars bloomed in the wilderness! Sales of unknown authors were snugged up alongside hallowed veterans. Amazon's philosophy is that if readers buy your book, your ranking goes up and Amazon will promote your book next to Tom Clancy or James North Patterson.

And, because I too heard the lonely call of the charging herd, I set up a Twitter account, FaceBook and a GoodReads author page. I promoted at Yahoo groups, Amazon forums, blog sites, author sites and review sites. I read and review for other mystery authors and post my reviews—with my by-line at the bottom—at places that allow me to do so. Then I watched as my ranking on Amazon climbed. At first slowly and then faster. I added three books in 2011 and plan to publish two more in 2012—a feat that was only wishful thinking a few short years before. I have readers, some who love my books, and some not so much—but that's the beauty of it. My books aren't for everyone and I make that clear in my posted biography that these are pure entertainment. If you want literary fiction, Steinbeck is down the hall, two doors on the left.

The changes have been exciting, and for this author, validation that I too can write books that readers enjoy. So, for all the august veterans who see the Internet as an encroachment onto their hard-won personal turf, let me paraphrase one of my favorite movie lines: Saddle up boys and girls; it's going to be a bumpy ride!

(R. P. Dahlke's website: http://www.rpdahlke.com/. She's also on Facebook: http://www.facebook.com/RPDahlke.)

Marja McGraw

A southern California native, Marja McGraw has served in both criminal and civil law enforcement. As a divorced, single parent she lived in a number of locations, including Wasilla, Alaska, and northern Nevada, where she worked for the Department of Transportation. She was also employed by the Jackson County sheriff's department while owning her own antique store/tea room. She's the author of the Sandi Webster and The Bogey Man mystery series.

Marja, has blogging helped your book sales?

To be honest, someone strongly suggested I start blogging and I went into it kicking and screaming. I really didn't want to blog. I was dead wrong. I enjoy writing these short articles or blogs, and now I'm glad I was pushed into it. However, I've learned that for the most part people like blogs that are down-to-earth so they come to know the author a little. And I've learned that I have no idea if a blog will help book sales or not, but that's not the only purpose. Marja's Mystery Blog is a great place to share information and to showcase my writing style and the style of others.

I've also learned how generous others can be with their blog sites, which allow me to spout off about new books, ideas, thoughts and whatever else comes to mind. I've met some wonderful authors and some great readers through blogging, and I've enjoyed hosting other authors on my site.

How did your two series come about?

I wanted to include some humor in my books, and I enjoy a good mystery, so I felt I needed character-driven stories. When I started writing I wanted a protagonist who people could relate to on some level. Sandi Webster is in her thirties, somewhat naïve, and who got into the business of private investigating for all the wrong reasons. She interacts with her partner, Pete (ex-cop), a menopausal mother, an elderly neighbor and Stanley, an employee who started out as a client. Sandi may be a bit naïve, but she's always up to the challenge when the chips are down. She's smart and she uses her common sense.

After four books, along came the Bogey Man Mysteries. I've always been a huge Humphrey Bogart fan, and I added a man (Chris Cross) with an uncanny resemblance to him as a character in *The Bogey Man*, one of the Sandi Webster mysteries. He was so popular with readers that I decided to give him his own series. It's turned out to be a lot of fun; much more so than I anticipated. He has a wife who partners with him, a stepson who wants nothing more than to be involved in one of the mysteries, and two "interesting" yellow Labrador retrievers. He swears he's not a gumshoe and yet frequently manages to become involved in mysteries.

What prompted you to use a 1940s backdrop for your novels?

Let me begin by saying that the stories take place today, not back in the forties. I don't want any confusion about that. With that said, how else could I do justice to a character looking like Bogey? He needs to use the old slang, and he demonstrates some of Bogey's mannerisms as they were in his movies. The forties were a fun time in a lot of ways, so I'm trying to keep that alive through the Bogey Man.

Sandi loves vintage movies and has a love for the "old days," too. She's become involved in a few capers involving cold cases; however, most of her work involves the present.

In what capacity did you work in law enforcement? And have you used your experiences in your novels?

I actually worked in a clerical capacity, but back in the day there weren't any female deputies in my department. If one was needed, we clerks filled in. Things were so different in the seventies. On one occasion I was asked to search a public women's restroom for a bomb, with no training. Thankfully, there was no bomb, or I wouldn't be writing this. Another time my life was threatened by a woman who'd applied for a job and wasn't hired. All I'd done was administer the typing test, and her typing wasn't why she was turned down. I may have been clerical, but I have lots of stories. I was very young and shy, and single at the time, and working with all those cops brought me out of my shell.

In the 1990s, I worked for a county sheriff's office in Oregon, and that was a different experience. Things had changed a lot by then. I do occasionally use my experiences in my books, but the stories also require a lot of research. As I've said, things have changed since I worked in law enforcement, so I've also made it a point to ask a lot of questions of those who still do.

How important are quirky characters in a mystery novel?

In my writing they're very important. My goal is to entertain the reader, and, realistically, murder isn't funny on any level. However, those quirky characters and their antics in solving the crimes can be quite humorous. For me, as a reader, humor and quirky characters give the story more character and make books even more memorable. I hope readers will remember my books with a smile on their face.

What's your writing schedule like?

I work about six hours a day, seven days a week, but that includes writing, marketing and promoting. It's hectic, but it's the most fun I've ever had while doing a job. It feels good to be able to say I like what I'm doing.

Why is writing important to you?

I've always been an avid reader, beginning with Dick and Jane. When I decided to write, it was because I wanted to entertain others as I'd been entertained. There's no sweeter music to the ears for an author than hearing a reader say they enjoyed the author's book, and it's even better when they say they took something away from it. It doesn't matter if they just got a smile out of it or if the story made them view something differently, as long as it had an effect on them.

Advice to aspiring mystery novelists?

Always begin your career by letting your skin thicken. No matter how good of a writer you are, not everyone is going to like your book.

Secondly, never apologize for your early work. I've done that, and I shouldn't have. Being a writer is like anything else you do in life. It's a learning process, and the more you do it, the better writer you become. I wouldn't have thought about that except that recently someone told me about their first book and commented that it wasn't all that great. Guess what? I loved it! Let the reader decide for themselves. If they see promise, chances are they'll come back and try your next book.

Last, when all else is said and done, make sure all of your periods and commas are in the right place, and that there are as few misspellings and typos as possible. Don't submit until the book is clean enough for the public to read. Be proud of what you submit.

Which author(s) influenced your own writing?

Harper Lee influenced me more than anyone else. I've read *To Kill a Mockingbird* a number of times, and each read I get something new out of it. Beyond her, every mystery writer I've ever read has had some impact on me. I especially enjoy authors who make the story come to life (even if there are a few typos). If a story is one-dimensional, I probably won't finish reading it. I like to set the book down feeling like I've come to know the characters.

A Little Humor, A Little Romance, A Little Murder

by Marja McGraw

I write two mystery series: The Sandi Webster Mysteries and The Bogey Man Mysteries. My logo is *"a little humor, a little romance, A Little Murder!"* It suits my books. They're lighter with a little humor, and while there is some romance, there are no sex scenes. They aren't necessary to my stories, and I'm old school—I've always felt that anticipation and imagination are much sexier that reading about it with the details all laid out for me.

Some books have sex thrown in just for shock value. It doesn't progress the story at all. I've also read stories where this element was pertinent to the story. In addition, there are books that don't have any sex and they're as entertaining as any story can be. I believe that the anticipation of what's to come can be very titillating, especially when you fill in the blanks yourself. Think about it. John Doe whispered something in Jane Smith's ear, and smiling, followed her through a door, pulling it closed behind him. Do you want someone to tell you what happened behind that door? Or would you rather dream up your own scenario? Hmmm. There are all kinds of possibilities there.

I have a friend, Shirley Kennedy, who wanted to write contemporary romances. Well, she wrote a good book and submitted it to a publisher. The publisher was interested, but only if she'd add sexual content. So Shirley sat down in front of her computer and started adding sex scenes. It turned out there was a problem.

She realized that as she wrote this graphic, sensual scene, she couldn't bring herself to look at the computer screen. She looked up, to the right, to the left, and out the window—anywhere except at the screen. She'd been asked to write something that she wasn't comfortable with. When she told me this story, I laughed. I could picture the whole thing in my mind. Still wanting to write romances, she changed from Contemporary to Regency romances, where she didn't have to include sex scenes. By the way, Shirley is a terrific writer and now writes other types of romance stories, too.

The thing is, when I laughed at this story and pictured it in my mind, the woman sitting in front of the computer unexpectedly turned into *me*. Talk about surprising yourself! I write mysteries, and my stories don't involve graphic sexual encounters. They're about mysteries and solving crimes. They center on the characters and their growth, and they include some humor.

I won't knock any author who writes graphic material, because there is a market for it–and some of it is extremely well-written. I simply prefer something entertaining and mysterious. I won't even try to change any minds here. However, I will add that a young woman approached me after reading my first book and told me two things. First, she said that she never, *ever* reads anything that doesn't contain graphic sex. Secondly, she said that it was two weeks after she read the book before she realized there wasn't any sex in it. So draw your own conclusions.

(Marja McGraw's website: marjamcgraw.com/, her blog site: http://blog.marjamcgraw.com/, and Facebook)

Susan Santangelo

A member of the Baby Boomer generation, Susan Santangelo served as a feature writer, drama critic and editor for daily and weekly newspapers in the New York metro area, including a stint at *Cosmopolitan Magazine*. A seasoned public relations and marketing professional, she designed and managed not-for-profit events and programs for over 25 years, and principal of her own public relations firm, Events Unlimited, in Princeton NJ for ten years.

Susan, why did you decide to become an independent writer-publisher?

I queried several top agents in New York with my first Baby Boomer mystery, *Retirement Can Be Murder*. Three of them absolutely loved it, but were unsure as to whether there was a market for it. As one of the 78.2 million Baby Boomers myself, I knew there was a market. So I decided to heed the advice of the books editor of our daily paper—if you're a new author, relatively unknown, take the leap of faith and do it yourself. I am blessed to live on Cape Cod, which has a wealth of talented artists and writers. Some of these folks and I now collaborate as Baby Boomer Mysteries Press. It's a win-win for all of us.

Why Boomer books?

It seemed to me that major attention was being paid to the Boomer generation, particularly to the financial aspects of hitting retirement age and beyond. Protecting/growing a nest egg, how to save for retirement, etc. But no one seemed to be addressing the emotional impact of growing older as a Boomer. For instance, what happens when a husband (or a wife), who has been out of the house for years at A Very Important Job, suddenly is at home, all the time. How does a couple deal with this re-defining of roles and not drive each other crazy? I decided to tackle these issues from the point of view of someone who's actually living it, using the cozy mystery format.

When did you begin writing?

I've written all my life. In my college years, I wrote a column for my school newspaper. Then I went to New York City and was lucky enough to land a job as editorial assistant to Victor Riesel, the labor columnist who was blinded by acid in the 1950s. What an experience. I learned so much about writing from him. From there, I went to *Cosmopolitan Magazine* (in the Helen Gurley Brown years) as a copy editor, then did freelance writing for years for newspapers and magazines while my children were growing up. I've also had my own public relations firm, and done my share of press releases and marketing materials. For the past 12 years, I've been in the nonprofit world with the Breast Cancer Survival Center, and written all their press materials and quarterly newsletters. I've never stopped writing, no matter what the genre.

How has your public relations background helped you in selling books?

I'm lucky to have made many media contacts over the years, all of whom I've called upon when the first Baby Boomer mystery came out. (Part of the proceeds from the books benefits the Breast Cancer Survival Center.) I've had to speak in public many times over the years, either for clients or for the cancer program, so I'm comfortable with that aspect of PR. I just think of myself as my own client now. But with the Internet, it's a whole new learning curve that I find very exciting. I'm not afraid to try something new. One of the things

I learned in PR was the value of a giveaway. With my first book, I had custom-designed socks made that I sent out with review copies. The socks had the title of the book on the cuff and the website on the instep. It made an impression.

What ratio of e-books have you sold to print books?

We are currently in our fourth printing for the first Baby Boomer mystery, *Retirement Can Be Murder.* The book was first released in traditional format in April 2009. The second book in the series, *Moving Can Be Murder,* was released on May 1, 2011. The first mystery went on Kindle at the end of January 2011. The second one was uploaded at the end of May 2011. I was resistant to the whole e-book phenomenon at first. But we topped 10,000 e-book sales in six months, which is twice as many as the traditional sales did in the same time frame. I never expected that. Both titles continue to sell well, and one book is definitely helping the other book sales-wise. Many people are buying both.

Tell us about your series.

The Baby Boomer mysteries (there are seven planned in the series) follow the lives of typical Boomers, Carol Andrews, and her husband, Jim, as they navigate the rocky road toward their twilight years. The first book dealt with Jim's impending retirement and Carol's reaction to it. The second book deals with downsizing and selling the family home. The third novel, which I'm currently working on, is *Marriage Can Be Murder,* and will feature a destination wedding on Nantucket. Each of the books also has a quiz in the back, to give readers something to think about. The first one has a retirement quiz. The second one has a moving quiz. The idea behind these quizzes is to help readers start conversations with his/or her partner to find out what's really important to both of you, to be sure you both want the same things. Communication and compromise are key.

Some Not-So-Secret Secrets of an Indie Author and Publisher

by Susan Santangelo

I never intended to become an indie author. My goal was to become a *published* author. But when it became clear to me that agents and major publishing houses were reluctant to take a chance on an unknown author, I made a giant leap of faith and started Baby Boomer Mysteries Press.

The first in the series, *Retirement Can Be Murder*, was published in traditional format on April 1, 2009. Every part of the book had been chosen with great care, including the style and size of the type font—not a large print book, but large enough so aging eyes could read without straining. And the cover art—a photograph of two rockers on a front porch—was chosen to symbolize the retirement stereotype.

Our local paper, the *Cape Cod Times*, also publishes a monthly magazine for Boomers and beyond called *Prime Time*. I contacted the editor before the first book came out, and she did a feature story about it and put me on the magazine cover. So the "buzz" began before the book actually came out.

I joined the National Association of Baby Boomer Women and got a back cover endorsement from its founder (which also publicized the book on its website), and another one from the author of a national Baby Boomer blog. I sent review copies to as many reviewers as I could find on the Internet, including Booklist (which did a 5-star review), and Midwest Book Review (another 5-star review).

I sold through indie book stores and gift shops, and did signings at stores, women's clubs, libraries, and book groups. My book has dogs in it, so I contacted our dogs' breeder, who arranged for me to do a signing at a major dog show, which was a huge success. I contacted retirement financial planners and did a series of joint events. Part of the book proceeds benefit a breast cancer survivors' program, so our hospital gift shop also sells the book. I found that cross-marketing increases book sales.

I had a web page, but I joined Facebook and Twitter. And I sold books in traditional format on Amazon and Barnes & Noble.

In January 2011, I took another leap of faith and had the first book formatted and loaded onto Kindle and Nook. When an author loads a book herself, you get to choose the search words that will lead readers to your book. I chose "baby boomer, retirement, women sleuths, cozy mystery, husbands and wives, and dogs." In the first month, I think I sold 25 on Kindle and three on Nook. Then I added "humor" to my search words, and the first book began to sell better, particularly on Kindle. By the time the second book, *Moving Can Be Murder,* came out in May 2011, I had developed a Kindle following, so I immediately published this as an e-book as well. Then, my numbers went through the roof. In three months, I sold over 8,000 books on Kindle alone. I couldn't believe it. One book's sales definitely helps the next one.

I use Facebook to publicize any events I'm doing, and I joined on-line book clubs like Sassy Girls, Authors Den, GoodReads, Readers Favorites, Must Read Mysteries, Lori's Reading Corner, Readers' Den, E-Reader Daily News, and The Frugal E-Reader. I've used all of them at one time or another to publicize my books. I also review cozy mysteries for *Suspense* magazine, which definitely helps my name recognition.

I don't think anyone can promote a book as well as its author can. And I take every opportunity I'm given to do just that!

(You can visit Susan Santangelo at her website: www.babyboomermysteries.com. She blogs at: http://murderousmusings.blogspot.com/, and is Grammasuze on Twitter. She also has a Facebook page.)

Ann Charles

Ann Charles, an award-winning novelist, writes humorous mysteries sprinkled with romance. The 2010 Daphne du Maurier Award winner for excellence in mystery/suspense fiction, she has a BA degree in English with an emphasis on creative writing from the University of Washington. When she's not writing fiction, she's sharing what she's learned about the craft of writing and conducting self-promotion.

Ann, tell us about your latest novel.

Dance of the Winnebagos is the story of Claire Morgan. When Claire's grandfather and his army buddies converge in the Arizona desert to find new wives, it's her thankless job to keep them out of trouble with the opposite sex. But when she finds a human leg bone and then partners with a reluctant geotechnician to dig up secrets from the past, trouble finds *her*. If she doesn't stop digging, she could end up dead.

How did your Jackrabbit Mystery series originate?

Once upon a time, I was playing hangman at work with one of my coworkers. It was her turn to come up with a word, and she added a lot of spaces on the white board. After I landed two consonants and a vowel, the board looked like this: T _ E _ _ _ N _ _ _ T _ E _ _ _ _ E _ _ _ _ _ E _. I was feeling pretty ambitious that day. I took one look at this puzzle and yelled, "The Dance of the Winnebagos!" (I know, the letters don't match up—I've never done well in spelling bees.) My coworker laughed and hung my poor stick man—the actual answer was *The Hound of the Baskervilles,* and she wondered what *The Dance of the Winnebagos* was.

I said, "I don't know, but it would make a great book title, don't you think?"

This game of hangman kick-started my brain. A weekend of plot-storming with my critique group fleshed out the story even more. Before I knew it, I had a fun cast, an intriguing mystery, and a book that practically wrote itself. This book landed me my agent, who asked me when I'd have book two in the series finished. I hadn't planned on a second book, but saw where I could tweak the story just a little and make it into a fun series, so I did. And that was all she wrote—well, not really, since I'm still writing this series.

How has the e-book revolution affected your sales?

I've sold over 17,000 e-books this year, my first year of publication. In comparison, I've sold around 1,000 print books. The e-book revolution has served me well, and I personally love reading e-books on my e-reader. As the co-owner of Corvallis Press, I can also say that e-books are much easier to publish, sell, and track.

Do you have a day job and what's your writing schedule like? Also, do you outline?

I am a technical writer by day and a fiction writer by night. Both are full-time jobs and keep me hopping—but not as much as my two young kids. My schedule is crazy, and I carve out moments to write and promote whenever I can, which is mostly at night after my family goes to bed because I am soooo not a morning person.

I am more of a right-brained, write-by-the-seat-of-my-pants author (aka a "pantser"), so my outline is very high level. I rarely stick to it. I like to write a scene and learn what comes next as it fills the pages. It makes the story more fun to build and share.

What are the best and worst aspects of writing?

Let's start with the bad stuff. The worst part is just the constant struggle to find time to write, not to mention do all of the promotion and marketing needed to find new readers. It's not a marathon—it's more like a triathlon. Some days I just want to hide under the covers. As for the best part, it's the peers, the friends, and the fans. I love meeting new people (even if it's just on the Internet) and building new relationships.

Advice to fledgling mystery writers?

Treat everything as an experiment, which allows you to use your failures as a learning device. Be patient and persevere. Remember, this is not a get-rich-quick business. The writing is just a piece of the whole endeavor—an important piece, mind you, but you will need to learn about all aspects of the business like any other entrepreneur.

Who most influenced your own work?

The list is long, but to name a few of the authors: Stephen King, Rachel Gibson, Dean Koontz, Janet Evanovich, and Jane Austen. I also am greatly influenced by movies, which I use to learn more about elements like dialogue and pacing.

In the event of 40 days of rain, which three objects would you save after your family and pets?

My husband has trained me to grab the hard drive that has all of our family pictures on it, so that's the first thing. Next, I'd probably save the printed photos of old. And third, I'd take my laptop to save me headaches later.

Ten Tips for Emerging Writers

by Ann Charles

There is so much more to being an author than just writing a book.

1. BE NICE!! All of the time. Bite your tongue. Use honey, not vinegar. It's a small world.

2. On the social networking front, approach other authors with the mindset of what you can offer them instead of what you can take/get from them.

3. Build a web presence, but do it with a plan. Decide where you want to concentrate your efforts and exactly what level of privacy you need.

4. Find a role model and emulate him or her—not their writing style and techniques, rather their business and promotion skills.

5. Build your business model. Remember that all businesses must have something to sell, so you can't neglect your inventory.

6. Learn how to multi-task, prioritize, and delegate.

7. Find your niche—or develop one—and then exploit it. Be original. Then use that niche to build your platform . . .

8. Treat everyone equally. Don't fawn over superstars in the business and ignore newbies. That newbie might be the next superstar.

9. Be professional. Treat your writing like a business and your book like a product, especially when interacting with agents and editors. You don't want to be labeled a 'prima donna.'

10. Learn constantly, and not just about craft. Learn about:

Promotion and marketing

Social networking venues (Facebook, Twitter, and more)

The software needed for your business
(Wordpress, Blogger, HTML, Microsoft Word)

What agents and editors do and don't like.

And ALWAYS keep broadening your horizons.

Ann's website: http://www.anncharles.com/, and her blog
sites: www.1stturningpoint.com and www.plotmammas.com

W. S. Gager

Wendy Gager began her writing career in Michigan, where she interviewed race car drivers and professional women golfers. She enjoyed the fast-paced life of a news reporter until deciding to settle down. Since then she has honed her skills by writing mystery novels. Her main series character is Mitch Malone, an edgy, crime-beat reporter who's always on the hunt for the next Pulitzer Prize, and reportedly won't let anyone stop him.

Wendy, did you pattern your crime beat reporter after anyone you've known?

Mitch is very much his own man. He came to me in a dream so you could say he's my dream man. I don't remember ever meeting anyone quite like Mitch. If he is closest to anyone it would be the opposite of me. Mitch isn't afraid to say exactly what's on his mind, which is something I only wish I could do.

How do you research your novels?

My bachelor's degree in journalism is from Central Michigan University. I worked at four different newspapers and did freelance writing for others as well as magazines. For research I still have friends in the business and I also have some police friends who check my manuscript for accuracy. For other items, I start with Google and go from there.

Why do you use your initials instead of your given name? Are readers more inclined to buy a crime novel written by a man?

I decided to use initials because Mitch is a male protagonist and would appeal to men. Many men I know won't read woman authors, so I didn't want to make it easy for them to figure out my gender. Funny thing is that many more woman love Mitch. I'm still trying to figure that out.

Tell us about *A Case of Hometown Blues.*

When my Pulitzer-winning reporter's editor presses him for a favor, Mitch Malone breaks his vow to never return to his hometown. It seemed simple enough—lead a seminar for the Flatville, Michigan, newspaper, keep a low profile and get back to the city post haste. But memories of his parents' death swarm him, and, to avoid solitude, he stops for a beer. In the crowded bar, Mitch is dismayed to see many of his former classmates—including the still-lovely Homecoming Queen, Trudy.

Once the object of his teenage crush, Trudy joins Mitch. He realizes she is upset and inebriated. Always the gentleman, Mitch sees Trudy safely home, and returns to his B&B, still trying to shake the memories of his parents' sad demise. The following day, he's stunned to learn that Trudy was murdered and he's the prime suspect. The locals treat the murder charge as a slam dunk, and Mitch realizes he must track down the real killer to keep himself out of jail. As he investigates, facts that he thought he knew about his family unravel, and danger ratchets up. Can Mitch discover the truth that will allow his parents to rest in peace, or will he be resting with them?

How are your print editions faring compared with your e-book sales?

It wasn't until just recently that I noticed a real uptick in e-book sales.

I've been selling a lot of print books at arts and crafts events and speaking engagements. Just in the last month or so I've had many people ask about whether it's in electronic form. Now, I'm giving away a lot of material to folks who have Nooks and Kindles with the link to Amazon or Barnes and Noble websites so they can download it. I think in the next royalty statement I will see them evening out as well.

What's your writing schedule like and do you aim for a certain amount of words per day?

I have children and whenever you plan a full day of writing, something happens. They are sick, forgot something they desperately needed or I am called into service for a volunteer project. I try to do 500 to 1,000 words a day normally. If I'm writing the first rough draft, I write much more and give myself permission not to edit at all. I try to get as much of the action down on paper and then go back and layer in setting and emotion and fill out the action.

Advice to novice writers.

Don't worry about selling, just write. Enjoy writing because once you sell, you have to do so much marketing and it is hard to get back to the writing. Keep writing and editing and find someone with experience to critique your work with constructive criticism to improve your manuscript. It will make a difference and help you get a salable project faster.

Aliteration

by Wendy Gager

Mary will never appear in my Mitch Malone mystery series, neither will a Mark or Mike. Why? Am I prejudiced against them? Or grew up with a scary Mike character? Did Mary steal my boyfriend in high school? Nothing as dramatic as that but having them appear could make readers angry.

In my mystery series, the main character is crime reporter Mitch Malone. I'm a big fan of alliteration. That being said I must alliterate in moderation. Too many mentions of many characters sharing a beginning moniker, whether manic or merry, can give readers bad memories. Okay, I will stop with all the M-words, just trying to make a point.

I love alliteration but authors must take care with multiple people's names starting with the same letter. I've given up reading a bestselling series because two of the main supporting characters have very similar names. I can't keep them straight and it's pivotal to the story. Experts say when using names in your books for characters you have to avoid duplicating first letters at all costs because it will confuse readers. Several authors told me they use the alphabet to keep track of names. For every book, each character's name goes next to the corresponding letter of the alphabet. Each book only gets one name that starts with that letter.

Research shows people read in groups and phrases, not individual words. Have you ever taken the test that removes all the vowels and just leaves consonants? It's still possible to figure out what the message is. Same applies to writing. Too many names that are alike will make your reader frustrated because they will have to slow down each time the similar names are mentioned to decipher what is going on. This will interrupt the flow and in frustration they may stab the book with a knife and chuck it across the room (A writer friend does this when authors make stupid or unbelievable things happen.)

It could be the best story in the world but if readers can't keep the characters straight, it won't matter. So, sorry Mary, Mike and Mark, Mitch Malone must remain the main man. (I couldn't help myself!)

(Wendy Gager's blog site: http://wsgager.blogspot.com/
She's on Facebook: http://www.facebook.com/wsgager.and
Twitter.

Chris Redding

Chris Redding earned a journalism degree from Penn State and has held a variety of jobs over the years, including pizza delivery and CPR Instructor. When not writing, she works part time at her local hospital.

Chris, when did you become serious about writing?

I began writing for publication 12 years ago. I hadn't written in a while and when I was pregnant with my second son I *had* to write. I had these stories bubbling over in me. So I began to write again. I figured if I was going to spend the time I might as well try to get published.

Why romantic suspense?

I've always been a mystery fan. My sister passed down her Nancy Drew books and my mother always had an Agatha Christie book lying around. I read three grades ahead of my age group and when I began writing, I started with straight romance, but I always ended up with a dead body. Thus, romantic suspense.

Tell us about your latest release.

A View to a Kilt is a humorous, romantic suspense novel about two people. One of them is trying to forget the past and the other *can't* forget the past. The heroine is an interior decorator who may have information about the murder of an ex-FBI agent's wife. He tries to get it out of her but she wants nothing to do with cops and investigations.

What's your writing schedule like with children at home and a part time job?

I tend to write five pages a day in the morning when I'm more awake and competent. There's also time to write after my last child gets on the bus and I leave for work.

Have you used your previous jobs as background for your novels?

I worked as an EMT for six years and have been involved in emergency medical services for a while in some form, so either EMT's or paramedics are in most of my stories.

Are any of your characters autobiographical?

There is always an element of me in any of my characters, but none of them are a true portrait of me. They are way more interesting and tough.

Advice to novice writers.

Hone your craft and be persistent. This can be a long road.

Why I write

by Chris Redding

Most writers will tell you that they can't *not* write. I know that's a double negative, but it's true. I write because I have to.

I write because when I'm inspired, I envision movies in my

head, which is called the film strip method of writing. The movies are IMAX, surround sound, and take up a lot of brain power. They make it hard to concentrate when I'm doing other things. I unload the dishwasher and put things away in the wrong places while the film strip is running.

I often forget what I'm doing at my day job, which doesn't make my boss happy. So to regain my concentration, I write down the movie currently playing in my head. While I'm writing, I'm able to download all that action, drama and dialogue that's been bugging me while I'm doing other things. Writing is a high that I imagine addicts experience while taking drugs. The endorphins flow and I love how I feel while I'm engaged in the act of writing. Very little bothers me for the rest of the day. How cool is that? I don't even have to exercise to feel that good. Writing does that for me.

What's not to love? It's a non-addictive high.

I write because that's what I've wanted to do since the age of ten. In fifth grade Sister Madonna assigned the class a story. If you received an "A," you were allowed to read your story in front of the class. I was chosen and my story was about a lady with a houseful of cats. When I read it to the class they were quiet and seemingly mesmerized. You have to understand that I was that weird kid with glasses who was always spouting facts. I was socially awkward and never knew when to shut up. But when I read my story to the class, the other students looked at me differently. The change in attitude didn't last, but for one moment I was that big-toothed, know-it-all kid with some writing talent.

That was one of the coolest moments of my life. And every time I sit down at my keyboard, I hope to have one of those moments again.

So I write.

(You can visit Chris Redding at her website: http://www.chrisreddingauthor.com/ or her blog site: http://chrisredddingauthor.blogspot.com/. She's also on Facebook and Twitter.)

Chapter Eleven: Cozies

Elizabeth Spann Craig

Elizabeth Spann Craig writes three diverse mystery series: her Myrtle Clover novels, her quilting, and culinary mysteries set in Memphis, written as Riley Adams.

Elizabeth, how did your Memphis Barbeque series and restaurant-owning grandmother-sleuth come about?

I think, like so many things in life, I was at the right place at the right time. Berkley Prime Crime was interested in acquiring *Pretty is as Pretty Dies* (I'd queried them with the manuscript), but it got buried in a slush pile and instead was published by Midnight Ink. But Berkley was interested in having me write a different book—a culinary mystery set in Memphis, a city they thought would provide a rich setting for a mystery. I set to work right away writing the book. Lulu is an amalgam of all the strong, southern women who helped raise me. I love her humor and common sense.

Why the pseudonym, Riley Adams?

As a writer with another series with a competing publisher, Berkley asked me to write under a pseudonym. My Myrtle Clover series and the Southern Quilting series are written under my own name, Elizabeth Craig.

Why, with young children at home, did you decide to write about senior amateur sleuths?

As a reader, I've always been drawn to older sleuths and love the wisdom they bring to the table when they investigate a crime. Miss Marple was one of my all-time favorites. My grandmother, who was strong and smart and funny, was also a tremendous inspiration for me. Currently, I'm working on writing the fourth Memphis barbeque book and also working on the second book for the Southern Quilting series, which I'm writing as Elizabeth Craig—and yes, it does involve an elderly sleuth. *Quilt or Innocence* debuts with a retired art museum curator as my sleuth.

How did you go about acquiring an agent?

It wasn't easy! I researched agents for weeks—checking their preferences and client lists against my manuscript to see if it was a match. I was rejected, probably fifty-sixty times over the course of a couple of years. Some agents were queried more than once, for different projects. I actually ended up with a publisher before I acquired an agent, and negotiated my own contract.

Fortunately, I found my agent, Ellen Pepus, before hazarding my negotiating abilities (more like inabilities) with a second publisher.

What's your schedule like and do you outline?

My writing schedule is nutty. There's actually no schedule at all—just a daily goal. As long as I make my goal, I fit my writing in where I can—in the carpool line at the elementary school, late at night, early in the morning, while taking my kids to the skate rink—wherever. I prefer not to outline my novels, but sometimes editors like to see a full synopsis. And I aim to please! But if left to my own devices, I make up my mysteries as I go along.

Do your family members serve as consultants and first readers?

My mother is my first reader and my father will read for me, too, time permitting. My mother is an avid reader and my father is an English professor. It really helps. My father and grandmother have always written—articles, newsletters, etc., but weren't novelists.

Tell us about your writing background.

Starting out, I worked as an intern at a magazine in London when I was studying abroad. After graduation, I married and moved to Birmingham, Alabama, and wrote articles (and did whatever else they needed—help selling ads or laying out copy) for an art magazine there.

Advice to fledgling writers?

My advice would be to figure out what you want, in terms of your writing. Are you happy just writing for yourself? Could you be happy just sharing your work with a small group of people? Once I figured out my direction and what my intent was for my writing, I was a lot more determined and treated it more seriously.

Promote Yourself, Not Just Your Book

by Elizabeth Spann Craig

Why should you promote yourself instead of merely your book? There are a couple of good reasons. One is because books, if you're pursuing traditional publishing, can have a fairly short shelf life. Another is that if you write *many* books and experiment with other genres, it's fairly futile to try to get the world to remember a particular book title. Better that they remember your name and look up the books you've written. That way you're giving readers only one thing to remember.

Which will ultimately be around the longest—a writer or a particular title? Unless we're as unfortunate as Stieg Larsson, we're the ones who'll be out there writing long after our books are gathering dust.

What does promoting yourself mean?

It really just means that we are present. We establish a presence where other writers and readers hang out—Facebook, Twitter, blogs, GoodReads. We create interesting content and share resources or information with others. It means that we don't have to cram our book down the world's collective throat.

I put my name out there. It's on Facebook, it's on Twitter. It's on my blog. And I have my covers right up there with me—they're splashed on my Twitter background, uploaded on Facebook, and are in my sidebar. I visit blogs and my name and comment stays behind to show that I was there. And I try very hard *not* to talk about my book. I mean—it's obvious I've written some books. If someone is interested, they'll check them out.

The nice thing about promoting our names is that it also gives our books exposure. I've gone into the bookstore *many* times and asked for "the latest Elizabeth George" or "the new M.C. Beaton" or "the last release from Deborah Crombie." I don't even *remember* the title of the book I'm looking for. But I sure remember *the authors*.

I'm definitely planning to promote my next release in the short term. But my *long-term* strategy is author branding. I'm hoping it's a strategy that will work for me for many years to come.

(Elizabeth Spann Craig's blog:
http://mysterywritingismurder.blogspot.com/
—chosen by *Writers Digest as* one of 101 Best Sites.
She's also on Twitter: @elizabethscraig.)

Anne K. Albert

Anne K. Albert's award-winning stories "chill the spine, warm the heart and soothe the soul—all with a delightful touch of humor." She's the recipient of the 2011 Holt Medallion Award of Merit for her mystery, *Frank, Incense and Muriel*. A diehard fan of Nancy Drew, Trixie Belden, the Hardy Boys, Agatha Christie and Erle Stanley Gardner, it's a given that she would write mystery and romantic suspense.

Anne, when did you decide to organize Mystery We Write Blog Tours?

After the release of my debut novel in 2010, I signed on to a blog tour with 20 other writers. Unfortunately, I dropped out within a few weeks for personal reasons, but knew another blog tour would be in my future.

In March 2011, Marilyn Meredith mentioned the high price advertising companies charge to arrange blog tours, so I asked if she would be interested in a blog swap. She was. It progressed from there from just the two of us. We sought out other mystery writers, and within days, the first Mystery We Write Blog Tour was born in 2011. It ran 12 weeks during the summer and was a great experience. We then did a second virtual tour in December.

Virtual tours are a lot of work, but the opportunity to rub elbows with some fantastic authors and meet new readers makes it all worthwhile.

Has teaching art and selling display advertising helped with writing fiction?

I believe everything I've experienced has affected my writing as well as my personality. It has also influenced how I choose to live each day. I'm the sum of all that's happened to me, and would not be who or where I am today if I'd chosen a different path. As a writer, I want to entertain my readers. I want to take them away from the cares and problems of the real world for just a few hours. If I succeed in providing them with a puzzle to solve, characters to care about, as well as bringing a smile to their faces, I've done my job.

What's the story behind *Frank, Incense and Muriel*?

My goal was to write a lighthearted mystery. I knew the story would take place the week before Christmas and I wanted the title to convey that timeframe. I already had the hero's name (Frankie Salerno), and I knew that he infuriated the heroine when they were in their teens. With a little tweaking I altered frankincense and myrrh to Frank, Incense and Muriel.

What makes your protagonist special?

Muriel Reeves is the intellectual in a family of thrill seekers. They live to win their annual D-DAY (Death Defying Act of the Year) award. Muriel's always felt like the black sheep of the family, but in reality the majority of her family are black sheep and she's the lone white one! Part of the fun in *Frank, Incense and Muriel* is watching her confidence grow as she steps out of her comfort zone and helps Frankie search for a missing woman.

Why did you decide to write mystery novels?

I've always loved reading cozy mysteries and when I decided to write a book I knew it would be a whodunit.

Who most influenced your own writing?

I'm unable to pick just one person, but Stephen Cannell's fast-paced writing style has always impressed me. I love it when I forget to analyze the author's writing style and become engrossed in the story. When that happens, I know I'm in the midst of genius!

Which author would you like to be trapped in an elevator with, past or present?

Trapped? Nope. Not gonna happen. I'm claustrophobic. All I would be capable of doing is focusing on getting out and remembering to breathe! However, if I could meet Mark Twain, Robert A. Heinlein or Ray Bradbury and chat, I'd love thirty minutes or so to pick their brains!

Advice for aspiring mystery writers?

Write. Finish what you write. Polish it until it shines. Read, then write some more. Oh, and never, never give up.

Write What You Know?

by Anne K. Albert

Writers are often advised to write what they know. From the beginning when my fingers first hovered above a keyboard, that suggestion made no sense to me.

Why?

In real life, I'm a wimp. I squirm at the sight of blood. I turn my head and look away when it's my blood filling a test vial. This will usually cause a snicker from the nurse, but I can't help it. My knees buckle at the slightest mention of scrapes, cuts or broken bones. I don't even have to see blood. All I have to do is *think* about it. Like I said, I'm a major wimp. (Or should that be wimpette?)

Still, in the fictional world, I murder people at the blink of an eye. With glee, I search for places to bury the bodies. Without the slightest hesitation, I'll crawl inside a killer's head and willingly see, hear, feel and sometimes even taste what these villainous characters experience. And, I do it all in the name of mystery.

The real me knows little about murder, murderers and murderous ways yet this desire to write a whodunit overpowers what I know, who I am, and what I feel deep, deep down inside.

Talk about a major disconnect!

How do I come to terms with it? One of my favorite quotes about this severed connection between the real person and the writer is attributed to W.P. Kinsella, author of *Shoeless Joe* (on which the movie "Field of Dreams" was based). He said an author does not have to commit suicide to write about it.

That statement, unlike the write-what-you-know advice, makes complete sense to me! So much so that I'll steal it, then alter it slightly. An author doesn't have to commit murder to write about it! I believe each writer selects a genre best suited to their personality. For example, being a wimp I write cozy mysteries and sweet romantic suspense stories. I also sprinkle a dash of humor in every book. Why? It's who I am. It's what I am. I write the kinds of stories I enjoy reading, and because I don't want (okay, let's be honest here, because I can't stomach) explicit or graphic details in the books I read, there is no way I will include such details in the books I write.

Bottom line? Write what you love. Write what you feel. Write what you imagine. Write!

(Anne's website: http://www.AnneKAlbert.com and her blog sites: http://anne-k-albert.blogspot.com, http://muriel-reeves-mysteries.blogspot.com)

Ron Benrey

Ron Benrey writes cozies with his wife, Janet. Together, they've written nine novels in three distinct series: The Royal Tunbridge Wells Mysteries, The Pippa Hunnechurch Mysteries, and The Glory North Carolina Mysteries. His first job was electronics editor at *Popular Science Magazine*. He then wrote speeches for senior corporate executives before becoming a novelist. He also authored ten non-fiction books, including *Know Your Rights—a Survival Guide for Non-Lawyers*. Benrey holds a bachelor's degree in electrical engineering, a master's degree in management, a law degree from Duquesne University, and he is currently a writing coach and instructor.

Ron, do you and Janet ever disagree while collaborating on a novel? If so, how do you resolve your differences?

We frequently disagree. But, because we jointly operated a marketing communications firm, we understand the need to create the best possible "product" whenever we write. Consequently, we've learned to make compromises and to rethink our initial creative decisions.

You've worn a variety of hats. Which job/profession has been the most difficult and which has given you the most satisfaction and pleasure?

In fact, my many careers have had a common thread. I have always thought of myself as a writer who writes interesting words about difficult subjects. That's even true about the novels I co-write with my wife today. It's ironic, but "simple writing" that explains how things work is the most difficult kind of writing to do successfully— at least for me. My latest non-fiction book took more time and effort than anything else I've written. A close second is *Understanding Christianity.* I'm always delighted when someone says, "I read your writing and now I understand."

Do you incorporate your background in engineering and law into your romantic suspense novels?

Frequently. When I develop plots, I often use the analytic thinking approaches I learned at both schools. Engineering thinking is great for zeroing in on precise solutions, while legal thinking is useful for dealing with the inevitable shades of gray in every story. I also feel comfortable dealing with technology in our storylines, and we often use legal issues to create dramatic conflict in our novels.

What are the biggest mistakes you've encountered from your students as a writing instructor?

I often find that students trying to write a novel will leave out one of the five key factors that make a manuscript publishable. 1. They don't write in a recognizable genre (and so they create a novel that can't be categorized—or sold). 2. They don't write with a strong, clear voice (this is the one aspect of publishability that probably can't be taught). 3. They have many errors of fact that stop readers cold. 4. They don't have a compelling story. 5. They don't know how to create a fictional dream for their readers.

In the days before self-published e-books, a serious problem in any of these areas would earn a flood of rejection letters from agents and publishers. Today, alas, an author can put an unpublishable novel "out there"—and many do. The few readers who buy them are usually disappointed, but may not be able to explain why.

Which elements of copyright law should authors know?

The key fact is that copyright attaches automatically when an author reduces his or her original words to a "writing" on paper or on a computer screen. There's no need to put © symbols all over your work or to register drafts with the Copyright Office in the Library of Congress or send yourself copies of the draft by Certified Mail (a truly worthless practice). Fledgling authors worry too much that their golden words will be stolen. Their unnecessary efforts to protect their work make them look like rank amateurs.

What advice do you give writers for presentations and new releases?

The one piece of advice I give to all of the presenters I coach is: Prepare! There is no such thing as a good off-the-cuff presentation. Even if you are reading words from a novel you've written, take the time to rehearse—several times. If you're giving a presentation, at the very least prepare a script outline and rehearse your comments—several times. The presenter's rule of thumb is that his or her preparation time should equal the time that the audience will invest in listening to the presentation. For example, if you expect 10 people to listen to a 30-minute presentation, you should spend at least 300 minutes (five hours!) creating an outline and rehearsing.

Tell us about one of your series.

Our Royal Tunbridge Wells Mysteries take place in and around the Royal Tunbridge Wells Tea Museum, a fictional institution located in a real English city. (Royal Tunbridge Wells is located roughly forty miles southeast of central London, England. It's a thriving "bedroom community" for well-to-do businesspeople who work in London.) Here's the synopsis of *"Dead as a Scone,"* the first book in the series:

Murder is afoot in the sedate English town of Royal Tunbridge
Wells, and the crime may be brewing in a tea pot! Nigel Owen is
having a rotten year. Downsized from a cushy management job at
an insurance company in London, he is forced to accept a temporary
post as managing director of the Royal Tunbridge Wells Tea Museum.
Alas, he regrets living in a small town in Kent. He prefers drinking
coffee (with a vengeance), and he roundly dislikes Flick Adams, PhD,
an American scientist recently named the museum's curator.

But then, the wildly unexpected happens. Dame Elspeth Hawker,
the museum's chief benefactor, keels over at a board meeting—
the apparent victim of a fatal heart attack. With the Dame's demise,
the museum's world-famous collection is up for grabs, her cats,
dog, and parrot are living with Flick and Nigel—and the two prima
donnas find themselves facing professional ruin.

But Flick, who knows a thing or two about forensic science, is
convinced that Dame Elspeth did not die a natural death. As Flick
and Nigel follow the clues—including a cryptic Biblical citation—they
discover that a crime perpetrated more than a century ago sowed
the seeds for a contemporary murder.

The Fine Art of Writing Mysteries Together

by Ron Benrey

My wife Janet and I write cozy mysteries together. Our two-
decades-long collaboration has resulted in three cozy mystery series:
the *Pippa Hunnechurch Mysteries, The Royal Tunbridge Wells
Mysteries,* and the Glory, North Carolina, Mysteries. It has also
given us some simple "rules" we live by when we collaborate.

The first thing we do when we set out to write a new novel is
to create a detailed outline. We believe a comprehensive outline is
essential to ensure that neither of us strays from the story, to solidify
the novel's theme in our minds, and to keep us focused on the four
(sometimes *five*) plots in the novel. Creating the outline also lets us
fight all the story battles before the actual writing begins.

On the other hand, this is hard for some people to believe: our outline is never a straightjacket. We feel free to make major changes as we move ahead. We use the classic three-act story model created by Aristotle about 2,500 years ago. We build a three-act structure for the main plot and for each subplot and then "weave" the various story elements together into a scene outline. It's typically 15 to 20 pages long.

A mystery story begins when the protagonist's world goes out of kilter. The rest of the novel shows how the protagonist restores the order of his/her world. Thus, the first question we have to answer when we start an outline is: *What will go wrong in the hero/heroine's world?*

Consider *Dead as a Scone* as an example. The unforeseen death of a wealthy benefactor threatens to remove the lion's share of the objects on display at the Royal Tunbridge Wells Tea Museum. This poses a major dilemma for Flick Adams, the museum's curator, and Nigel Owen, the managing director.

Janet and I often analogize our novel-writing approach to creating a clay sculpture. Our outline is analogous to the wooden skeleton ("armature") that's inside the sculpture. It's my job to build it; most take about a month.

Janet takes the finished skeleton and piles on the first layer of "clay." In fact, she works quickly to produce a very rough first draft—typically a chapter at a time. Fortunately, she doesn't mind facing a blank word-processor screen. Then I refine and rewrite each chapter as necessary, invariably adding new material and evolving details we established in the outline.

We don't squabble when I "cavalierly" change words that Janet has written (an act that has started World War III between many collaborators); because our years of dealing with hard-nosed marketing-communications clients who demanded things are done their way made us realize that words on a word-processor screen aren't permanent. That was a remarkably liberating lesson to learn. A novel isn't set in concrete until it's published. Consequently, it's foolish for either of us to be overly "word proud" during the writing process.

(You can learn more about Ron and Janet Benrey at their website: www.benrey.com, and his blogs: benrey.com, greenbrierpatch.com)

Maggie Bishop

Maggie Bishop's cozies are set in the Appalachian Mountains and feature hiking, skiing, horseback riding, adventure and romance. She has been touted as the Appalachian Agatha Christie and was chosen as one of East Carolina University's "Incredible Women."

Maggie, how have the honors affected your writing life?

After the champagne celebration, I decided to concentrate on "giving back" by teaching writing workshops. When I attended workshops given by members of Romance Writers of America and Sisters in Crime, I bought their books but couldn't find a way to express my appreciation for the knowledge and direction given in the craft of writing. Since I could not repay the individual teachers, I'm passing on the favor with the workshops.

Which of your awards means the most to you?

Being declared one of "100 Incredible ECU Women," for literature and leadership has helped me acknowledge that mystery writing is a worthwhile endeavor. Making up something that others enjoy reading can be difficult, especially when that little voice says "this is awful." I'm honored that East Carolina recognized my work.

How did your Appalachian series originate?

Appalachian Adventures started with romance, then turned to murder. The original concept was four books, four male cousins, four seasons and four different sports. I had to get the romance out of my system. *Appalachian Paradise* is romance and backpacking. *Emeralds in the Snow* concerns romance, downhill skiing and a cold case mystery. *Murder at Blue Falls*, my third novel (third male cousin, third season and third sport–horseback riding) changed everything. My publisher, Ingalls Publishing Group, fell in love with the two main characters and the following books are based on the fictional Blue Falls Guest Ranch in the real Triplett Valley outside the real cozy mountain town of Boone, NC.

Do you consider your blog and your contributions to the Dames of Dialogue blog team important to your writing career?

It plays a strong role in keeping my name and titles in the public viral landscape. The Dames (there are five of us) of Dialogue interview authors and celebrities and host guest bloggers. It is another way we can "give back" to the writers and entertain the readers.

Have you found that Internet promotions or speaking engagements are more effective in getting one's name and work before the public?

I wish I could pick one. My best paperback book sales are at craft fairs. I live deep in the mountains with the nearest city an hour and a half away. Since Boone is a tourist destination (skiing, hiking, biking, climbing), craft fairs are popular. The beauty of online is that potentially more people can find out about my books from the comfort of their home. My e-book sales are increasing since the price of each book is now at $2.99 (less than a latte) in anticipation of the release of my latest mystery. When another popular author interviews me, it helps sales in both categories. And, in today's publishing environment, both Internet and in person appearances are important.

Tell us about your novel, *One Shot Too Many*.

This time Detective Tucker is the main character and we find out more about his past. Yesterday's regret; today's deadly fix.

Impulsive acts during emotional upheavels from the past return to haunt, ending in the death of a photojournalist near the cozy mountain town of Boone, NC. Detective Tucker must deal with his past while investigating the secrets of suspects determined to keep from facing their own histories. Jemma Chase, trail ride leader and CSI wannabe, follows clues, even though her interference may cost Tucker his job. *One Shot Too Many*—suspects aplenty for Detective Tucker when someone kills the newspaper photographer who took one too many photos. Everyone has something to hide. The nurse—too many injections. The judge—too many attempts. The retired army man—too many guns. And then there's the dental hygienist who has too many ejac—lovers, the grandmother who loves too much, the sports medicine professor who drinks too much. When Tucker's own past comes back to haunt, Jemma Chase, his CSI wannabe girlfriend, has to make a choice.

Advice to fledgling writers.

Just write the story and give yourself permission to be bad on the first draft. Play with it. Keep asking "what if?" Enjoy the flow and agony of the lives you create.

What would you be doing, if not a writer?

See the USA! We'd like to spend a month in each state to hike and explore the National and State Parks, to eat the local favorite foods, to see how people decorate their yards, to listen to the cadence of speech, to feel how people react to strangers. I'm itching to experience other places.

The most influential writer in your life?

I come from a family of readers so picking one author is impossible.

For learning the craft, I salute Romance Writers of America. The craft workshops gave me the courage to embark on a life of writing.

A Writing Exercise

by Maggie Bishop

This technique applies to both fiction and non-fiction. Starting point: attitude.

Writing your first draft exercises a part of the brain that encourages those "feel good" endorphins that enhance all aspects of your life.

In this attitude, give yourself permission to be bad. Remember the first time you sang. Were you good? Your first dance step. Your first plunge into water, could you swim? Turn off that editor, the critic. For memoirs, this is a way to figure out who you used to be and how you got to be who you are now. The same can be applied to fictional characters.

Look at your lifestyle and decide when and how much time you can write each day. Commit to this. Tom Wolfe (Bonfire of the Vanities) dressed in business clothes, walked to the curb and back to begin his work day. He wrote three hours a day from 9:00 until noon.

Answer these questions:(Two minutes)

How much time do you spend writing?

Time of day?

For how long?

The number of days you spend each week writing?

Where you write?

Do you record hours you spend writing?

How do you reward yourself after two months?

Write fast to submerge yourself in the writing zone and get carried away by the story. You live the story, which becomes infused with your energy and your excitement. Write fast. Sylvester Stallone wrote the screenplay for *Rocky* in 18 days.

How do you or your characters tell time in life? Not by the clock but by "before the divorce" or "my first job" or "the year of the hurricane." Which time frame strongly marked your character, for good or bad?

List six pivotal points in your story or your life. (Five minutes)

Let's narrow down to one scene. Not necessarily the first scene but work with the one that is bugging you. You need a working title for the scene you want to work on. Be specific, not generic. This will help you focus. Which do you prefer, "Elder Rage" or "Taking Care of Mom"?

Write down a title. (Two minutes)

Write three sentence description of this scene. Remember, no "editor." This is brainstorming. (Two minutes.)

Who: players, clothes (designer, sloppy, old), music (now and then, is it the same?), food (likes, dislikes, allergies) (Two minutes)

Emotion: What are you or character feeling at beginning of scene? Anger with clinched jaw. Frustration with tight gut. Joy and want to sing. (Two minutes)

Setting: (inside/outside, year, season, events, era) (Two minutes)

Now, close your eyes and think of your scene. Who is there? Listen to the voices. What are they saying? Is there jargon or slang or twang? What is about to happen? Open your eyes and write. (Five minutes)

Get something down on paper. Show no one, especially not your inner critic. I believe the energy of the story leaks out if you show it before the third draft.

Think about the next scene before you go to bed. See yourself writing in the time and place you agreed upon.

(You can learn more about Maggie at her webpage: maggiebishop1.tripod.com, as well as her previously mentioned blogs. She's also on Facebook and Twitter.)

Chapter Twelve: Amateur Sleuths

John M. Daniel

John M. Daniel was born in Minnesota, raised in Texas, and educated in Massachusetts and California. He was a Wallace Stegner Fellow in Creative Writing at Stanford University and a Writer in Residence at Wilbur Hot Springs. He taught fiction writing at UCLA Extension and Santa Barbara Adult Education and was faculty member of the Santa Barbara Writers Conference for nearly twenty years. He now teaches creative writing at Humboldt State University Extended Education in northern California. His stories have appeared in dozens of literary magazines. His thirteen published books include four mysteries: *Play Melancholy Baby, The Poet's Funeral, Vanity Fire,* and *Behind the Redwood Door.*

John, when were you first interested in literature?

When I was five-years-old my mother read to me from *The Wonderful Wizard of Oz*. She explained the irony in that remarkable book, and I knew then that forevermore I would be a reader. About ten years later I started reading the novels of Richard Bissell, and I knew then that, whatever it took, I would be a writer.

You've worked in a number of jobs. Which did you enjoy most and which would you rather forget?

I think I got my highest moments as an innkeeper and a bookseller, because in both cases I was dealing with people and supplying them with what they most wanted at the time. Teaching, too, come to think of it. My least favorite job was as an academic editor for the Stanford University Press. I essentially flunked out, because I wasn't good enough. That job was hard, borrrrring, and I wasn't up to the task.

Have you incorporated your work experiences into your novels?

Of course. I've written fiction about hotel managers and bar musicians, and my newest one is about a bookstore clerk. My main work experience, as a small press publisher, is what fuels the Guy Mallon mystery series, or at least the first two books thereof, *The Poet's Funeral* and *Vanity Fire*.

Who most influenced your own work?

I've already mentioned Richard Bissell, my favorite writer because of his honest, humorous, wry, cynical yet compassionate voice. He writes about simple folk and makes them into small-time heroes. I should also give a nod to science fiction writer Ray Russell, with whom I corresponded weekly. He was my mentor during my thirties, and he helped me become the writer I became. I also must acknowledge Wallace Stegner and Nancy Packer of the Stanford Creative Writing Program.

How did your small press come about?

I moved to Santa Barbara in 1983 with the goal of being an entertainer, singing old standards and accompanying myself on the guitar. I had a few gigs, but I needed a day job. I'd worked as an editor and a bookseller, so I hired on at Capra Press, a distinguished independent publisher. My position was assistant to the sales manager, Susan Winton. Within a few months, Susan and I were a couple, and we left Capra, pooled our meager resources, and started our own publishing business which—after we married in 1987—became Daniel & Daniel. We've never looked back, even in moments when the business drives us nuts.

Have you published any of your own books and how do you feel about indie publishing?

I have a lot of respect for indie publishing, which comes in many flavors. I've published three books under one of our own imprints, Fithian Press: *Confessions of a Small-Press Publisher*; *Structure, Style and Truth: Elements of the Short Story*; and *The Ballad of Toby and Lark: A Cat Fantasy*. I've also e-published three novels with Kindle and Nook: *Swimming in the Deep End*, *Geronimo's Skull*, and *Elephant Lake*.

Advice for aspiring writers?

Write for the joy of writing. Other reasons to write are for money or fame, which may not pay off, but if you love the pleasure of telling stories, you've already won the game.

What are the biggest mistakes your writing students have made?

The word "very" in every other sentence. Beginning writers tend to think the word "very" strengthens a sentence, when in fact it more often than not does the exact opposite.

What inspired *Behind the Redwood Door*?

When Susan and I moved to the North Coast of California, famous for its rocky shores, its towering Redwood trees, its mountains inland, and (yes, for better or for worse) its illegal cash crop, I was enchanted. Then I started hearing gossip about the area's shady past: exploitative lumber barons, the poor treatment of native peoples, family feuds, etc. I got hooked. I knew I had to write about this place. And I knew I had to make the murder take place behind our favorite bar, which I renamed the Redwood Door.

What is a Story? An Etude in the Key of C

by John M. Daniel

I took [the letter] up, and held it in my hand. I was a-trembling, because I'd got to decide, forever, betwixt two things, and I knowed it. I studied a minute, sort of holding my breath, and then says to myself:
"All right, then, I'll go to hell"—and tore it up.
It was awful thoughts, and awful words, but they was said. And I let them stay said; and never thought no more about reforming.
—Huck

Rust Hills summed it up thus: "Something happens to someone." That's it. Plot (something happens) and *character* (to someone).

Okay, but what happens? *Change.* Our someone is, at the end of the story, a different person from the one who she or he was at the beginning.

How does that come about? It could be because of *chance* (a trolley runs over his foot, so he will never be able to tap dance again); but more often, and more interestingly, it's because the character has made a *choice.*

The choice arises from a *conflict.* Remember: no conflict, no story. Conflict resolution, which comes in many forms, is what results in choice, and therefore in change. By the way, the conflict is often the outcome of a *crisis* of *conscience,* and results in a shift in the balance of power.

Yes, the choice itself has a *consequence.* The change, yes, we talked about that. But maybe a greater change. The moral *center of gravity* may have shifted. To make our story important, make that choice consequential. Write about what matters: the human condition. Write about love and death.

This *critical moment* of change, this *catharsis,* for reasons as old as the *creative process,* the recreative process, and even the *procreative* process, usually happens at the *climax* of the story.

If you don't believe me, ask Huck Finn.

So as we write our stories, let us remember all of these ingredients, listed here in alphabetical order:

Catharsis, Center of Gravity, Chance, Character, Change, Choice, Climax, Condition (human), Conflict, Conscience, Consequence, Creative Process, Crisis, Critical Moment...and I'm sure I've forgotten a few—

(John M. Daniels website: http://www.danielpublishing.com/ jmd/index.html, his blog site: http://blog.johnmdaniel.com/, and Facebook: http://amazon.johnmdaniel.com/)

Margaret Koch

When Psychologist Margaret Koch retired, she decided to write mystery thrillers instead of self-help books. Fortunate to live near the University of Iowa, where the famous creative writer's workshop is housed, she was unable to connect with an agent, so she decided to publish her books: *Blonde Joke, Camp Soul, Song of the Soul, Stark Raving, To Kill an Echo* and *Power in the Blood* in various formats.

Margaret, when did the writing bug bite you?

I've been writing my entire life—but usually in conjunction with the job I had at the moment. When I worked at Redstone Arsenal as a recreation director, I wrote a newspaper column and I did a lot of community service type writing. As a grad student and psychologist, I wrote some scientific papers and a dissertation. But when I retired, I wanted to write for fun. I wanted to write books that would entertain people. That's when writing took over my life and I could say I'd been "bitten." My characters will not leave me alone now. They are having so much fun taking over my life that occasionally I need to kill one just for the peace and quiet.

Why do you think it strange to have a double major in art and English for someone raised in Alabama?

It took a lot of effort to be allowed to do that double major. It was unusual enough so that I had to get permission all up and down the line. This was quite a while ago—maybe it's different now. But it's interesting how things work out—now I can write the book and do the cover sketch.

Why grad school to study psychology after a failed 20-year marriage? And has the experience found its way into your novels?

I was in my early forties—too old to be accepted into medical school, so I could not be a psychiatrist, even though the time span to a Ph.D. and a practice in psychology actually was longer than the route to the M.D. I was really interested in human behavior. I could not explain what happened to my marriage after all those years. I needed to study people.

And yes, my life experience does show up in my series of mystery novels. My protagonist is a psychologist, divorced from a physician, and for the same reasons. I have a good group of retired psychologists from my old practice, who go over my books thoroughly, and we make sure no actual persons or ex-clients show up in the books. But there are types—and trends that I ran into through the years that do show up in my books.

After retiring from your practice in Iowa, why did you decide to write mysteries instead of self-help psychology books?

I wanted to have fun, and not be accountable. If you write self-help books, the ethics of the profession follow you into your new writing career. I will readily admit that I might have had more publishers willing to take a chance on a self-help book, but I needed to be free.

Did the e-book revolution change your conception of the publishing business?

It wasn't the revolution so much as it was the sudden awareness that no matter how happy traditional publishing was to have you, it was going to take years to get five books out there and available to the public. I started writing in 2006, and now I have five books published—one per year, with the sixth one out last Christmas. If I had kept at the traditional route, I'd be lucky to have one or two out by now.

Tell us about your Barb Stark series as well as your latest release.

Barb Stark's routine life as a small resort-town psychologist changed forever when the bastard son of an international crime family walked into her office requesting marital therapy with the wife he intended to kill. Her battle of wits and wills with him threw her into a dark world of ever-escalating challenges.

One of my priorities is to show how people learn and change when they are confronted with the unexpected and the dangerous. The scramble to learn and cope when the stakes are life and death makes for riveting reading. The series is also focused on relationship changes, with plenty of romantic intrigue. I try to make my villains dimensional. In each book, the reader gets to see what made the villain go down his dark path.

And courage and humor are necessary in my books. There has to be lots of courage and humor.

How do you promote your books and are you planning anything special in the near future?

I haven't promoted my books. I put the titles and links under my signature on lists like DorothyL or the Sisters in Crime's listserve, but that's about it. The rest has been word-of-mouth. I hope to do better at marketing.

Who most helped your writing career?

Other authors—people like Sue Grafton, Charlaine Harris, Joan

Hess, Margaret Maron, and many others—who inspired me enough to try to emulate them. Also, very good friends who eagerly read every page I write. They have helped to convince me that I'm not just doing a self-indulgent exercise. People are enjoying my books.

Advice for fledgling mystery writers?

It's a brutal world. You have to be able to bear criticism without folding, and you have to stick with it to produce enough product so that people know you are serious. One book probably won't do it these days. The first book is probably a learning exercise. Tenacity above all else seems to be the required characteristic.

Another required characteristic is that you cannot get too focused on thinking that people will judge you based on what you write. If a character would ordinarily curse, I'd suggest you let them curse. You can't care what people will think.

Life's Too Short to Ignore Dreams

By Margaret Koch

I wanted to be a writer—to call myself a pro, not just write memoirs for friends and family. I wanted to entertain people with fast-paced mysteries—tales of courage and humor, romance, intriguing puzzles and derring-do. My words would dance, leap and shine, sucking readers in until all they could do was turn the next page and gasp, then pant for air and relax. They would sigh and smile when the book was done, satisfied.

I was a psychologist, with a successful practice. I'd heard plenty about life's adventures, but I couldn't use those stories, nor did I want to write research-style—with lots of colons and multi-syllabic words documenting minutia. The joke about research writing is that many colons are needed because material is over-digested, then expelled. And much of it should be flushed. I would write no self-help books, either. I had no life-fixing thoughts I cared to share. So I had no experience with that glittering mix of excitement I wanted in my books. And I was overly mature. An unkind person might even say I was old. There I was, a fast-aging wannabe, totally ignorant of what I was getting into. Scary.

I hitched up my brain and dove headfirst into the buzzsaw of writing and publishing. No guts, no glory. During the next five years, as I wrote and published my mystery-thriller series of six (so far) novels, this is what I learned—in simple form, no colons.

1. The business is brutal, as are most businesses allied to arts. If you want respect and due consideration, get over it. You'll likely batter at the gates, unacknowledged. Unless you are struck by lightning you'll be dismissed. It's a business. They don't trust wannabes, especially old ones writing a series. You might be spectacular, but the first lesson is "Get over yourself." Start young, if possible.

2. A single book traditionally published will take at least two years to get to a reader—too slow, if you've started late. Your life will slip away while publishing proceeds at a snail's pace. By the time you're offered a contract, your brain will have departed. You can't do a series of one, anyway.

3. There's another way. The e-book revolution arrived. The odds of success increase with each e-book you publish, if you turn out a quality product. And it's fast. But e-book publishing is like diving into a stormy maelstrom where many good writers perish unknown. Each e-book gives readers another chance to find you. With six out, I'm selling enough to know that I'm valued by readers. People thank me. I like my reviews. I like royalty checks. I believe that I'm a good writer. That's heady.

4. Writing fiction requires courage. You're exposed. You cannot worry about what people will think. You'll be praised, ignored and critiqued. You'll be emotionally tossed from highs to lows. Do it anyway. Life's too short to ignore dreams.

(Margaret Koch is on Facebook and Amazon:
http://www.tinyurl.com/margaretkoch, Smashwords:
http://tinyurl.com/7d6eznr and Barnes & Noble:
http://tinyurl.com/7atjknx)

Jacqueline King

Jacqueline King loves books, words, and writing tall tales. She especially enjoys murdering the people she dislikes on paper. King is a full-time writer who occasionally teaches writing at Tulsa Community College. Her latest novel, *The Inconvenient Corpse,* is a traditional mystery. She has also written five novellas as co-author of the Foxy Hens Series. *Warm Love on Cold Streets* is her latest novella and is in an anthology, *The Foxy Hens Meet an Adventurer.* Her first nonfiction book is *Devoted to Cooking.*

Jackie, how did *The Inconvenient Corpse* evolve?

Oddly enough, *The Inconvenient Corpse* was birthed in its setting, a charming Bed and Breakfast Inn. I plotted the book by playing every writer's favorite game: "What if?"

What if I'd found a dead man in this bed? What if he were naked? What if his clothes were nowhere to be found? What if the police thought I was the killer and told me that I couldn't leave town? And then, what if I learned that I had no money, no available credit, and no resources at all? What if I'd been born with a silver spoon in my mouth and had previously spent my days as a Junior League member? Could I survive on just my own moxie? I felt impelled to answer these questions.

What in your background prepared you to write?

My mother was a natural born storyteller. One night (at the end of the great depression) there was nothing for supper. Mother never told us this grim fact. She smiled (bravely) and said, "Let's have stories for supper!" My brother, sister and I clapped our hands with joy. Stories for supper? What could be more wonderful? I must have been close to three at the time. After that, I think stories (and later books) became a part of my DNA.

What's your writing work space like?

Shabby, overflowing with papers and magazines and books, and writing supplies. Probably sounds awful, but for me it's heaven on earth. I'm living my life's dream and am happy beyond belief.

Do you have a writing schedule and do you outline your work?

I write every day that it's humanly possible, but not on any particular schedule. I love to write first thing in the morning, but this goal seldom happens. I do outline my work, sort of. I start a spiral notebook for each novel and jot down anything I can think of that comes to mind about my new project. I play a lot of "what if?" as I described earlier. I'm envious of outliners who stick to their exact outlines, but I seem to be totally incapable of such a plan. I'm a "pantser." (As in flying by the seat of your pants.) It requires a huge amount of rewriting, but luckily I love what I fondly call: wordsmithing.

Who taught you the language of fiction?

Although I've had many excellent teachers of fiction (mainly Peggy Fielding), I think I absorbed the language of fiction by reading and reading and reading. I mentally inhaled other writers' wonderful novels, which has helped improve my own writing.

Have your children followed in your keystrokes?

My youngest daughter, Jennifer Sohl, co-authored my only nonfiction book, *Devoted to Cooking,* a collection of family stories and their own special recipes. My granddaughters, Lauren Keithley and Morgan Sohl, are prepublished writers.

How do you feel about the e-book revolution?

I guess I'm a book rebel, (I'm American, after all) because I love e-readers and e-books. I also love paper books. If you write good prose on the sidewalk in front of my house, I'll read that, too.

What's the best way you've found to promote and market your work?

I love promoting my books in the CyberWorld! What a joy it is to become acquainted with readers who live all over the world. Readers are extremely smart, witty, and interesting folk and I can "talk" to any of them who own a computer. Lucky me, I can promote worldwide, day and night (if I choose) in my jammies.

Advice for aspiring writers?

Don't let anyone discourage you. I hate to go to a writer's conference where a well-known writer tells how hard it is to get published at this time, thus intimating those poor souls who have not yet found a publisher and will probably be left out in the cold. THIS IS A LIE! You can do it if you follow the tried and true recipe of success: (1) Write every day. (2) Submit what you write. (3) Never give up.

The Three Rules of Writing

By Jacqueline King

Rule 1: Don't allow yourself to be intimidated. Books are written one word at a time, one sentence at a time, and one paragraph at a time. Each day remind yourself that all you have to do is write one sentence, and then one more, and then one more . . .

Rule 2: Give yourself permission to write a bad first draft. This removes the fear of failure. You can't fail because it's okay to write sucky pages. What's hard is putting your heart on paper. Don't listen to your internal monitor that says, "You can't even spell." (Like that makes any difference? Many successful writers can't spell. That's why God made dictionaries and spell checkers.)

Rule 3: Write every day. Determine to write even in chaos or tragedy, because life is seldom perfect. No matter how busy you are, you have a right to sometime of your own; learn to recognize and grasp these moments. Keep either index cards or a notebook close at all times. (I prefer index cards and always carry some in my purse, pocket and car.

Modern men and women spend a huge amount of time standing in lines, waiting at the doctor's office, or the dentist or hairdresser, or for a child at private lessons or activities. Use these moments to make character sketches, brainstorm writing ideas, or write a scene or part of a scene. It's possible to write a scene in 20 minutes. I know one author who wrote her second book waiting at the airport for her next plane.

Get a large collapsible file to keep all your notes, character sketches, newspaper clippings, etc., together. Writing time shouldn't be wasted searching for lost notes. Keep that file somewhere handy and drop each scrap of paper or index card into it.

Writing a book doesn't always happen in an organized way. Writers are creative folk and there are different ways to begin. Many things can trigger a germ of an idea from which a novel can develop: an overheard snatch of conversation; a newspaper or magazine article; a scene flashing through your mind unexpectedly.

Trust yourself and follow your intuition while writing. This brings out that precious quality called "voice."

Discipline is primary.

Talent is secondary.

Luck is nice, but persistence can overcome a lack of luck.

Use your experiences plus your imagination.

(You can visit Jackie King at her website: www.jacqking.com as well as her blog site: http://bnbmysteries.blogspot.com. She's also on Facebook.)

Lou Allin

Born in Toronto, Lou Allin's family moved to Cleveland when her film-broker father relocated there. She earned her PhD in English renaissance literature for her study of murdered spy, Christopher Marlow, and she later taught in Ontario's bush country, before moving to Canada's "Caribbean Island" where she continues to write mysteries.

Lou, what was life like in Canada's nickel capital?

I taught English courses at Cambrian College—as well as a few Canadian literature courses, but mostly practical stuff like business and tech writing. Finally I wrote reports for Criminal Justice students, which was timely because I had finally begun to publish mysteries. Sudbury is 250 miles north of Toronto, smack in the middle of the bush. It's a sizable enough town, with 95,000 at the core and another 50,000 in the environs. In the late 19th century, most of its tall timber went to Chicago to rebuild after the fire.

Then nickel was found, so the next eighty years were spent in ravaging the landscape for wood to smelt the ore. An area the size of New York City was reduced to barren black rock. It was so bleak that the astronauts went there to train for the moonwalk, or so the legend goes. But just as I arrived in 1977, a super stack had been built to clean the air and prevent acid rain. Over the next thirty years, a reforestation program included business; government, students, and townspeople who helped plant over twenty million pine trees and regreen the rocks with soil and rye grass (rye on the rocks). It was one of the most successful environmental initiatives in history. I'm proud to have been a part of it in showcasing the community to the world.

Where I lived far north of the city, it was drop-dead gorgeous with boreal forest. From my novels, *Northern Winters are Murder* to *Blackflies are Murder* to *Bush Poodles are Murder* to *Murder, Eh?* to the final book, *Memories are Murder*, my work is a love story to a place which welcomed and nurtured me for thirty years.

What inspired your Belle Palmer mystery series?

In 1986 I was living in a cottage on a gigantic lake north of the city. With no television, and six-month winters, there was little to do but read. I devoured mysteries—about eight to the weekend. I'd already started publishing poetry (mostly in small magazines), but a few paying slots like *National Enquirer* as well as short stories, so I took the leap with the wilderness as my inspiration. A snowmobile chase concludes my first book. I'll never forget the rush of flying across that frozen lake and seeing my house's windows lit up like gold by the setting sun's reflection. No way did I want anyone to be identifying my characters, so a college setting was out. A realtor with cottage property as a specialty seemed a good choice. But it took until book four to allow her to find a body in a house she was selling.

Why did you relocate to Vancouver, Island?

After decades of -35C winters, I wanted to go to the warmest spot in Canada. What else but the magical island? I didn't know at the time that the summers were so temperate. It rarely gets over 75F on the coast here with the winds across the strait. In the interior it's a bit hotter. They call the Cowichan Lake area the Warmlands.

Why have you been setting your latest novels in the U.S.?

I had a couple of standalones that were written after the first two series books. I didn't want to invest more time until I found a publisher. So one book, *A Little Learning is a Murderous Thing*, is set in a university in Michigan's Upper Peninsula and the other, *Man Corn Murders*, in the Grand Staircase Escalante wilderness in Utah. I have travelled in both places. They're from Five Star, which does limited library print runs. Now the rights are mine, and I have them on Kindle. My newest book from Orca Press in Victoria begins in the California desert when an older woman with a classic Mustang meets a young male drifter. But they head right back over the border to northern Ontario and her hunting lodge.

Tell us about your latest mystery?

I have two books submitted and pending, but you know the publishing climate. One is the third in my Vancouver Island series, a police procedural "lite." My RCMP corporal cannot do much detective work on her own. She's with a small detachment of three in Fossil Bay on the coast. I like to be authentic. To make her a detective, she'd have to be posted to a larger city with about fifty officers. So Cpl. Holly Martin has cases when an *accidental death* turns out to be a murder, or a long-ago murder surfaces, or the law enforcement agencies just plain give up and put the case on a back burner. The other I sent off to Orca Press, who published my Rapid Reads novella for adults with literacy weaknesses, called *That Dog Won't Hunt*. The second and, as yet unaccepted book, is titled, *Contingency Plan* and deals with a young widow and her daughter, who run into a very dangerous man on Vancouver Island.

I'm also a sixth of the way in on a young adult novella called *Two by Four*, which stars Chloe Cooke, an overweight and spunky twelve-year-old who has to spend the winter with her eccentric aunt in Yukon. On my far back burner is an historical mystery set in 1895 Victoria here on the island.

What's the most difficult aspect of writing for you and the most pleasurable?

Like most authors, I don't like flogging my books at stores. The only way you can take it is by making it a game. Keep a smile on your face and be happy that one out of fifteen people do buy a book. Or maybe the next one will say, "Hey, I've read your books, and I love them."

As for the pros, I cherish fan mail. Notice that I have not mentioned money. That's because there's precious little of it for small press authors.

Who most influenced your own work?

I feel that my work is closest to the early books of Nevada Barr, U.S. park ranger. Setting is one of her strongest points, that and the fact that the reader learns something about each national park.

Advice for fledgling mystery writers?

You need the Three T's: Tools, talent, and tenacity. Easy to get the tools, like grammar and structure. Harder to have the talent, though you can learn much from reading. and you must always have the "what if?" mentality. But anyone can develop the tenacity to keep going. You'd be surprised how many "overnight success" authors spent years and years building their careers. I know some who have five books "in the closet." They learned something from each one.

Layering the Landscape

by Lou Allin

There are 1001 ways to write fiction. I agree with Ortega y Gasset, who said, "Tell me the landscape in which you live, and I will tell you who you are." Setting is critical to me. In the diverse environments where I have lived since I left Ohio, ignoring nature can easily kill a person. I seek to traverse, transpose, and then transport the reader to my world: once the wilderness of Northern Ontario and currently

Vancouver Island.

In my first visit, I write only the bare essentials. Who's there and what they are doing. Conversation is at a minimum because later the scene may whisper more and increase my options. At this point, I may complete only one or two pages. The next time, I add sensory details, starting with sight. I'm not the kind of a person who painstakingly writes a scene inch by inch, savoring everything in my path, perfecting one sentence before moving to the next. Some sensations I don't think about. Others don't occur to me until the fifth or sixth draft. Adding hearing, touch, smell, and even perhaps taste, I visit and revisit and revisit until I am satisfied. Layer upon layer, the painting emerges. Each time, another ten percent on average is added to the text.

Both of my literary homes have had four distinct seasons. And as each season emerges, it offers different opportunities. Northern Ontario has very severe winters, but only during the winter does the land open for travel by snowshoe, skis, or snowmobile. Summer is humid and frantic with high temperatures and murderous bug invasions. It's hard to imagine -40C in *Northern Winters are Murder* when it's 40C in *Blackflies are Murder*. Solid walls of rain during Vancouver Island's winters stand far apart from the droughts and forest fires of summer. The seasons change as I go through my drafts, and at a leisurely pace of a book a year, usually I come full circle. I always live where I write. The one exception was my standalone novel, *Man Corn Murders*, which took place in the red rock desert of Utah. For that I depended on a month-long trip to the canyons.

My reference library includes books on birds, animals, plants, fungi, geology, history, astronomy, fossils, everything important about my landscape. I've purchased topographic maps to guide me. I'd rather not construct a road where there isn't one or stick a river in the middle of a bog. Once I did make an old brewery into a grow-op near an abandoned rail line designed to carry shipments of marijuana. I got a big laugh out of the aptly-named Budd car (a single coach with engine on board used in the far north).

My Clintonias don't bloom in early September when the yellow flower has become a purple fruit. April is the time for skunk cabbage. Salmonberries ripen before blackberries. Wherever I have lived,

I keep a monthly diary of emerging plants. Nor do I want to make a mistake about local animals. There are no foxes on Vancouver Island, nor moose, but you may see an elk. There are plenty of black bears, but very few grizzlies.

Instead of the devil, the angel is in the details. By the time I reach the final version of the scene, the readers know whether sweat is evaporating on skin, what the wind is like, what's on the path, what's singing in the stillness, which trees are in leaf in what order, and if bare, how the snow on branches is behaving in the thaw. How does the frosty air feel in the nose and are the hairs prickling? Is the rock face granite or sandstone? The final process begins when the sensory experience is complete. That's when I add subtleties like an analogy between nature and the individual. Some may call this the "pathetic fallacy," but nature often reflects the way I feel.

(You can learn more about Lou at her website: www.louallin.com, at Facebook and Twitter as @louallin.)

Karen E. Olson

Karen Olson worked as a journalist for twenty years before retiring from news gathering to edit a Yale medical journal. Her two mystery series feature a tattoo artist-sleuth and journalist Annie Seymour. Her quirky characters have been compared to those of Janet Evanovich.

Karen, how did you research your tattoo artist? And why was the series set in Las Vegas?

Since I don't have any tattoos, I had to start from scratch with Brett. I visited a tattoo shop with a friend's daughter, who *is* tattooed. I spent a lot of time online: YouTube is great for "learning how to tattoo." I also learned all the parts of a tattoo machine online. I spoke with many friends, who are tattooed, about their experiences. I also read a fascinating book about the history of women and tattoos, which was invaluable in understanding Brett, a woman in a typically male profession. As for Las Vegas, well, my editor wanted the locale to be one that was warm with palm trees. Miami and Southern California were tossed about, but I finally decided on Vegas because everything in Vegas is just bigger than life and I could write some really fun stories that might only happen in a place like Las Vegas.

**Have your quirky characters have been compared to those
of Janet Evanovich?**

My Annie Seymour series has been compared to Janet Evanovich's
work, although I think the secondary characters in my tattoo shop
series are much more Evanovich-like!

**In your first series, Annie Seymour is a journalist. Tell us
about your protagonist.**

My protagonist, Annie Seymour, is a police reporter in New Haven,
Connecticut. The plots in all four books were gleaned from the
headlines, as you might expect a series set in a newsroom to be.
Annie is tough, but vulnerable, and she believes that everything is
black and white, there's no gray area at all. I was a journalist for more
than 20 years, so creating a journalist-protagonist was relatively
easy. Annie is a compilation of many reporters I've worked with over
the years, not based on just one or on myself at all. She is also a native
New Havener and lives a block away from Wooster Street, which has
great pizza restaurants and a very colorful past. I loved bringing my
city to life through Annie's eyes.

When did your writing begin?

I always wanted to be a writer and I began writing stories when I
was nine. I was an English major in college, but realized I couldn't
support myself writing fiction, so I became a newspaper reporter.
When I was about 30, I decided to write my first mystery novel, the
first book I completed, and no one will ever read it. It was my learning
book. It took two more tries before I wrote *Sacred Cows*, which won
the Sara Ann Freed Memorial Award for a best first novel.

How difficult was it for you to find an agent?

I went through the query process and it was incredibly frustrating.
I finally decided to take the bull by the horns and called a writer I'd
interviewed ten years earlier and asked if he would be willing to help
me. He read the book, then called me with his agent's name and

number. That was not *Sacred Cows*, though, that was the second mystery I attempted. The agent did not agree to represent me but encouraged me to try again. When I sent him my *Sacred Cows*, he did agree to represent me.

How long did it take to complete the book?

It took me two years to write *Sacred Cows*. I started it in 1999. My agent agreed to represent it in 2001—two weeks before 9/11. Publishing virtually shut down, the rejections began pouring in. I wrote another book. In 2004 I heard about the Sara Ann Freed Memorial Award competition and submitted the manuscript. It won. The book was published in 2005.

What's your writing schedule like?

I work part time in the mornings and get home around 1:30 in the afternoon. I usually write for an hour before my daughter gets home from school, or when she's at her various after-school activities— about two hours a day, or as long as it takes me to write five pages. I try to write every day, but sometimes it's just not possible, and I don't beat myself up over it.

What are the best and worst aspects of writing?

I love starting to write a book, when the story is fresh and the characters are new. I love placing my characters in different situations to see how they handle them. But I hate writing the endings. Not because I have to leave everything behind, but because I have to figure out how to wrap everything up. I don't outline, so sometimes my plots take twists and turns that might not be so easy to wrap up and I end up rewriting and moving whole chunks of the book around. Maybe I should outline, but I like the freeness of just seeing where the story goes.

Advice to fledgling writers?

Perseverance pays off. It may take a long time, but it will pay off eventually.

Stretching My Wings

by Karen Olson

When you start writing fiction, everyone tells you to write what you know. So, because I've lived in the New Haven area all my life and was a longtime reporter and editor for various Connecticut newspapers, I created Annie Seymour, a police reporter who lives and works in New Haven. Annie was easy; I knew who she was, everything about her life. For research, I went downtown and ate at a lot of restaurants and made sure I had the right streets intersecting.

But after four books with Annie, my editor asked me if I wanted to write a series about a tattoo shop owner. I began to hyperventilate. I have no tattoos. I had never considered getting a tattoo. Okay, so I have friends with tattoos, but it's not exactly the same thing.

And then my editor said maybe I should stretch my wings even further by setting the book somewhere other than Connecticut. More hyperventilating. I lived in Miami for two years way back in the early 1980s. It's a little different there now. I went to college in southwestern Virginia. Not exactly sexy. My editor suggested a place with palm trees. After some discussion, I finally settled on setting the book in Las Vegas.

I had been to Vegas exactly once. For two days. Twelve years earlier. I was breaking the ultimate rule of writing. I was going to write a book about everything I didn't know. I found myself on YouTube, where I watched a video of a man demonstrating how to tattoo by tattooing a grapefruit. I downloaded PDF images of the parts of a tattoo machine. I read a book by Margot Mifflin about the history of women and tattoos. I visited a tattoo shop and talked to my friends who have tattoos. I began to read tattoo blogs and exchanged emails with people who offered their expertise and pictures of their tattoos and other types of body modification.

Halfway through writing *The Missing Ink*, the first book in the series, I told my husband that I needed to go to Las Vegas, where I had decided to set the series' tattoo shop, *The Painted Lady*, in the

Grand Canal Shoppes at the Venetian on the Strip. Trying to make sense of the map of the place online just wasn't cutting it.

Slowly, the series came to life. I wrote the first book, then the second, *Pretty in Ink*, and the third, *Driven to Ink*. I went back to Vegas a second time and hiked Red Rock Canyon, admired the vistas at Lake Mead, ate at Thomas Keller's Bouchon at the Venetian and the In-'N-Out Burger just a block from the Strip off Tropicana, admired the glass flower sculpture in the Bellagio's lobby and saw real flamingos at the Flamingo Hotel. Research doesn't have to be hard.

When I started writing *Ink Flamingos*, the fourth in the series, I realized I was no longer having any hyperventilating moments. The words flowed easily.

I was writing what I knew.

(You can visit Karen Olson at her website: http://www.kareneolson.com/ and her blog site: http://kareneolson.blogspot.com/)

Pat Browning

A veteran traveler, Pat Browning's globetrotting of the 1970s led to her work as a travel agent and correspondent for *TravelAge West*, a trade journal published in San Francisco. During the 1990s, she served as a newspaper reporter and columnist. Her mystery novel, *Full Circle*, first of her Penny McKenzie mystery series, was later republished as *Absinthe of Malice*. She's currently hard at work on the second novel in the series.

Pat, when did you realize you were a writer?

I can't remember when I didn't write. Scribble would be more accurate, but from an early age I exhibited something every writer needs—unabashed confidence that people want to read what I write.

In the fifth or sixth grade, I wrote one-page, illustrated haunted house stories (in pencil, on notebook paper) and passed them around the classroom. That summer, I wrote a "book," a blatant knock-off of the Bobbsey Twins, and passed it around the neighborhood. When I was about 12, I sat under a pear tree in our front yard and wrote a story about fairies living in a tree stump. I mailed it to *The Kansas City Star*; they printed it, and sent me a check for something like 50 cents. I was always a writer. If you don't count my 50 cents from *The Kansas*

City Star, I really knew I was on to something when *The Fresno Bee* hired me as a stringer and began publishing my feature articles back in the 1960s. They hired me to do routine society news, weddings and such, but I started doing features like they were going out of style and never looked back.

Which awards have you won?

"Got Those Ol' Call Me Fat, Diet Time Blues," a feature I wrote for the *Bee* in 1964, won third place in California Press Women's annual writers contest. I gave that up for the travel business and wrote for *TravelAge West,* a trade journal published in San Francisco. No awards, just some fantastic travel assignments.

In the 1990s, I signed on full time as a newspaper reporter and columnist at *The Selma Enterprise* and *Hanford Sentinel* in California's San Joaquin Valley. While at the *Enterprise,* my lifestyle coverage placed first two years in a row in the California Newspaper Publishers Association Better News-papers Contest. As co-writer of a feature on AIDS, I was a finalist for the 1993 George F. Gruner Award for Meritorious Public Service in Journalism. At *The Sentinel,* my feature story about a Hanford man, who was one of the Japanese-American "Yankee Samurais" of World War II, placed second in the CNPA contest.

In 2000, the first chapter of my mystery novel, *Full Circle,* won *Futures Magazine's* second annual Karen Besecker Memorial Award. The award was named for the late Karen Besecker of Fresno, California, who founded the San Joaquin Chapter of Sisters in Crime.

When did you decide to write your first novel, and how did the story evolve?

While I was working for *The Hanford Sentinel,* the editor decided the lifestyle pages needed a book review column. I went to the library and pulled books off the shelves. They turned out to be mysteries, and I thought, how hard can it be to write one? Ten years later I can say, it's not as easy as it looks.

It became *Absinthe of Malice* almost overnight when an online friend decided to start his own publishing company, read *Full Circle*, and made me an offer I couldn't refuse. Three months later the new book was revised and reissued. It was a mad, mad merry-go-round and I loved every sweaty minute of it.

How have your various jobs influenced your writing?

Everything I've done has turned up in my writing in one form or another, especially the newspaper columns and features. My Penny Mackenzie mystery series reflects the small newspaper offices and law office where I worked, as well as the small California town where I lived for almost 50 years.

Do you feel that the current publishing market will force major publishers to streamline their methods?

Major book publishers seem to be turning into foreign-owned conglomerates that are only interested in the bottom line, and it's difficult to know who's publishing what any more. Pearson (UK) owns Penguin Putnam Inc. and all of its imprints. Bloomsbury (UK) owns Walker and its imprints. Holtzbrink (Germany) owns Macmillan and its imprints, and also St. Martin's. Hachette Livre (France) owns Warner Books/Little, Brown and their imprints. But Kensington/ Zebra is one fairly large U.S. publisher, which I think is still independent.

The smart publishers are getting on the e-book bandwagon. HarperCollins, with numerous imprints, has a Browse Inside section on its web site (www.harpercollins.com). The blurb reads "HarperCollins Browse Inside lets you start reading books before they go on sale with a sneak peak and offers full access on selected titles, where you can read the entire book for free online."

I clicked on the cover of *The Gradner Shift* by Ulrich Boser, which went on sale in hardcover and e-book formats—the true story of the world's largest unsolved art theft—several chapters of the book are there to read. It certainly piqued my interest.

What are the most difficult aspects of writing and what do you enjoy most about the creative process?

The most difficult aspect is sitting down to do it. Once I'm into it, I lose all track of time. The creative process is like breathing to me. I couldn't live without it.

Has blogging increased your book sales?

I don't usually blog about my book. My blog is just a personal thing, not a marketing tool. As for other blogs I show up on, who knows? It does keep your name before the public but I can't even guess how it relates to sales.

Tell us about your memoir, "*White Petunias*," which was published in the *Red Dirt Festival Anthology*.

It's basically about a summer night when a boy walked me home from church, but in a larger sense about a small rural community in Oklahoma that was changed forever by World War II. I first wrote the church scene in the 1960s, planning to turn it into a novel. Didn't happen. But it was near and dear to my heart, so I filed it away and got it out again about every 20 years, wondering what to do with it, rewrote it, and filed it away. A couple of years ago I rewrote it again, and it won second place in the Memoir category of the 2007 Writers Competition, "Frontiers in Writing," sponsored by the Panhandle Professional Writers, Amarillo, Texas. A year ago I rewrote it once more, and it was accepted for inclusion in the *Red Dirt Book Festival Anthology*. The anthology and festival are sponsored by the Oklahoma Humanities Council and the Pioneer Library System.

Advice for fledgling writers?

We'd need another book for that!

My Favorite First Lines

by Pat Browning

The first question I have is always: What is this book about? You can't depend on cover blurbs to tell you. Often they're so much gush. I'm not impressed when some famous author says the book in question is the best book ever written. How do I know the famous author even read it?

For me, the easiest way to find out what a book's about is to check online at Amazon.com. If a book has been published it will be listed there with some kind of story line or a summary. Yet even when I know what a book's about, I like to hold it in my hand. I like to riffle through the pages to get a feeling for writing style, characters, dialogue.

I always open a book to the first page. A funny first line gets my attention. Other than that I can't really say why the first few lines pull me into a book or turn me off, but here are some opening lines that I love, for whatever reason.

My favorite first line of all time:

"He loved to watch fat women dance." ~ From *Goodnight, Irene* by Jan Burke.

Some others I like:

"I was a nice Jewish boy who had gone astray." ~ *Tropic of Murder* by Lev Raphael.

"My mind was on Steinbeck; my foot was on a hand." ~*Till the End of Tom* by Gillian Roberts.

"Afterwards, Sarah could never be quite sure whether it was the moonlight or that soft, furtive sound that awakened her." ~ *Death in Kashmir* by M.M. Kaye.

"Through the slit in the closed drapes, a thin bar of afternoon sunlight fell across the soldier's chest, highlighting the small, dark bullet hole." ~ *Some Welcome Home* by Sharon Wildwind.

"My back's broken," I said. "I'm too old to sit in a cotton field in the middle of the night." *~Absinthe of Malice* by Pat Browning.

Not a complete list, but it's a start. Writers take note: The first line is the hardest but it may sell your book.

(You can learn more about Pat Browning at her blog site: http://browningpat.wordpress.com/ She's also on Facebook.)

Lesley Diehl

Lesley Diehl retired as a psychology professor and reclaimed her country roots by moving to a small cottage in the Butternut River Valley of upstate New York. In the winter she migrates to "old Florida"—cowboys, scrub palmetto, and open fields of grazing cattle. She goes to the "Big Lake" to write, hang out in cowboy bars, and immerse herself in the Florida of the past. "No beaches, no bikinis, no sand. Just cows, horses, and gators."

Lesley, how did you find your winter haven in Florida where cowboys herd cattle among the scrub palmetto.

We stumbled upon this part of Florida by accident, looking for a place to buy that was more reasonable in price than where we were wintering in Key Largo. Rural Florida drew us because it is unpretentious and undeveloped. Aside from the sounds nature provides, such as frogs croaking in our canal or coyotes howling when the train passes, human noises seldom interfere. The city of Okeechobee is the only place for shopping for over thirty miles in any direction and, once you leave the city, you encounter only pastures, live oaks hung with Spanish moss, scrub palmetto and sabal palms. Nothing is manicured, everything grows wild. This is old Florida, before the interstates and rampant development. Eagles nest here.

Caracaras settle alongside the roadways. There are more cattle in Okeechobee County than people, and I think there are probably more alligators. This place is not pretty, but it is beautiful.

Did you hang out in cowboy bars to research your latest novel?

There is nothing better than a bar filled with cowboys, some right off the range still wearing their spurs and manure on their boots, others dressed up for a Saturday night on the town, lean, maybe mean, faces shaved close enough that the skin shines, hair still wet from their showers and the smell of aftershave, and I don't mean the designer stuff.

I got the idea for my protagonist tending bar from a woman I saw serving drinks one New Year's Eve. She wasn't very big, but everyone in the bar knew she could keep order. She had a ponytail which flipped around as she worked and a pair of dangly earrings that threatened to toss you on your butt if you got too close. I'll bet she could free pour a shot within a millimeter of it being legal. She was an inspiration.

You hold book signings in unusual settings.

I sold well at breweries because my first book, *A Deadly Draught*, was set in upstate New York and featured a woman microbrewer accused of killing off her competition. Doing the research for it was fun, and it's only natural that I'd sign in microbreweries.

I've held signings at the usual places such as bookstores and libraries. I also found an appreciative audience in an old inn and hotel recently reopened and restored. When people are happy, filled with food and good drink, they seem to like buying books. I also set up a table in my front yard for the community yard sales in my town. Since we're new to the village, it was a fun way to get to know people.

How did your *Dumpster Dying* book come about?

I know many retired people whose spouses have died and who find another person to love. Couples may not want to marry again for various reasons, some of which may be financial, so I thought to myself, "but what happens if one of them dies and everything is in *his* name?" And what if he left a will naming his ex-wife as sole beneficiary? Does the partner have any legal recourse; especially in a conservative community where it is expected couples are legally wed? That's the situation Emily Rhodes confronts. To earn money she becomes a bartender at the local country club. She's barely making ends meet when she finds the body of a rancher in the club's dumpster. He just happens to be someone with whom she's had several fights. Guess who the authorities think killed him?

Why did you decide to reclaim your country roots after retiring as a psychology professor?

I was born and raised on a dairy farm in the Midwest. I love what cities have to offer in the way of shopping, culture, dining and excitement, but I'm really a country girl at heart. I adore cows and love the smell of horse manure. My most pleasurable dream is of swimming in a field of golden, ripe wheat. Heavenly. In Florida, we live only 30 miles from the coast, so I can get my coastal "fix" easily and then slide right back into my country life. In the summer in upstate New York I have to travel much further to find a city, and I don't do it often because it's difficult to pull me away from my trout stream. And there's also work to do on the cottage.

Tell us about your writing schedule and whether you outline extensively before you begin?

I write and plot by the seat of my pants. I do not outline, which surprised several of my friends because they find my plots complex. I have a general idea of where I want the story to go, and I love being surprised when it goes in another direction. I write everyday if I can, but do not keep a rigid schedule.

For whom do you write?

Both men and women read me, young and older. My target audience is probably women over 30 and under 100. Yet I don't think of the audience when I'm writing, so you could say I'm writing for myself because I have to write.

Which writer most influenced your own writing?

Reading Janet Evanovich has given me permission to write spunky, outrageous protagonists. I enjoy a good laugh, and I try to write funny stuff, although my first book was serious. I find that my latest manuscripts kind of "gallop" with humor, at least they do to me.

The writers I love to read probably influence me in ways I'm unaware of. I love Robert Parker, Elizabeth George, Nevada Barr, yet they are not funny. I recently read several of Tom Dorsey's books. His humor can get grisly, but he writes with regard for old Florida, so I respect him.

Advice to fledgling writers?

Keep writing. Join critique and writing groups as well as organizations such as Sisters in Crime and Mystery Writers of America. Spend your money on one conference a year, a good one where you can meet other writers, editors, agents and bask in that atmosphere where you're sharing your love of writing with others who feel the same way.

Programs and Signings: A Beer, A Muffin and A Book

by Lesley Diehl

What do libraries and bars have in common? I like both and they like me. I do signings and programs in them. Both places have interesting people in them so, if you don't sell a book, at least you have some cracking good conversations with the folks there.

Friends of the library—not all libraries have them, but once you find libraries that do, you've uncovered the mother lode. Libraries love local authors, and often the friends group arranges author programs. And they usually provide food after the program. Oh yum!

I did a book launch for my novel set in rural Florida, in the local library. I wanted to do something different so I made up baskets themed around my protagonist's journey in the book and that of four other characters. I think this works best with a humorous story, which mine was. One basket was the "Clara Gets Out of Jail" basket. It included bath salts, fancy soap, a loofah sponge, a bath pillow, a very classy champagne glass and a split of champagne.

Wouldn't you want this when you got out of lock-up? I had my attendees drop their names in a cowboy hat, and we pulled winners of five baskets out after my short program. Many of the baskets held some kind of beverage (the one for guys had a beer glass and a bottle of beer and was fashioned around one of my male characters). I spent little money making them up as I went to yard sales and the dollar stores for the items.

Another great place where I've signed is a nearby restaurant featuring local microbrews. Since one of my books features a microbrewer accused of murder, it was a perfect setting for people to grab a brew and snack on food I've provided. I don't do programs here, just book signings. The protagonist of my Florida book is a bartender at a country club, so I'm now moving on to golf and country clubs for book events. My signing at restaurants, bars, country clubs, breweries and golf courses sell my books as well as promote the businesses. They seem to love having me there, and I certainly enjoy several hours of chatting with their patrons.

Who cares if I sell a book? Well, I do, but I never feel cheated if I don't because I've spent an enjoyable evening with some entertaining people. I usually give the business a complimentary copy of my book, and they often display it somewhere on the premises. One brewery bought a dozen of my books to sell.

My philosophy is if a reader complains it's impossible to hold a drink in one hand, a muffin in the other and buy one of your books, offer to hold the muffin.

(You can visit Lesley anytime at her website: http://www.lesleydiehl.com/ as well as her blog site: http://anotherdraught.blogspot.com/)

Sunny Frazier

Sunny Frazier is a former Ma Bell operator, Navy dental technician, photojournalist and a narcotics secretary at the Fresno County Sheriff's Department. All that before turning to fiction writing. After solidifying her reputation with short stories, she moved on to writing novels. Her Christy Bristol astrology mysteries include *Fools Rush In* and *Where Angels Fear*, both based on real cases. Frazier has been dabbling in astrology since 1970, and is a small press acquisitions editor.

Sunny, when did your interest in astrology come about and why did you incorporate it into your novels?

I describe the incident in *Fools Rush In*. I passed a dusty bookstore and *Astrology for the Aquarian Age* was in the window. I was drawn to the book. When I opened it, despite that all I saw were strange symbols and numbers, it all felt very familiar. Past life, perhaps?

I have some very strong views of astrology and have never been happy with how it's been portrayed in books. Casting horoscopes takes a toll on astrologers because we can't help but absorb energy from the person, both good and bad. Also, I do the future and some people have so much sadness on the horizon. I think of astrology as a tool, not a toy. I try to let readers know, through Christy, what it feels like from the inside. I try my best to be honest and to give something I've never read in any book.

When did you begin your writing career?

I started in high school and was the editor of the newspaper. I continued writing for military publications while in the Navy, and attended college on the GI Bill. My degree is in journalism.

Why do you write?

It comes very natural to me. I'm not very good at anything else.

Who most influenced your work?

My father. Although moderately educated, he was from the South and had a gifted way of telling stories.

What was most difficult about making the transition from journalism to writing fiction?

I would have to argue that the way newspaper reporting is done these days, it's hard to tell journalism from fiction. That being said, I tried to base my first two books as close to the cases they were actually based on. *Fools Rush In* is about a methamphetamine case we did; *Where Angels Fear* is about a sex club we busted. By remembering that story comes before fact, I feel I had an easy time constructing plots.

Why mystery novels?

My last job was working with an undercover narcotics team for 11 years. I lasted longer than any secretary they'd ever had, longer than many of the detectives. With so much first-hand material, it seemed a shame to waste it.

Tell us about your latest novel.

The one I'm working on is called *A Snitch in Time*. Based loosely on the strange people and crazy incidents that occur in the Sierra Nevada foothills, I'm having a ball killing off people at a rather quick rate.

What's your writing schedule like and do you hold down a day job?

I gave up my job with the sheriff's department to take care of my dying father. I now write full-time.

I get up when the cats want to eat. The first thing I do is check my email and get that out of the way. Then I work on the book. In the early afternoon, I tackle query emails and read manuscripts. From 8 p.m. on it's TV time. I do love TV. I end the day with "The Daily Show," a cup of chamomile and a good book.

How has the e-book revolution affected your book sales?

My sales are healthier with e-books. I love the royalties.

What's the best way to promote your books?

I believe that promotion starts when a writer decides to write a novel. If they wait until after publication, they are already behind. Because I realize that many authors are intimidated or overwhelmed by the Internet, I started "The Posse." This is a group I contact when I find a good marketing site. I send them over to support good blogs and to support each other when anyone from the group gets interviewed or blogs. Anyone can be in the Posse by contacting me. I now have Posse Posts over on my website so people can catch up and improve their marketing strategies.

How are you involved in your area writers' group?

I have the list of all Central Valley authors and have used the list to put together a Book Fest and speaker program for the Kings County Library. A new group is forming over in Tulare County, and I'm going to become part of that organization. I have also supported the Madera County writers' group as well.

Advice for novice writers?

Learn as much as you possibly can about the publishing industry, especially small presses and e-publishing. Carve your own path and career, one that suits you, not one others say is the only way. There have never been so many opportunities and options for writers as exist today.

Establish name recognition early. Get involved with writers' forums in your genre. Learn the names of the movers and shakers. Network your butt off.

Please learn craft. Craft is not just plot, it's how you use words to tell the story. I don't think it's taught in schools. Craft is the nuts and bolts of good writing—and I'm not talking punctuation. It's what makes sentences sing, what makes you stop in your reading to admire the author's talent with words. Craft separates good writing from great writing.

Acquisitions: The Good, Bad and the Ugly

by Sunny Frazier

If you love to read, the job of acquisitions editor for a small press is a dream come true. If you hate to dash dreams, are easily swayed or thin-skinned, find another occupation.

I'm the gatekeeper who stands between you and the publisher. The publisher concentrates on production and relies on me to take queries and make decisions based on the needs of the publishing house. We share a vision and it's my job is to find manuscripts for that vision. So, read the guidelines and study titles we've published. Get an idea of what we're looking for. We concentrate on our strongest genres and have marketing expertise.

Note our word length. Larger outfits can produce huge books and charge more; we have to keep production costs down and make books affordable.

If it's a mystery, kill somebody already! The days of long literary passages are over. This is a TV generation, so grab my interest and do it quickly. Show me craft. Anyone with a computer can write a novel, but few realize that writing needs to be studied like any other profession. Craft is more than punctuation.

Here are the authors who get a rejection slip:

The Braggart: "This is the best book you'll ever read. All of my relatives say so." I'm not impressed, nor am I going to let the opinions of others sway me.

The Beggar: "Please publish my book before I die. I just want to see my name on the cover." I sympathize, but that's not a good reason for me to send a contract. That's what vanity press is for.

The Demander: "Have you read my book yet? Will you read it in the next 24 hours?" No, so don't bug me every week. The more you ask, the longer it takes.

The Sensitive: "You don't like my book? You don't like me!" I'm not rejecting you, and I will take the time to tell you why your book didn't make the cut.

The Impatient: "I got the contract a year ago. Where's my book?" Publishing is slow. We do our best, but we get the flu, have the occasional crisis and sometimes get overwhelmed with the workload. I work on Christmas and Thanksgiving—do you?

The Slob: "I wrote the book, now you can fix the punctuation, grammar and spelling errors." Nope. I'm going to pick manuscripts that are clean.

The Inflexible: "My words are precious, so don't change them." I respect your opinion, but it will probably cost you a contract.

The Lazy: "Me, market? That's for underlings. I'm an author!" We need authors with marketing savvy and a willingness to promote.

The Clueless: "I want to be on Oprah's book list. And I hear Hollywood calling." Make sure your expectations are realistic.

The Bait and Switch: "Thanks for doing all the work on my book, but now I'm going to give it to another publisher." Time and money wasted. Plus, some deserving author lost an opportunity.

(You can learn more about Sunny Frazier at her website:
http://www.sunnyfrazier.com as well as her blog site:
http://otpblog.blogsppot.com/)

Jinx Schwartz

Raised in the jungles of Haiti and Thailand, with return trips to Texas, Jinx Schwartz followed in her father's steel-toed footsteps into the construction and engineering industry in the hope of building dams. Finding all the good rivers taken, she traveled the world, and like the protagonist in her mystery series, Hetta Coffey, Jinx was a woman with a yacht who wasn't afraid to use it when she met her husband, "Mad Dog" Schwartz. After their marriage, they sailed under the Golden Gate Bridge and headed for Mexico. They now divide their time between Arizona and Mexico's Sea of Cortez.

Jinx, how did you deface landscapes in Alaska, Japan, Mexico, New Zealand and Puerto Rico?"

I went into the petrochemical field. We built large chemical plants, refineries and pipelines.

How did you meet Robert "Mad Dog" Schwartz? And how long after your marriage did you decide to live in Arizona and Mexico?

I was single, working hard and supporting a three-story Victorian in the Bay Area when my dog up and died. I decided to change my life, so I bought a 42 foot power boat (my first ever boat) and moved aboard. Six months later, I met Mad Dog at a yacht club, and three years later we married and left for Mexico in what was supposed to be a honeymoon trip, but we decided to stay.

Tell us about your Hetta Coffey series.

My protagonist, Hetta Coffey, is an engineer, with her own one-woman consulting company. She takes on somewhat iffy projects from a legal and ethical standpoint. When her dog dies (sound familiar?) she decides to change her life, so she sells her home and buys a boat to live on. Hetta has a penchant for iffy men, as well, and her world travels have left a string of bad boys in her wake. She's hoping to change all that, but her human foibles keep getting in the way.

How did your YA series in Haiti evolve?

All of my Hetta Coffey books, and *Land of Mountains* I would classify as "fictography" (a term I stole from the back cover of John Grisham's *A Painted House*.) I never set out to write a series, it just happened.

What's the most difficult aspect of writing and what do you enjoy most about the publishing industry?

I am not the most disciplined writer in the world, and it is difficult for me to write when I'm not in the mood. I write humor, for the most part, and you've got to be "on" to do it. I also love book signings and meeting people.

How do you promote your books?

I'm a lousy promoter. When I was working I could sell a client on a multimillion dollar project, but I have difficulty asking people to buy my books although I do well one-on-one at signings.

Which of your novels was the most difficult to research and write?

Without a doubt, my historical novel, *The Texicans*, required the most research. The other books were easy; I lived it.

Advice to novice mystery writers?

I cannot emphasize enough the importance of editing. Of course, now you can go back into a Kindle version and fix your mistakes, but why make them in the first place?

WHAT A CHARACTER!

by Jinx Schwartz

How many times have we heard that phrase, what exactly does it mean, and how does it apply to my writing?

For starters, I have a lot of characters in my life. Not the ones in my books, but living, breathing *characters,* the kind defined by Webster as a person with many eccentricities.

I admit that my lifestyle fairly screams for character encounters. We live half the year in Mexico's Sea of Cortez aboard our boat, and there cruisers abound from all over the world and all walks of life. One thing they have in common is that they are adventurous types who have chosen a life *way* outside the box. I can pick up enough material from one potluck on the beach (which happens at the drop of a hat) to fuel many a book. When in port, a walk down the dock or a beer at a local watering hole and I have new best friends from, well, everywhere. Tuning into the daily ham radio nets, with boaters checking in from all over Mexico and the Pacific Coast with the tale of the day, has me jotting notes for future plots, or idiosyncratic scenarios.

And then there is the other half of my life, living smack dab on the Arizona/Mexico border. Not only do we make the headlines frequently, the city of Bisbee has been named by a national organization as one of the quirkiest places to live in the United States, and they are right. My *gardener* packs a .380 in his boot, my Zumba instructor is a retired, gay, exotic dancer, and my nearest neighbor is a Rottweiler who lives alone. Her owner shows up with food and water once a day and I give her lots of treats, but otherwise she has the house and the yard to herself most of the time. Rosa is an equal opportunity barker; she targets illegal crossers and Border Patrol agents with equal hostility. She's the best dog I never owned.

Even my more normal friends (you notice I used the word *more*?) are great book fodder. When one of them was barred from visiting the Kremlin because she set off the radiation detectors (she'd recently had a nuclear stress test), I filed that away, *et voila*, it became part of a plot point in *Just Deserts,* fourth in my Hetta Coffey mystery series.

And then there is Hetta Coffey. She's a woman with a yacht, and she's not afraid to use it. Okay, so she isn't real, but boy, sometimes it doesn't feel that way. Many of my readers actually think I *am* Hetta, or that Hetta is me. Since almost everyone says I am a real character, maybe we are one? The plot thickens.

(You can find Jinx Schwartz at her website: www.jinxschwartz.com as well as Facebook, Twitter, Google and a number of writer forums, including Murder Must Advertise and DorothyL.)

About the Editor

Jean Henry Mead is a mystery/suspense novelist as well as a national award-winning photojournalist who has been published domestically as well as abroad. She also writes western historical novels and the Hamilton Kids' mystery series. *The Mystery Writers* is her fifth book of interviews and second collection of mystery writers.

Her Logan & Cafferty series features *A Village Shattered, Diary of Murder* and *Murder on the Interstate*. Children's titles are *Mystery of Spider Mountain* and *Ghost of Crimson Dawn*. Her western historicals include *Escape, A Wyoming Historical Novel* to be followed during the summer of 2012 by *No Escape: The Sweetwater Tragedy*. She's also written a number of non-fiction books for a total of 17 in all.

You can learn more about the former news, magazine and small press editor at her website: www.jeanhenrymead.com.

She also blogs at five sites: http://mysteriouspeople.blogspot. com/, http://theviewfrommymountaintop.blogspot.com/, http://theviewfrommymountaintop.blogspot.com/, http:// makeminemystery.blogspot.com/, http://writersofthewest. blogspot.com/, and is on Facebook and Twitter.

www.ingramcontent.com/pod-product-compliance
Lightning Source LLC
LaVergne TN
LVHW051448080426
835509LV00017B/1694